Pizza

Anytime

Also by JoAnna M. Lund

The Healthy Exchanges Cookbook
HELP: The Healthy Exchanges Lifetime Plan
Cooking Healthy with a Man in Mind
Cooking Healthy with the Kids in Mind
Diabetic Desserts
Make a Joyful Table
Cooking Healthy Across America
A Potful of Recipes
Another Potful of Recipes
The Open Road Cookbook
Sensational Smoothies
Hot Off the Grill: The Healthy Exchanges Electric Grilling Cookbook
Cooking Healthy with Splenda®
Cooking Healthy with a Microwave
The Diabetic's Healthy Exchanges Cookbook
The Strong Bones Healthy Exchanges Cookbook
The Arthritis Healthy Exchanges Cookbook
The Heart Smart Healthy Exchanges Cookbook
The Cancer Recovery Healthy Exchanges Cookbook
String of Pearls
Family and Friends Cookbook
JoAnna's Kitchen Miracles
When Life Hands You Lemons, Make Lemon Meringue Pie
Cooking Healthy with Soy
Baking Healthy with Splenda®
Cooking for Two
Cooking Healthy with a Food Processor

Pizza

Anytime

A HEALTHY EXCHANGES® COOKBOOK

JoAnna M. Lund

with
Barbara Alpert

A Perigee Book

A PERIGEE BOOK
Published by the Penguin Group
Penguin Group (USA) Inc.
375 Hudson Street, New York, New York 10014, USA
Penguin Group (Canada), 90 Eglinton Avenue East, Suite 700, Toronto, Ontario M4P 2Y3, Canada
(a division of Pearson Penguin Canada Inc.)
Penguin Books Ltd., 80 Strand, London WC2R 0RL, England
Penguin Group Ireland, 25 St. Stephen's Green, Dublin 2, Ireland (a division of Penguin Books Ltd.)
Penguin Group (Australia), 250 Camberwell Road, Camberwell, Victoria 3124, Australia
(a division of Pearson Australia Group Pty. Ltd.)
Penguin Books India Pvt. Ltd., 11 Community Centre, Panchsheel Park, New Delhi—110 017, India
Penguin Group (NZ), 67 Apollo Drive, Mairangi Bay, Auckland 1310, New Zealand
(a division of Pearson New Zealand Ltd.)
Penguin Books (South Africa) (Pty.) Ltd., 24 Sturdee Avenue, Rosebank, Johannesburg 2196, South Africa

Penguin Books Ltd., Registered Offices: 80 Strand, London WC2R 0RL, England

While the author has made every effort to provide accurate telephone numbers and Internet addresses at the time of publication, neither the publisher nor the author assumes any responsibility for errors, or for changes that occur after publication. Further, the publisher does not have any control over and does not assume any responsibility for author or third-party websites or their content.

PIZZA ANYTIME

For more information about Healthy Exchanges products, contact:
Healthy Exchanges, Inc.
P.O. Box 80
DeWitt, Iowa 52742-0080
(563) 659-8234
www.HealthyExchanges.com

First edition: February 2007

Perigee trade paperback ISBN: 978-0-399-53311-2

An application to register this book for cataloging has been submitted to the Library of Congress.

PRINTED IN THE UNITED STATES OF AMERICA

10 9 8 7 6 5 4 3 2 1

PUBLISHER'S NOTE: The recipes contained in this book are to be followed exactly as written. The publisher is not responsible for your specific health or allergy needs that may require medical supervision. The publisher is not responsible for any adverse reactions to the recipes contained in this book.

Most Perigee Books are available at special quantity discounts for bulk purchases for sales promotions, premiums, fund-raising, or educational use. Special books, or book excerpts, can also be created to fit specific needs. For details, write: Special Markets, The Berkley Publishing Group, 375 Hudson Street, New York, New York 10014.

Dedication

This book, as always, is dedicated in loving memory to my parents, Jerome and Agnes McAndrews. Pizza was just gaining popularity in the early sixties as my mother's days of daily cooking and baking for her family were beginning to slow down. But I know if the ingredients of today were available to her back then, she'd have been making "homemade" pizza for us at least once a week, each offering better than the week before! Mom was exceptionally creative when it came to cooking and Daddy was appreciative of everything she made. My sisters and I felt safe and secure as we sat together every night at the kitchen table as a family and said our prayer of thankfulness before we enjoyed another wonderful meal prepared with love by our mother.

However, my mother was just as creative and prolific when it came to writing poetry as she was in the kitchen. I'd like to share one of her beautiful poems with you. My prayer is that you enjoy both Mom's poem and my "common folk" healthy pizza recipes!

When the Sun Goes Down

I sit here by my window and watch
    as the golden sun sinks into the west,
It envelops the earth into darkness,
    while the day slowly goes to rest.
All life seems to follow this same pattern,
    just as night succeeds the day,
Old age follows youth, spreading happiness
    and sunshine along the way.
And now in the hush of the evening
    while all nature seems to stand still,
My thoughts slowly begin to wander,
    although it's really against my will.
I recall the days of my childhood and
    go back through memory lane,
Remembering so many happy moments—
    but some sad ones, too, remain.
These precious memories are like little
    sunbeams, each one a bright ray of light.
Next will come the beautiful sunset,
    then the dark curtain of night.
And someday, when the sunglow of my life
    fades into knowing I tried to do my best,
From the portals of eternity, I pray that
    my Maker welcomes me home to rest.

—Agnes Carrington McAndrews

Acknowledgments

I t takes many ingredients to make a good pizza. And so it is with writing a good pizza cookbook, too! For helping me do just that, I want to thank:

Shirley Morrow, Rita Ahlers, Phyllis Bickford, Cheryl Hageman, Gina Griep, and Jean Martens—my employees. Some typed, some cooked, some tasted, and some washed the dishes! But they all had to agree that the pizza was beyond "this is good," or the recipe wasn't included!

Cliff Lund—my husband. Even though Cliff is on the road more than he is home, when he pulls that truck into our driveway, I know he's going to be mighty happy if I greet him with a kiss—and a tasty pizza!

Barbara Alpert—my writing partner. Barbara has a lot on her plate—with working full-time teaching and mentoring school children—but she saved enough space to fit my pizza project into her busy schedule. Without her, this book might have gone "cold" before it ever got baked!

Coleen O'Shea—my literary agent. She is the one who suggested I take my idea of sharing a few of my favorite Healthy Exchanges pizza recipes in my newsletter and turning them into a whole book filled with all kinds of family-pleasing pizza ideas. Just as a good pizza needs a good oven, an author needs a good agent!

John Duff—my publisher and editor. I am so thankful that he, too, thought there would be enough interest in my "common folk" healthy pizza recipes to turn my idea into a real book. When you no longer have to call for pizza delivery, thank John!

God—my creator and savior. When He blessed me with the ability to create healthy recipes, I think He doubly blessed me when it comes to pizza ideas. I wonder what kinds of pizza are served in the main dining hall of Heaven—surely any in this collection are candidates!

Contents

Please Pass the Pizza!   1
A Peek Into My Healthy Exchanges Pantry   9
JoAnna's Top Tips for Perfect Pizzas   13
Yes, But How Much Should It Be? A Healthy Exchanges
   Chopping Chart   15
JoAnna's Ten Commandments of Successful Cooking   19

THE RECIPES

How to Read a Healthy Exchanges Recipe   25
Appealing Appetizer Pizzas   27
Exciting Entrée Pizzas   65
Dazzling Dessert Pizzas   147
Pizza-Inspired Delights   237
Pizza Parties with Pizzazz!   307
Making Healthy Exchanges Work for You   309
Index   311

Please Pass
the Pizza!

Did you ever notice that when you walk by a pizza parlor, everyone inside is smiling and munching away on their pizzas? Families are sitting together sharing a pie or two. Kids are getting along. People are talking to each other, and there's rarely a frown in sight.

That, to me, is the power of pizza.

Maybe it's because we eat it with our hands, so it just seems like more fun than other foods.

Maybe it's because it comes to the table fresh—and we get to choose *exactly* what we want on it.

And maybe, just maybe, it creates its own sense of community. Sure, you can enjoy an individual pizza, but much of the time, eating pizza calls for company: a friend, or your whole family, or half your department at work.

Pizza seems to me to speak a rare universal language that reaches across the generations. Little kids, teenagers, young adults, twentysomethings just starting out, working parents, grandparents—they all love pizza!

I can still recall the first pizza I ever tasted. It was way back around 1955, when I was eleven years old. My older sister and her date had driven down to the "cities" to eat at one of the first pizza parlors in Davenport. She brought back the leftovers for the rest of us to try. (Oh, yes, that's another reason to love this food—there are almost always leftovers!)

That pizza was just a flat yeast crust with some tomato sauce and cheese sprinkled over the top. But it was almost like eating food from another planet, it was so different from what we were used to eating. As basic as that pizza was, I was hooked with my very first bite.

And just a few years later, there were pizzerias almost everywhere, including the small Iowa town where I grew up.

Who Made the First Pizza?

It's been fun to use the Internet to research the history of the pizza, but what I've learned is that people don't agree about a number of the "facts." We think of pizza as an Italian food, but its origins are likely quite ancient. Several sites I visited suggested that a forerunner of pizza was eaten by the Babylonians, the Israelites, the Egyptians, and other Middle Eastern cultures. This flat unleavened bread, much like the pita bread of today, was topped with olive oil and spices and cooked in mud ovens.

Another source noted that anyone could have invented pizza, once they figured out that mixing flour and water and cooking it on a hot stone would produce a rustic bread that could hold all kinds of toppings and soak up gravy or broth. Some say the idea of using bread as a plate came from Greece, where working-class and nobles alike ate a flat, round bread called *plankuntos*. Another story I particularly liked said that during the reign of the Persians, the armies of Darius the Great (around 500 BC) baked a flat bread using their metal shields, then covered it with dates and cheese to eat on their long marches.

There is actual evidence that there was pizza in ancient Rome. Cato the Elder's history of the city described people eating "flat rounds of dough dressed with olive oil, herbs, and honey baked on stones." They even found flat, round breads in the ruins of Pompeii after Vesuvius erupted!

But the real story of pizza as we know it begins in the 1500s, when the tomato arrived in Italy from the New World (from Peru!). People first thought these red spheres were poisonous but eventually the people of Naples began adding them to their rounds of yeast dough, along with cheese, herbs, and oils. Visitors to the city would visit the poorer neighborhoods in search of this

Neapolitan specialty, made at home by thrifty housewives unwilling to let bits of leftovers go to waste, and in shops by men known as "pizzaioli."

Finally, royalty gave its approval to this peasant dish: first, when Queen Maria Carolina, wife of Ferdinando IV, the King of Naples, had a special oven built in Capodimonte, their summer palace, so that their cook could prepare pizzas for her and her guests; and second, when the King of Italy, Umberto I, and his wife, Queen Margherita, visited Naples in the 1880s. While there, the most popular pizza chef of the time, Raffaele Esposito, was summoned to the palace to prepare his best-loved versions of pizza. One was topped with garlic, olive oil, and tomatoes; another featured pork fat, cheese, and basil; and a third used tomatoes, basil, and mozzarella (in the red, green, and white of the Italian flag). The Queen's favorite was the third, and to this day, it bears her name.

Just think: The world's first true pizzeria, Antica Pizzeria Port'Alba, opened in 1830 and is still in business today in Naples.

How Pizza Conquered America

As Italians immigrated to the United States during the later years of the nineteenth century, pizza came along for the ride. There's a story that Chicago first learned about pizza from a peddler who walked up and down Taylor Street, a metal tub on his head filled with pizzas, which he sold at two cents apiece. Pizza sellers in Naples had originated the method, selling pizzas from copper drums with false bottoms packed with charcoal from their ovens to keep the pizzas hot.

Who was New York City's pizza pioneer? Signore Gennaro Lombardi, who opened his pizzeria on Spring Street in 1905, claims that honor. (His restaurant is still in business today.) Mostly it was Italian immigrants, hungry for a taste of home, who enjoyed those first "store-bought" pizzas.

When did pizza become a true American phenomenon? Demand grew like crazy after servicemen who'd spent World War II in Italy returned home, hungry for the savory pies they'd enjoyed overseas.

The rest, as they say, is history! (And yes, that history includes the development of homemade pizza kits, frozen pizzas, and eventually, fast food pizza from companies like Pizza Hut (launched in Wichita, Kansas, in 1958), and delivery to your door by individual owners and franchises like Domino's (first pizza delivered in 1960, Ypsilanti, Michigan).

A Few Fun Facts About Pizza

According to some published calendars, National Pizza Week is celebrated in January, but October is National Pizza Month. Could it be that Americans can't get enough of a good thing?

There are some fascinating bits and bytes of information about pizza out there in cyberspace. Here are just a few:

1. Americans eat more than 11 billion slices of pizza each year, which works out to about 100 acres of pizza each day, or 350 slices per second!

2. Pizza in America is a $32+ billion per year industry.

3. Pizzerias represent 17 percent of all restaurants and they continue to outpace overall restaurant growth of any kind.

4. Ninety-three percent of Americans eat at least one pizza per month.

5. A study by the USDA found that in a three-day survey, 42 percent of children between the ages of six and eleven ate pizza during that period.

6. By numbers alone, thin-crust pizzas are preferred over thick-crust pizzas. (But one site I checked out noted there were really three regional styles of pizza in the United States: the East, where people prefer "New York style," the thin-crust Neapolitan type, topped with tomato sauce, mozzarella, vegetables and/or meat; the West, where peo-

ple opt for more sophisticated, chewy-crusted pizzas with elegant toppings like sundried tomatoes, gourmet cheeses, and asparagus; and the Midwest, which favors Chicago's deep-dish style pizza, piled high with every possible topping.)

7. The favorite pizza topping is pepperoni. The least favorite is anchovies. And gourmet toppings are gaining ground in some areas of the country. Imagine a pizza topped with chicken, oysters, crayfish, dandelions, sprouts, eggplant, Cajun shrimp, artichoke hearts, or tuna. Other recent trends include game meats such as venison, duck, and Canadian bacon.

8. Saturday night is the biggest night of the week for eating pizza out.

9. The Guinness Book of Records states that the largest pizza ever made and eaten was created in Havana, Florida, and was one hundred feet and one inch across!

10. More than $1 billion was spent on frozen pizza in a recent year, making it one of the fastest-selling prepared foods in America.

11. Italian food ranks as the most popular ethnic food in America.

12. You'll find pizza not just in the flat round shape these days. There's also deep-dish pizza, stuffed pizza, pizza pockets, pizza turnovers, rolled pizza, and yes, pizza-on-a-stick!

Now, if you're curious, people around the world love pizza, too, though they choose very different toppings as their favorites:

- Brazil—green peas

- Pakistan—curry

- Japan—eel and squid

- Russia—"mockba," a combination of sardines, tuna, mackerel, salmon, and onions

Well, let me calm your fears—there is absolutely no eel or squid in any of my Healthy Exchanges recipes! (No sardines, either.) But be brave—and be prepared to try some combinations you may never have thought of before.

Opting for variety when choosing your toppings is one of the great joys of making your own pizzas. I've let my imagination run wild when creating the pizzas and pizza-inspired recipes that fill this book. Now it's up to you to take full advantage of that freedom!

But Is Pizza Really Healthy?

Let's look at the components of a basic pizza: a flour-based crust, tomatoes and/or tomato sauce, and cheese. The U.S. government's dietary guidelines encourage people to consume grains, low-fat dairy products, and vegetables, so pizza sounds like a winner on all counts.

But let's go a little deeper. Takeout and fast-food pizzas generally use high-fat cheeses instead of the reduced-fat kind I recommend. They also frequently use oil during the baking process, both for the flavor and to make the finished product really crisp. Healthy Exchanges recipes don't require an infusion of oil, so I can keep the fat content low in that way, too.

What about carbs, white flour, or the negative publicity about how those ingredients drive up your blood sugar and make it harder to lose weight? All of my Healthy Exchanges recipes are reviewed by a dietitian who also provides the Diabetic Exchanges for each dish. Every pizza and pizza-inspired recipe in this book is designed to be eaten by people who want to lose weight, control cholesterol, improve cardiac health, and maintain a healthy blood sugar level.

The answer for me has always been *moderation*. I don't expect you to eat pizza three times a day, every single day, for months at a time. I also don't recommend that you *only* eat pizza; that's just not my style. I hope that you will enjoy these pizzas as part of a lifetime healthy eating plan, that you will serve them alongside complementary dishes—salads, soups, non-pizza entrees—and that your daily menu will include a healthy number of fruit and vegetable servings as well.

I created Healthy Exchanges to share my "common folk" healthy recipes and common sense approach to healthier living. These pizza recipes are part of that plan, but only you and your health-care provider can decide what's right for you.

Eating for Pleasure

While I was working on this book, I thought a lot about how good it feels to enjoy pizza, especially as part of a healthy eating plan that allows you to lose excess weight. Eating pizza gives me a lot of pleasure, and I've served it to enough other people to know that I'm not the only one who loves this food category.

It's not just the basic ingredients that bring me pleasure, either, though I do use the best products I can find, as well as the best fresh foods. It's more a state of mind that I—and others—get into when pizza is on the menu.

I call it "eating for pleasure," and I'm convinced that when we focus on eating the foods we love that are also good for us, we get more from eating than just the nutrients those foods contain.

When we eat for pleasure, I believe that we also get a boost of emotional energy that is felt throughout our bodies. That "energy effect" contributes to an overall positive attitude about our lives, which research has shown makes a substantial difference in our physical and mental health.

So as you turn the pages of this cookbook, looking for the pizzas that will give *you* the most pleasure, let yourself experience happy anticipation. Plan meals with people who will share your positive feelings. Use this book to help make your life the best that it can be, *as you measure it*, and I will feel amply rewarded.

Is It Time for Pizza Yet?

There is nothing like the aroma of a freshly made pizza baking in the oven to alert your taste buds that something really good is on its way! When, minutes later, that pizza comes out of the oven you'll discover that "homemade in the Healthy Exchanges Way" is just as fast as calling to have one delivered to your home.

Not only that, but it's the quickest way I know to get your family running into the kitchen, wondering when dinner will be on the table—and ready to eat!

The pizzas featured in this collection, are healthy, tasty, inexpensive, fun to make, and great to eat! In fact, once you start baking your own pizzas, the takeout delivery person may think you've left town!

Jo Anna

Please note:

In many of my cookbooks, I've included my Healthy Exchanges eating plan, which explains how to use my version of the "exchange" system for planning what to eat and how much to eat for optimum health and weight loss (or maintenance). Because this is a "special-interest" cookbook, I've chosen to focus just on the recipes in this volume. If this is your first Healthy Exchanges cookbook, please check one of my other books for an explanation of the exchange system and an abundance of healthy cooking tips! Good recent choices include *The Open Road Cookbook* or *Cooking Healthy with a Man in Mind.*

A Peek Into My Healthy Exchanges Pantry

I do almost all of my shopping at a supermarket in my small town of DeWitt, Iowa. If I can't find it there, I don't use it in my recipes. I want you to be able to make any and all of these dishes without struggling to locate a particular ingredient. That's what it means to cook *The Healthy Exchanges Way*.

That said, I have tested brands from many different manufacturers, looking for the healthiest, tastiest, and easiest to get items that deliver the most flavor for the least amount of fat, sugar, or calories. I update this list for every cookbook and for my newsletter readers every year in the March issue. If you find others you like as well *or better*, please use them. This is only a guide to make shopping and cooking easier for you.

Here are my preferred ingredients and brands, as of this time:

Egg substitute—*Egg Beaters*
Fat-free plain yogurt—*Dannon*
Nonfat dry milk powder—*Carnation*
Evaporated fat-free milk—*Carnation*
Fat-free milk
Fat-free cottage cheese
Fat-free cream cheese—*Philadelphia*
Fat-free half & half—*Land O Lakes*
Fat-free mayonnaise—*Kraft*

Fat-free dressings—*Kraft*
No-fat sour cream—*Land O Lakes*
"Diet" margarine—*I Can't Believe It's Not Butter! Light*
Cooking sprays
   Olive oil– and butter-flavored—*Pam*
   Butter-flavored—for spritzing *after* cooking—*I Can't Believe
   It's Not Butter!*
Cooking oil—*Puritan Canola Oil*
Reduced-calorie whipped topping—*Cool Whip Lite* or *Free*
White sugar substitute—*Splenda*
Baking mix—*Bisquick Heart Smart*
Quick oats—*Quaker*
Graham cracker crumbs—*Nabisco Honey Maid*
Sugar-free pancake syrup—*Log Cabin* or *Cary's*
Parmesan cheese—*Kraft Reduced Fat Parmesan Style Grated*
Reduced-fat cheese (shredded and sliced)—*Kraft 2%
   Reduced Fat*
Processed cheese—*Velveeta Light*
Shredded frozen potatoes—*Mr. Dell's* or *Ore Ida*
Reduced-fat peanut butter—*Peter Pan, Skippy,* or *Jif*
Spreadable fruit spread—*Welch's* or *Smucker's*
Chicken and beef broth—*Swanson*
Dry beef or chicken bouillon—*Wyler's Granules Instant
   Bouillon*
Tomato sauce—*Hunt's*
Canned soups—*Healthy Request*
Tomato juice—*Healthy Request*
Ketchup—*Heinz No Salt Added*
Pastrami and corned beef—*Carl Buddig Lean*
Luncheon meats—*Healthy Choice* or *Oscar Mayer*
Ham—*Dubuque 97% Fat Free* or *Healthy Choice*
Bacon bits—*Oscar Mayer* or *Hormel*
Kielbasa sausage and frankfurters—*Healthy Choice* or *Oscar
   Mayer Light*
Canned white chicken, packed in water—*Swanson*
Canned tuna, packed in water—*Starkist*
Canned salmon, packed in water—*Starkist*
95 to 97% lean ground sirloin beef or turkey breast

Crackers—*Nabisco Soda Fat Free* and *Ritz Reduced Fat*
Reduced-calorie bread (40 calories per slice)
Small hamburger buns (80 calories per bun)
Rice—instant, regular, and wild—*Minute Rice*
Instant potato flakes
Noodles, spaghetti, macaroni, and rotini pasta
Salsa
Pickle relish—dill, sweet, and hotdog
Mustard—Dijon, prepared yellow, and spicy
Unsweetened apple juice—*Musselman's*
Reduced-calorie cranberry juice cocktail—*Ocean Spray*
Unsweetened orange juice—*Simply Orange*
Unsweetened applesauce—*Musselman's*
Fruit—fresh, frozen, and canned in fruit juice
Vinegar—cider and distilled white
Lemon and lime juice (in small plastic fruit-shaped bottles,
    found in produce section)
Diet lemon-lime soda pop—*Diet Mountain Dew Caffeine Free*
Instant fruit beverage mixes—*Crystal Light*
Reduced-calorie chocolate syrup—*Hershey's Lite Syrup*
Sugar-free and fat-free ice cream—*Wells' Blue Bunny*

Remember, these are my suggestions. You are always free to use other national or local brands. Just keep in mind that if your choice is higher in fats and carbs, then you must adjust the recipe nutritional data accordingly.

If you keep your pantry stocked with these products, you can whip up any recipe in this cookbook. I suggest you start a running list, and whenever you use up anything (or start to run low), remember to make a note of it. Your shopping trips will become quicker and thriftier!

JoAnna's Top Tips
for Perfect Pizzas

1. If the recipe calls for an 8-ounce can of refrigerated crescent rolls, do NOT use the inexpensive store brands! It really is a case of penny-wise and pound-foolish, as the generic store brands often don't cover the pan completely. Trust me, if you try to make it "fit," you'll end up with an ugly mess instead of a smooth crust.

2. If the recipe calls for an 11-ounce can of refrigerated Pillsbury's Crusty French Loaf, it usually works best to lightly spray the "crust" and then bake for 6 to 8 minutes, to "set" the crust. This helps keep the bottom from getting soggy at serving time.

3. Speaking of soggy bottoms, it is very important to not skip the step of placing the baking sheet on a wire rack and allowing the pizza to set for a few minutes. This lets the heat escape from the bottom of the pan, thereby not allowing it to seep up through the top and making the crust "soft" in the process.

4. While it may be harder to find in smaller grocery stores, the refrigerated Pillsbury Pizza Crust may be used in place of French Loaf. However, it's not quite as thick and a bit "tougher" to cut than French Loaf. The French Loaf weighs 11 ounces and the Pizza Crust is only 10 ounces, but the nutrients are almost the same.

5. When chopping veggies for your pizza, you may prefer using a cutting board and knife instead of a food processor or

chopping gadget. When you use a processor or chopper, it's very easy to cut the veggies too fine. Be careful that you'll still be able to recognize what you chopped after it's cooked!

6. Most of the entrée pizzas can be turned into appetizers if you wish to include them in party menus. Also, many of the appetizer pizzas can be cut into larger pieces and served at suppertime, if you're not planning on hosting a party.

7. If you have leftover pizza, you can refrigerate it for a day or two, covered in plastic wrap or inside a storage container. Then, when you're ready to enjoy it all over again, you have several options for reheating. First, you may want to purchase one of those special microwave dishes that crisps the bottom of whatever you're cooking or baking. Or, if you own one of those electric pizza baking machines (like the Presto Pizzazz Pizza Oven) that goes around in circles and both heats the top and crisps the bottom, use that. Now, if you're *very* careful, you can put your pizza on a paper plate and microwave it for a short time—start with thirty seconds. Check it, and repeat as necessary. You can also use your regular oven or toaster oven, placing your pizza slice on a metal cookie sheet for reheating. Preheat first to 350 degrees and watch the leftovers carefully so they don't burn.

Yes, But How Much Should It Be? A Healthy Exchanges Chopping Chart

Ever since I began sharing recipes all those years ago, readers have asked me to clarify what I mean by a particular size vegetable. They've also wanted to know if it was okay to use a little bit more of this or that in a specific recipe, rather than throw it away or freeze it.

I decided to provide you with a chart based on my experience preparing thousands of recipes over the years. I hope this will make it even easier to stir up Healthy Exchanges recipes each and every day. Now, everyone's idea of what a medium onion is might be slightly different. Some may think that it should chop up to ½ cup; others may believe that it produces at least a cup or even more. So to help you get a sense of a realistic "output" for my recipes, I've compiled the following chopping chart.

Just remember that in most cases we're talking about veggies with very minimal calorie counts. If your "medium" onion chops up to more than I suggest it should, you have my blessing to use it all. However, that does *not* mean that you can replace a small head of cabbage with a large one and expect the final quantity of the recipe to be the same!

Fruits
 Apple:
  Medium = 1 cup chopped
 Pear:
  Medium = 1 cup chopped
 Peach:
  Medium = ¾ cup chopped

Vegetables
 Broccoli:
  Small = 3 cups chopped
  Medium = 5 cups chopped
  Large = 7 cups chopped
 Cabbage:
  Small = 4 cups chopped
  Medium = 6 cups chopped
  Large = 8 cups chopped
 Cauliflower:
  Small = 3 cups chopped
  Medium = 5 cups chopped
  Large = 7 cups chopped
 Carrots:
  Medium = ⅓ cup chopped
  Large = ⅔ cup chopped
 Celery:
  Medium stalk = ⅓ cup chopped
 Cucumber:
  Small = 1 cup chopped
  Medium = 2 cups chopped
 Green or Red Bell Pepper:
  Small = ⅓ cup chopped
  Medium = ½ cup chopped
  Large = ¾ cup chopped
 Lettuce:
  Small = 4 cups shredded
  Medium = 6 cups shredded

Onion:
  Small = ½ cup chopped
  Medium = ¾ cup chopped
  Large = 1 cup chopped
Potato:
  5-ounce raw = ¾ cup chopped
Tomato:
  Medium = ¾ cup chopped
  Large = 1 cup chopped
Turnip:
  Medium = ¾ cup chopped
Zucchini:
  Small = 1 cup chopped
  Medium = 2 cups chopped

JoAnna's Ten Commandments of Successful Cooking

A very important part of any journey is knowing where you are going and the best way to get there. If you plan and prepare before you start to cook, you should reach mealtime with foods to write home about!

1. **Read the entire recipe from start to finish** and be sure you understand the process involved. Check that you have all the equipment you will need *before* you begin.

2. **Check the ingredient list** and be sure you have *everything* and in the amounts required. Keep cooking sprays handy—while they're not listed as ingredients, I use them all the time (just a quick squirt!).

3. **Set out** *all* **the ingredients and equipment needed** to prepare the recipe on the counter near you *before* you start. Remember that old saying *A stitch in time saves nine*? It applies in the kitchen, too.

4. **Do as much advance preparation as possible** before actually cooking. Chop, cut, grate, or do whatever is

needed to prepare the ingredients and have them ready before you start to mix. Turn the oven on at least ten minutes before putting food in to bake, to allow the oven to preheat to the proper temperature.

5. **Use a kitchen timer** to tell you when the cooking or baking time is up. Because stove temperatures vary slightly by manufacturer, you may want to set your timer for five minutes less than the suggested time just to prevent overcooking. Check the progress of your dish at that time, then decide if you need the additional minutes or not.

6. **Measure carefully.** Use glass measures for liquids and metal or plastic cups for dry ingredients. My recipes are based on standard measurements. Unless I tell you it's a scant or full cup, measure the cup level.

7. **For best results, follow the recipe instructions exactly.** Feel free to substitute ingredients that *don't tamper* with the basic chemistry of the recipe, but be sure to leave key ingredients alone. For example, you could substitute sugar-free instant chocolate pudding for sugar-free instant butterscotch pudding, but if you used a six-serving package when a four-serving package was listed in the ingredients, or you used instant when cook-and-serve is required, you won't get the right result.

8. **Clean up as you go.** It is much easier to wash a few items at a time than to face a whole counter of dirty dishes later. The same is true for spills on the counter or floor.

9. **Be careful about doubling or halving a recipe.** Though many recipes can be altered successfully to serve more or fewer people, *many cannot.* This is especially true when it comes to spices and liquids. If you try to double a recipe that calls for 1 teaspoon pumpkin-pie spice, for example, and you double the spice, you may end up with a too-spicy taste. I usually suggest increasing spices or liquid by 1½ times when doubling a recipe. If it tastes a little bland to you, you can increase the spice to 1¾ times the origi-

nal amount the next time you prepare the dish. Remember: You can always add more, but you can't take it out after it's stirred in.

The same is true with liquid ingredients. If you wanted to **triple** a main dish recipe because you were planning to serve a crowd, you might think you should use three times as much of every ingredient. Don't, or you could end up with soup instead! If the original recipe calls for 1¾ cups tomato sauce, I'd suggest using 3½ cups when you **triple** the recipe (or 2¾ cups if you **double** it). You'll still have a good-tasting dish that won't run all over the plate.

10. **Write your reactions next to each recipe once you've served it.**

Yes, that's right, I'm giving you permission to write in this book. It's yours, after all. Ask yourself: Did everyone like it? Did you have to add another half teaspoon of chili seasoning to please your family, who like to live on the spicier side of the street? You may even want to rate the recipe on a scale of 1 ☆ to 4 ☆, depending on what you thought of it. (Four stars would be the top rating— and I hope you'll feel that way about many of my recipes.) Jotting down your comments while they are fresh in your mind will help you personalize the recipe to your own taste the next time you prepare it.

The Recipes

How to Read a Healthy Exchanges Recipe

The Healthy Exchanges Nutritional Analysis

Before using these recipes, you may wish to consult your physician or health-care provider to be sure they are appropriate for you. The information in this book is not intended to take the place of any medical advice. It reflects my experiences, studies, research, and opinions regarding healthy eating.

Each recipe includes nutritional information calculated in three ways:

Healthy Exchanges Weight Loss Choices or Exchanges
Calories; Fat, Protein, Carbohydrates, and Fiber in grams;
    Sodium and Calcium in milligrams
Diabetic Exchanges
Carb Choices for those who prefer to count their carbs

In every Healthy Exchanges recipe, the Diabetic Exchanges have been calculated by a registered dietitian. All the other calculations were done by computer, using the Food Processor II software.

25

When the ingredient listing gives more than one choice, the first ingredient listed is the one used in the recipe analysis. Due to inevitable variations in the ingredients you choose to use, the nutritional values should be considered approximate.

The annotation "(limited)" following Protein counts in some recipes indicates that consumption of whole eggs should be limited to four per week.

Please note the following symbols:

☆ This star means read the recipe's directions carefully for special instructions about **division** of ingredients.

❋ This symbol indicates **FREEZES WELL.**

Appealing
Appetizer Pizzas

I t's party time, and what better way to get a party going than to serve your guests a selection of delectable pizza dishes? They're perfect for eating while mingling, they can be eaten with one hand (in case you're holding a drink in the other hand!), and instead of filling you up, they simply and deliciously "awaken" the appetite! Of course, if your guests gobble down enough of them, they'll not only be sure they've had a meal, they'll know they've dined on fresh, flavorful foods that surpass anything you could get with a phone call to your local pizza joint.

Just as you always assemble your guest list with care, it can be fun to figure out which of these recipes will dazzle your friends and family at a festive buffet or impromptu party. If you're feeling a little "South of the Border," choose from *Mexican Pizza Bites* or *Mini Mexican Pizza Appetizers;* if you want to impress new friends or show old pals how much you cherish their friendship, go for *Pineapple Chicken Salad Appetizers* or *Shrimp Cocktail Pizza Bites.* And you can never go wrong serving *Grande Bacon Pizza Bites* or *Gazpacho Appetizer Pizza*—they're tasty, fun, and fabulous!

Tex-Mex Appetizer Pizza

For a Super Bowl party or after-school snack, what could be better than these spicy treats? They're ready fast, and they're full of flavor!

◐ Serves 12 (2 pieces each)

> 1 (8-ounce) can Pillsbury Reduced Fat Crescent Rolls
> 1 (8-ounce) can Hunt's Tomato Sauce
> ½ cup chunky salsa (mild, medium, or hot)
> ½ cup finely chopped onion
> 1 tablespoon Splenda Granular
> 1 teaspoon chili seasoning
> 1 cup frozen whole-kernel corn, thawed
> ½ cup sliced ripe olives
> 1½ cups shredded Kraft reduced-fat Cheddar cheese

Preheat oven to 375 degrees. Spray a rimmed 9-by-13-inch baking sheet with butter-flavored cooking spray. Unroll crescent rolls and carefully pat into prepared baking sheet, being sure to seal perforations. Bake for 5 minutes. Meanwhile, in a small bowl, combine tomato sauce and salsa. Stir in onion, Splenda, and chili seasoning. Spread sauce mixture evenly over partially baked crust. Sprinkle corn, olives, and Cheddar cheese evenly over top. Continue baking for 7 to 9 minutes or until crust is golden brown and cheese is melted. Place baking sheet on a wire rack and let set for 5 minutes. Cut into 24 pieces.

HINT: Thaw corn by rinsing in a colander under hot water for 1 minute.

Each serving equals:

HE: ¾ Bread • ⅔ Protein • ½ Vegetable • ¼ Fat • 7 Optional Calories

147 Calories • 7 gm Fat • 6 gm Protein • 15 gm Carbohydrate • 385 mg Sodium • 118 mg Calcium • 1 gm Fiber

DIABETIC EXCHANGES: 1 Starch • 1 Meat • ½ Vegetable • ½ Fat

CARB CHOICES: 1

Mini Mexican Pizza Appetizers

Here's a way to combine two food-loving cultures in one tasty dish—the crispy crust from Italy, and the topping from south of the border! *Olé!* ☻ Serves 5 (2 pieces each)

> 1 (7.5-ounce) can Pillsbury refrigerated buttermilk biscuits
> ½ cup reduced-sodium ketchup
> 1 teaspoon taco seasoning
> ½ cup finely chopped green bell pepper
> ½ cup finely chopped fresh mushrooms
> ¼ cup finely chopped onion
> 1¼ cups shredded Kraft reduced-fat Cheddar cheese

Preheat oven to 450 degrees. Spray a large baking sheet with butter-flavored cooking spray. Separate dough into 10 biscuits. Place biscuits on prepared baking sheet and flatten each into a 4-inch circle. Slightly turn outside edge of each circle up, forming a rim. In a small bowl, combine ketchup and taco seasoning. Evenly spread about 1½ tablespoons ketchup mixture over top of each biscuit. In a small bowl, combine green pepper, mushrooms, and onion. Evenly sprinkle 2 tablespoons vegetable mixture over top of each appetizer. Sprinkle 2 tablespoons Cheddar cheese over top of each. Bake for 6 to 8 minutes or until biscuit cups are golden brown and cheese is melted. Serve at once.

Each serving equals:

HE: 1½ Bread • 1 Protein • ½ Vegetable • ¼ Slider • 5 Optional Calories

250 Calories • 10 gm Fat • 12 gm Protein • 28 gm Carbohydrate • 501 mg Sodium • 224 mg Calcium • 1 gm Fiber

DIABETIC EXCHANGES: 2 Starch/Carbohydrate • 1 Meat • ½ Vegetable

CARB CHOICES: 2

Grande Bacon Pizza Bites

What a fun, light meal these would make, as well as a spirited change from a grilled cheese sandwich. I always use real bacon bits—just enough to supply that "nothing-else-will-do" tangy flavor.   ☻   Serves 4 (4 each)

 ¼ cup Kraft fat-free mayonnaise
 1 cup chunky salsa (mild, medium, or hot)
 ¼ cup Oscar Mayer or Hormel Real Bacon Bits
 1 teaspoon taco seasoning
 4 (6-inch) flour tortillas
 ½ cup shredded Kraft reduced-fat Cheddar cheese

Preheat oven to 415 degrees. Spray an 11-by-15-inch jelly-roll pan with butter-flavored cooking spray. In a small bowl, combine mayonnaise, salsa, bacon bits, and taco seasoning. Evenly spread mayonnaise mixture over tortillas. Sprinkle 2 tablespoons Cheddar cheese over top of each. Place tortillas on prepared pan. Bake for 10 to 12 minutes or until golden brown and cheese is melted. Cut each into 4 wedges. Serve at once.

Each serving equals:

HE: 1 Bread • 1 Protein • ½ Vegetable • 10 Optional Calories

184 Calories • 8 gm Fat • 8 gm Protein • 20 gm Carbohydrate •
764 mg Sodium • 126 mg Calcium • 2 gm Fiber

DIABETIC EXCHANGES: 1 Starch • 1 Meat • ½ Vegetable

CARB CHOICES: 1

Vegetable-Cheese French Pizza Snacks

"Eat your vegetables," Mom always said, but I bet even she would be surprised at how easy it is to get kids to gobble them up when they're served as part of a delectable pizza topping! Yum, yum! Or should I say "Ooh-la-la?" ☻ Serves 4 (2 slices each)

⅓ cup Kraft fat-free mayonnaise
1 teaspoon Italian seasoning
1 teaspoon dried onion flakes
¾ cup shredded Kraft reduced-fat mozzarella cheese
½ cup finely shredded carrots
¼ cup finely diced celery
8 slices reduced-calorie French or white bread, toasted

Preheat oven to 350 degrees. Spray a large baking sheet with butter-flavored cooking spray. In a medium bowl, combine mayonnaise, Italian seasoning, and onion flakes. Add mozzarella cheese, carrots, and celery. Mix well to combine. Spread a full 1 tablespoon of cheese mixture over each slice of toast. Arrange toast slices on prepared baking sheet. Bake for 5 to 7 minutes or until cheese is melted. Serve at once.

Each serving equals:

HE: 1 Bread • ¾ Protein • ⅓ Vegetable • 13 Optional Calories

157 Calories • 5 gm Fat • 10 gm Protein • 18 gm Carbohydrate • 528 mg Sodium • 186 mg Calcium • 1 gm Fiber

DIABETIC EXCHANGES: 1 Starch • 1 Meat

CARB CHOICES: 1

Veggie Pizza Appetizers

Talk about a super salad on a crust, and you've described these va-va-va-voom vegetable pizza delights! These taste oh-so-good—and they're good for you, too!　　●　　Serves 12 (2 pieces each)

> 1 (8-ounce) can Pillsbury Reduced Fat Crescent Rolls
> 1 (8-ounce) package Philadelphia fat-free cream cheese
> ½ cup Land O Lakes no-fat sour cream
> ½ cup Kraft fat-free mayonnaise
> 1 teaspoon dried dill weed
> 1 teaspoon dried onion flakes
> 1 cup finely chopped fresh broccoli
> 1 cup grated carrots
> 1 cup finely chopped fresh cauliflower
> ¼ cup finely chopped green onion
> ¼ cup finely chopped red bell pepper
> ¾ cup shredded Kraft reduced-fat Cheddar cheese

Preheat oven to 375 degrees. Spray a rimmed 9-by-13-inch baking sheet with butter-flavored cooking spray. Unroll crescent rolls and carefully pat into prepared baking sheet, being sure to seal perforations. Bake for 8 to 10 minutes or until crust is golden brown. Place baking sheet on a wire rack and allow to cool completely. In a medium bowl, stir cream cheese with a sturdy spoon until soft. Stir in sour cream, mayonnaise, dill weed, and onion flakes. Spread mixture evenly over cooled crust. In a large bowl, combine broccoli, carrots, cauliflower, green onion, and red pepper. Arrange vegetable mixture evenly over cream cheese mixture. Sprinkle Cheddar cheese evenly over top. Refrigerate for at least 30 minutes. Cut into 24 pieces.

Each serving equals:

HE: ⅔ Bread • ⅔ Protein • ⅔ Vegetable • 16 Optional Calories

125 Calories • 5 gm Fat • 6 gm Protein • 14 gm Carbohydrate • 351 mg Sodium • 128 mg Calcium • 1 gm Fiber

DIABETIC EXCHANGES: 1 Starch • 1 Meat • ½ Vegetable

CARB CHOICES: 1

French Salad Pizza Appetizers

Surprised to find lettuce and tomato on top of your pizza? It's popular with people who enjoy a little extra crunch with their munchies! I think the peas are maybe the most unexpected flavor in this dish—but I think they work.

◐ Serves 12 (2 pieces each)

> 1 (8-ounce) can Pillsbury Reduced Fat Crescent Rolls
> 1 (8-ounce) package Philadelphia fat-free cream cheese
> ⅓ cup Kraft fat-free mayonnaise
> 1 tablespoon dried onion flakes
> 3 cups shredded lettuce
> 1 cup shredded carrots
> 1 cup frozen peas, thawed
> ¼ cup diced green onion
> ⅓ cup Kraft Fat Free French Dressing
> 1 (2-ounce) jar chopped pimiento, drained
> ½ cup shredded Kraft reduced-fat Cheddar cheese
> ½ cup shredded Kraft reduced-fat mozzarella cheese

Preheat oven to 375 degrees. Spray a rimmed 9-by-13-inch baking sheet with olive oil–flavored cooking spray. Unroll crescent rolls and carefully pat into prepared pan, being sure to seal perforations. Lightly spray top of crust with olive oil–flavored cooking spray. Bake for 8 to 10 minutes or until crust is golden brown. Place baking sheet on a wire rack and allow to cool completely. In a small bowl, stir cream cheese with a sturdy spoon until soft. Add mayonnaise and onion flakes. Mix well to combine. Evenly spread mixture over cooled crust. In a large bowl, combine lettuce, carrots, peas, and green onion. In a small bowl, combine French dressing and pimiento. Drizzle evenly over lettuce mixture. Toss gently to coat. Evenly spread lettuce mixture over cream cheese mixture. Sprinkle Cheddar and mozzarella cheeses evenly over top. Refrigerate for at least 1 hour. Cut into 24 pieces.

HINT: Thaw peas by rinsing in a colander under hot water for 1
    minute.

Each serving equals:

HE: ⅔ Bread • ⅔ Protein • ½ Vegetable • 16 Optional Calories

141 Calories • 5 gm Fat • 8 gm Protein • 16 gm Carbohydrate •
423 mg Sodium • 166 mg Calcium • 2 gm Fiber

DIABETIC EXCHANGES: 1 Starch • 1 Meat • ½ Vegetable

CARB CHOICES: 1

Stuffed Cheese Pita Pizza Snacks

Instead of commercial stuffed crust pizza, which is high in fat and calories, why not please your taste buds and your tummy by trying these? Pick the pita bread you enjoy most, turn up the salsa heat if that's your thing, and mmm-mmm!   ○   Serves 4 (2 each)

2 pita bread rounds
½ cup chunky salsa (mild, medium, or hot)
2 tablespoons reduced-sodium ketchup
1 teaspoon pizza or Italian seasoning
1 cup shredded Kraft reduced-fat Cheddar cheese

Plug in and generously spray both sides of double-sided electric contact grill with olive oil–flavored cooking spray and preheat for 5 minutes. Meanwhile, cut pita breads in half and then cut each half in half again to form 8 wedges. In a small bowl, combine salsa, ketchup, pizza seasoning, and Cheddar cheese. Evenly spread about 1½ tablespoons sauce mixture between each wedge. Arrange wedges evenly on prepared grill. Lightly spray tops with olive oil–flavored cooking spray. Close lid and grill for 4 to 5 minutes. Repeat, if necessary. Serve at once.

Each serving equals:

HE: 1 Bread • 1 Protein • ¼ Vegetable • 8 Optional Calories

187 Calories • 7 gm Fat • 10 gm Protein • 21 gm Carbohydrate • 572 mg Sodium • 227 mg Calcium • 1 gm Fiber

DIABETIC EXCHANGES: 1½ Starch • 1 Meat

CARB CHOICES: 1½

Bacon, Lettuce, and Tomato Appetizers

If your idea of heaven is a perfect BLT, then you might want to start your pizza pleasure odyssey with these appealing yummies. They're great for one of those nights when all you want to do after work is watch *CSI* and nibble on a light supper!

☻ Serves 12 (2 pieces each)

> 1 (8-ounce) can Pillsbury Reduced Fat Crescent Rolls
> ¾ cup Kraft fat-free mayonnaise
> 2 teaspoons dried onion flakes
> 1½ teaspoons dried basil
> 2 cups finely shredded lettuce
> 2 cups chopped unpeeled fresh tomatoes
> ½ cup Oscar Mayer or Hormel Real Bacon Bits
> 2 slices reduced-calorie bread, toasted and made into
>   crumbs

Preheat oven to 375 degrees. Spray a rimmed 9-by-13-inch baking sheet with butter-flavored cooking spray. Unroll crescent rolls and carefully pat into prepared baking sheet, being sure to seal perforations. Bake for 8 to 10 minutes or until crust is golden brown. Place baking sheet on a wire rack and allow to cool completely. In a medium bowl, combine mayonnaise, onion flakes, and basil. Evenly spread mixture over cooled crust. Sprinkle lettuce, tomatoes, bacon bits, and bread crumbs evenly over top. Refrigerate for at least 1 hour. Cut into 24 pieces.

Each serving equals:

HE: ⅔ Bread • ½ Vegetable • ⅓ Protein • 10 Optional Calories

163 Calories • 5 gm Fat • 4 gm Protein • 13 gm Carbohydrate •
406 mg Sodium • 11 mg Calcium • 1 gm Fiber

DIABETIC EXCHANGES: 1 Starch • ½ Vegetable • ½ Fat • ½ Meat

CARB CHOICES: 1

Italian Salad Appetizer Pizza

Ciao, baby, are you hungry for a little taste of Rome tonight? Take a quick trip abroad, culinary style, when you fix these flavorful bits of crisp pleasure. ☉ Serves 12 (2 pieces each)

1 (11-ounce) can Pillsbury refrigerated low-fat French Loaf
1 teaspoon Italian seasoning
¼ cup Kraft Reduced Fat Parmesan Style Grated Topping
4 cups torn romaine lettuce
1½ cups chopped fresh tomatoes
½ cup chopped red onion
½ cup sliced ripe olives
1¼ cups shredded Kraft reduced-fat mozzarella cheese
¼ cup Kraft Fat Free Italian Dressing
1 tablespoon Splenda Granular

Preheat oven to 375 degrees. Unroll French loaf and pat into an ungreased rimmed 10-by-15-inch baking sheet and up sides of pan to form a rim. Lightly spray top with olive oil–flavored cooking spray. Evenly sprinkle Italian seasoning and Parmesan cheese over crust. Bake for 8 to 12 minutes or until crust is golden brown. Meanwhile, in a large bowl, combine lettuce, tomatoes, onion, olives, and mozzarella cheese. Add Italian dressing and Splenda. Mix well to coat. Remove baking sheet from oven and place on a wire rack. Evenly arrange salad mixture over hot crust. Drizzle any remaining dressing evenly over top. Cut into 24 pieces. Serve at once.

Each serving equals:

HE: ¾ Bread • ⅔ Vegetable • ½ Protein • 10 Optional Calories

124 Calories • 4 gm Fat • 5 gm Protein • 17 gm Carbohydrate • 378 mg Sodium • 111 mg Calcium • 2 gm Fiber

DIABETIC EXCHANGES: 1 Starch • ½ Vegetable • ½ Meat

CARB CHOICES: 1

Tomato Mozzarella Bites

It's the classic cheese that stretches and bubbles and makes pizza irresistible. Combined with fresh tomatoes and some fresh basil, it's a true aphrodisiac—or at the least, a supremely satisfying snack.

○ Serves 8 (3 pieces each)

> 1 (11-ounce) can Pillsbury refrigerated low-fat French Loaf
> 1 cup Kraft fat-free mayonnaise
> ¼ cup Kraft Reduced Fat Parmesan Style Grated Topping
> 2 teaspoons dried onion flakes
> 4 cups peeled and chopped fresh tomatoes
> ¼ cup finely chopped fresh basil
> 2¼ cups shredded Kraft reduced-fat mozzarella cheese

Preheat oven to 375 degrees. Spray a rimmed 10-by-15-inch baking sheet with olive oil–flavored cooking spray. Unroll French loaf and pat into prepared baking sheet and up sides of pan to form a rim. Lightly spray top of crust with olive oil–flavored cooking spray. Bake for 6 minutes. Meanwhile, in a medium bowl, combine mayonnaise, Parmesan cheese, and onion flakes. Evenly spread mixture over partially baked crust. Arrange tomatoes evenly over mayonnaise mixture. Sprinkle basil and mozzarella cheese evenly over top. Continue baking for 6 to 8 minutes or until crust is golden brown and cheese is melted. Place baking sheet on a wire rack and let set for 5 minutes. Cut into 24 pieces.

Each serving equals:

HE: 1¼ Protein • 1 Bread • 1 Vegetable • ¼ Slider

211 Calories • 7 gm Fat • 11 gm Protein • 26 gm Carbohydrate • 661 mg Sodium • 214 mg Calcium • 2 gm Fiber

DIABETIC EXCHANGES: 1½ Starch • 1 Meat • 1 Vegetable

CARB CHOICES: 2

Olive Pizza Appetizers

They're the "fruit" of the Mediterranean, and they come in so many scrumptious varieties, it's tempting to put some on every pizza I prepare! Yes, they're a bit salty (if you're watching your sodium), but since I divide one cup among twelve servings, you won't be eating too much! ☉ Serves 12 (2 pieces each)

> 1 (11-ounce) can Pillsbury refrigerated low-fat French Loaf
> 1 (8-ounce) can Hunt's Tomato Sauce
> 1½ teaspoons pizza or Italian seasoning
> 1 tablespoon Splenda Granular
> ½ cup Kraft Reduced Fat Parmesan Style Grated Topping
> 1 cup sliced ripe olives

Preheat oven to 375 degrees. Spray a rimmed 10-by-15-inch baking sheet with olive oil–flavored cooking spray. Unroll French loaf and pat into prepared baking sheet and up sides of pan to form a rim. Lightly spray top of crust with olive oil–flavored cooking spray. Bake for 6 minutes. Meanwhile, in a medium bowl, combine tomato sauce, pizza seasoning, and Splenda. Evenly spread mixture over partially baked crust. Sprinkle Parmesan cheese evenly over sauce. Arrange olives evenly over top. Continue baking for 8 to 10 minutes or until crust is golden brown. Place baking sheet on a wire rack and let set for 5 minutes. Cut into 24 pieces.

HINT: Good warm or cold.

Each serving equals:

HE: ⅔ Bread • ⅓ Fat • ⅓ Vegetable • 11 Optional Calories

99 Calories • 3 gm Fat • 3 gm Protein • 15 gm Carbohydrate • 413 mg Sodium • 34 mg Calcium • 2 gm Fiber

DIABETIC EXCHANGES: 1 Starch • ½ Fat • ½ Vegetable

CARB CHOICES: 1

Mediterranean Appetizers

The growing season in countries who share a coastline with the Mediterranean Sea is long, and the typical menu enticing. Enjoy these festive delights and imagine you're sailing in a yacht, the wind in your hair, and all your stress left far behind!

○ Serves 8 (3 pieces each)

1 (11-ounce) can Pillsbury refrigerated low-fat French Loaf
1 (8-ounce) package Philadelphia fat-free cream cheese
¼ cup Kraft fat-free mayonnaise
½ teaspoon dried minced garlic
½ teaspoon dried oregano
2 cups finely shredded fresh spinach
1 cup finely chopped tomatoes
½ cup sliced ripe olives
1½ cups crumbled feta cheese

Preheat oven to 375 degrees. Spray a rimmed 10-by-15-inch baking sheet with olive oil–flavored cooking spray. Unroll French loaf and pat into prepared baking sheet and up sides of pan to form a rim. Lightly spray top of crust with olive oil–flavored cooking spray. Bake for 8 to 10 minutes or until crust is golden brown. Place baking sheet on a wire rack and allow to cool completely. In a medium bowl, stir cream cheese with a sturdy spoon until soft. Stir in mayonnaise, garlic, and oregano. Evenly spread mixture over cooled crust. Arrange spinach, tomatoes, and olives evenly over cream cheese mixture. Sprinkle feta cheese evenly over top. Cut into 24 pieces.

Each serving equals:

HE: 1¼ Protein • 1 Bread • ½ Vegetable • 5 Optional Calories

195 Calories • 7 gm Fat • 11 gm Protein • 22 gm Carbohydrate • 751 mg Sodium • 203 mg Calcium • 1 gm Fiber

DIABETIC EXCHANGES: 1 Meat • 1 Starch • ½ Vegetable

CARB CHOICES: 1½

Gazpacho Appetizer Pizza

Instead of liquefying all these luscious veggies, I've topped some piquant pizza treats with them—and what a treat that is! They're beautiful to look at, too.   ● Serves 8 (3 pieces each)

1 (8-ounce) can Pillsbury Reduced Fat Crescent Rolls
1 (8-ounce) package Philadelphia fat-free cream cheese
2 tablespoons Kraft fat-free mayonnaise
½ teaspoon Italian seasoning
1½ cups peeled and diced cucumber
½ cup chopped red bell pepper
1½ cups diced fresh tomatoes
½ cup chopped green onion
2 tablespoons chopped fresh parsley
½ cup Kraft Fat Free Italian Dressing

Preheat oven to 375 degrees. Spray a rimmed 9-by-13-inch baking sheet with olive oil–flavored cooking spray. Unroll crescent rolls and carefully pat into prepared baking sheet, being sure to seal perforations. Bake for 6 to 8 minutes or until crust is light golden brown. Place baking sheet on a wire rack and allow to cool completely. In a medium bowl, stir cream cheese with a sturdy spoon until soft. Stir in mayonnaise and Italian seasoning. Evenly spread mixture over cooled crust. In a large bowl, combine cucumber, red pepper, tomatoes, green onion, and parsley. Add Italian dressing. Mix gently to combine. Sprinkle vegetable mixture evenly over top. Refrigerate for at least 30 minutes. Cut into 24 pieces.

Each serving equals:

HE: 1 Bread • 1 Vegetable • ½ Protein • 11 Optional Calories

128 Calories • 4 gm Fat • 6 gm Protein • 17 gm Carbohydrate • 552 mg Sodium • 84 mg Calcium • 1 gm Fiber

DIABETIC EXCHANGES: 1 Starch • 1 Vegetable • ½ Meat

CARB CHOICES: 1

French Onion Appetizers

If you enjoy the wickedly cheesy classic French onion soup, these "minis" will win your heart as well. These are ideal party food to accompany an evening of conversation with friends and a hot new DVD starring that "Frenchman-by-marriage" Johnny Depp!

◐ Serves 8 (3 pieces each)

> 1 (11-ounce) can Pillsbury refrigerated low-fat French Loaf
> 1 tablespoon + 1 teaspoon I Can't Believe It's Not Butter!
>   Light Margarine
> 4 cups thinly sliced onion
> 1 cup Kraft fat-free mayonnaise
> ½ cup Kraft Reduced Fat Parmesan Style Grated Topping
> 1 tablespoon dried parsley flakes
> 8 (¾-ounce) slices Kraft reduced-fat Swiss cheese

Preheat oven to 375 degrees. In a large skillet sprayed with butter-flavored cooking spray, melt margarine. Stir in onion. Sauté for 6 to 8 minutes. Meanwhile, spray a rimmed 10-by-15-inch baking sheet with butter-flavored cooking spray. Unroll French loaf and pat into prepared baking sheet and up sides of pan to form a rim. Lightly spray top of crust with butter-flavored cooking spray. Bake for 6 minutes. In a medium bowl, combine mayonnaise, Parmesan cheese, and parsley flakes. Evenly spread mixture over partially baked crust. Arrange browned onion evenly over mayonnaise mixture. Evenly arrange Swiss cheese slices over top. Continue baking for 6 to 8 minutes or until crust is golden brown and cheese is melted. Place baking sheet on a wire rack and let set for 5 minutes. Cut into 24 pieces.

Each serving equals:

HE: 1¼ Protein • 1 Bread • 1 Vegetable • ¼ Slider

224 Calories • 8 gm Fat • 10 gm Protein • 28 gm Carbohydrate • 593 mg Sodium • 261 mg Calcium • 2 gm Fiber

DIABETIC EXCHANGES: 1½ Starch/Carbohydrate • 1 Meat • 1 Vegetable

CARB CHOICES: 2

Beet and Feta Appetizers

You don't have to spend a dime on airfare to get the gorgeous taste of the Greek Islands; just pick up a package of feta cheese at your supermarket and combine it with rosy red beets. These are lovely to look at and even more luscious to gobble down!

☻ Serves 8 (3 pieces each)

> 1 (8-ounce) can Pillsbury Reduced Fat Crescent Rolls
> ½ cup Kraft fat-free mayonnaise
> ½ cup Kraft Fat Free Ranch Dressing
> 1 teaspoon dried onion flakes
> 2 teaspoons dried parsley flakes
> 2 teaspoons Splenda Granular
> 2 cups finely shredded lettuce
> 1 (15-ounce) can diced beets, rinsed and drained
> 1 cup frozen peas, thawed
> 1 cup crumbled feta cheese

Preheat oven to 375 degrees. Spray a rimmed 9-by-13-inch baking sheet with butter-flavored cooking spray. Unroll crescent rolls and carefully pat into prepared baking sheet, being sure to seal perforations. Bake for 8 to 12 minutes or until crust is golden brown. Place baking sheet on a wire rack and allow to cool completely. In a medium bowl, combine mayonnaise, Ranch dressing, onion flakes, parsley flakes, and Splenda. Evenly spread mixture over cooled crust. Layer lettuce, beets, and peas evenly over dressing mixture. Sprinkle feta cheese evenly over top. Refrigerate for at least 30 minutes. Cut into 24 pieces.

Each serving equals:

HE: 1¼ Bread • ¾ Vegetable • ½ Protein • ½ Slider • 15 Optional Calories

191 Calories • 7 gm Fat • 6 gm Protein • 26 gm Carbohydrate • 765 mg Sodium • 70 mg Calcium • 2 gm Fiber

DIABETIC EXCHANGES: 1½ Starch/Carbohydrate • 1 Vegetable • ½ Meat

CARB CHOICES: 2

Springtime Appetizers

I promised you pizza all year long, so here's my candidate for a patio party in May, fresh and flavorful and featuring that "taste-of-spring" veggie, fresh asparagus! You can show your friends how much you care by serving these splendid squares.

☻ Serves 8 (3 pieces each)

> 1 (8-ounce) can Pillsbury Reduced Fat Crescent Rolls
> 1 cup Kraft fat-free mayonnaise
> 1 tablespoon lemon juice
> 1 tablespoon Splenda Granular
> 1½ tablespoons chopped fresh parsley or 1½ teaspoons dried parsley flakes
> 3 cups chopped fresh asparagus, cooked, rinsed, and cooled
> ½ cup crumbled feta cheese
> ½ cup Oscar Mayer or Hormel Real Bacon Bits

Preheat oven to 375 degrees. Spray a rimmed 9-by-13-inch baking sheet with olive oil–flavored cooking spray. Unroll crescent rolls and carefully pat into prepared baking sheet, being sure to seal perforations. Lightly spray top of crust with olive oil–flavored cooking spray. Bake for 8 to 12 minutes or until crust is golden brown. Place baking sheet on a wire rack and allow to cool completely. In a medium bowl, combine mayonnaise, lemon juice, Splenda, and parsley. Evenly spread mixture over cooled crust. Sprinkle asparagus, feta cheese, and bacon bits evenly over top. Cut into 24 pieces.

HINT: Do not overcook asparagus!

Each serving equals:

HE: 1 Bread • ¾ Protein • ¾ Vegetable • ¼ Slider • 1 Optional Calorie

193 Calories • 9 gm Fat • 8 gm Protein • 20 gm Carbohydrate • 801 mg Sodium • 66 mg Calcium • 2 gm Fiber

DIABETIC EXCHANGES: 1 Starch • 1 Meat • 1 Vegetable • 1 Fat

CARB CHOICES: 1

Egg Salad Snack Pizza

I know, I know, it's a little off the beaten track when it comes to pizza, but if you love egg salad as much as I do, you'll definitely want to try these! Use your favorite tangy mustard and the best pickle relish you can find for a wonderful result.

◑ Serves 8 (3 pieces each)

> 1 (8-ounce) can Pillsbury Reduced Fat Crescent Rolls
> 8 hard-boiled eggs
> ¾ cup Kraft fat-free mayonnaise
> ¼ cup sweet pickle relish
> 2 teaspoons prepared yellow mustard
> 1 cup finely chopped celery
> 2 cups finely shredded lettuce

Preheat oven to 375 degrees. Spray a rimmed 9-by-13-inch baking sheet with butter-flavored cooking spray. Unroll crescent rolls and carefully pat into prepared sheet, being sure to seal perforations. Bake for 8 to 12 minutes or until crust is light golden brown. Place baking sheet on a wire rack and allow to cool completely. Meanwhile, finely chop eggs. In a large bowl, combine chopped eggs, mayonnaise, pickle relish, mustard, and celery. Evenly spread mixture over cooled crust. Sprinkle shredded lettuce evenly over top. Refrigerate for at least 30 minutes. Cut into 24 pieces.

Each serving equals:

HE: 1 Bread • 1 Protein • ½ Vegetable • ¼ Slider • 3 Optional Calories

198 Calories • 10 gm Fat • 9 gm Protein • 18 gm Carbohydrate • 545 mg Sodium • 40 mg Calcium • 1 gm Fiber

DIABETIC EXCHANGES: 1 Starch • 1 Meat • ½ Vegetable • ½ Fat

CARB CHOICES: 1

Cheesy Tuna Party Squares

If the combination of tuna and cheese rings your chimes, put these on the menu ASAP! What could be tastier than your favorite fish holding hands with yummy cheese and perfectly baked in your oven? Mmm-mmm . . .   ◐   Serves 8 (3 pieces each)

> 1 (8-ounce) can Pillsbury Reduced Fat Crescent Rolls
> ¼ cup Kraft fat-free mayonnaise
> 1 teaspoon lemon juice
> ⅛ teaspoon black pepper
> 1 (6-ounce) can white tuna, packed in water, drained and
>   flaked
> 1 cup shredded Kraft reduced-fat Cheddar cheese
> ¼ cup finely chopped green onion
> 1½ teaspoons dried parsley flakes

Preheat oven to 375 degrees. Spray a rimmed 9-by-13-inch baking sheet with butter-flavored cooking spray. Unroll crescent rolls and carefully pat into prepared baking sheet, being sure to seal perforations. Bake for 6 minutes. Meanwhile, in a medium bowl, combine mayonnaise, lemon juice, and black pepper. Add tuna, Cheddar cheese, onion, and parsley flakes. Mix well to combine. Evenly spread mixture over partially baked crust. Continue baking for 6 to 8 minutes or until crust is golden brown and cheese is melted. Place baking sheet on a wire rack and let set for 5 minutes. Cut into 24 pieces.

Each serving equals:

HE: 1 Protein • 1 Bread • 4 Optional Calories

181 Calories • 9 gm Fat • 11 gm Protein • 14 gm Carbohydrate • 302 mg Sodium • 126 mg Calcium • 1 gm Fiber

DIABETIC EXCHANGES: 1 Meat • 1 Starch • ½ Fat

CARB CHOICES: 1

Shrimp Cocktail Pizza Bites

It's the glamorous appetizer on so many menus, but for once you don't have to eat out to dine well. These are a scrumptious choice for a cocktail party, but they're also great for a family evening at home.

☾ Serves 8 (3 pieces each)

1 (8-ounce) can Pillsbury Reduced Fat Crescent Rolls
1 (8-ounce) package Philadelphia fat-free cream cheese
¼ cup Kraft fat-free mayonnaise
½ cup chili sauce
1 tablespoon prepared horseradish sauce
2 cups finely shredded lettuce
¾ cup finely chopped celery
¼ cup finely chopped green onion
2 (5-ounce) packages frozen shrimp, cooked, cooled, peeled,
    and coarsely chopped
2 tablespoons lemon juice

Preheat oven to 375 degrees. Spray a rimmed 9-by-13-inch baking sheet with butter-flavored cooking spray. Unroll crescent rolls and carefully pat into prepared baking sheet, being sure to seal perforations. Bake for 8 to 12 minutes or until crust is light golden brown. Place baking sheet on a wire rack and allow to cool completely. In a medium bowl, stir cream cheese with a sturdy spoon until soft. Stir in mayonnaise, chili sauce, and horseradish sauce. Evenly spread mixture over cooled crust. In a large bowl, combine lettuce, celery, and green onion. Sprinkle lettuce mixture evenly over dressing mixture. In same bowl, combine shrimp and lemon juice. Evenly sprinkle shrimp over top of lettuce mixture. Refrigerate for at least 30 minutes. Cut into 24 pieces.

Each serving equals:

HE: 1¾ Protein • 1 Bread • ½ Vegetable • ¼ Slider • 6 Optional Calories

193 Calories • 5 gm Fat • 16 gm Protein • 21 gm Carbohydrate •
938 mg Sodium • 102 mg Calcium • 1 gm Fiber

DIABETIC EXCHANGES: 2 Meat • 1 Starch • ½ Vegetable • ½ Fat

CARB CHOICES: 1½

Shrimp and Feta Appetizers

You'll find fabulous feta cheese in many Greek-inspired dishes, but adding shrimp to the mix reminds us that Greece is a country that lives by and off the sea! Enjoy the delectable bounty of the ocean in this sparkling dish! ☻ Serves 8 (3 pieces each)

> 1 (8-ounce) can Pillsbury Reduced Fat Crescent Rolls
> 2 tablespoons olive oil
> 1 (6-ounce) package frozen cooked shrimp, thawed
> ½ teaspoon dried minced garlic
> 1½ cups shredded Kraft reduced-fat mozzarella cheese
> ½ cup sliced ripe olives
> ½ cup crumbled feta cheese
> 1 tablespoon snipped fresh rosemary or 1 teaspoon dried
>   rosemary

Preheat oven to 375 degrees. Spray a rimmed 9-by-13-inch baking sheet with olive oil–flavored cooking spray. Unroll crescent rolls and carefully pat into prepared baking sheet, being sure to seal perforations. Bake for 6 minutes. Meanwhile, pour olive oil into a large skillet sprayed with olive oil–flavored cooking spray. Add shrimp and garlic. Mix well to combine. Cook over medium heat for 2 to 3 minutes or until shrimp turns pink, stirring often. Sprinkle mozzarella cheese evenly over partially baked crust. Evenly spoon shrimp mixture over mozzarella cheese. Sprinkle olives, feta cheese, and rosemary over top. Continue baking for 6 to 8 minutes or until crust is golden brown and cheese is melted. Place baking sheet on a wire rack and let set for 5 minutes. Cut into 24 pieces.

HINT: Good served warm or cold.

Each serving equals:

HE: 2 Protein • 1 Bread • ½ Fat

198 Calories • 10 gm Fat • 13 gm Protein • 14 gm Carbohydrate •
546 mg Sodium • 199 mg Calcium • 1 gm Fiber

DIABETIC EXCHANGES: 2 Meat • 1 Starch • 1 Fat

CARB CHOICES: 1

Crab Appetizer Pizza

If you've never tried what manufacturers call "imitation crab," I think you'll be pleasantly surprised by how tasty it is—and how the texture will win you over. This "surimi," which means "minced fish" in Japanese, is often prepared from mild-flavored fish caught off the coast of Alaska, and does a remarkable job of imitating the real thing.   ◐   Serves 8 (3 pieces each)

1 (8-ounce) can Pillsbury Reduced Fat Crescent Rolls
1 (8-ounce) package Philadelphia fat-free cream cheese
¼ cup Kraft fat-free mayonnaise
2 cups finely shredded fresh spinach
¼ cup chopped green onion
1 teaspoon lemon pepper
1 (6-ounce) package cooked frozen imitation crab, thawed
    and finely chopped

Preheat oven to 375 degrees. Spray a rimmed 9-by-13-inch baking sheet with butter-flavored cooking spray. Unroll crescent rolls and carefully pat into prepared baking sheet, being sure to seal perforations. Bake for 8 to 12 minutes or until crust is golden brown. Place baking sheet on a wire rack and allow to cool completely. Meanwhile, in a large bowl, stir cream cheese with a sturdy spoon until soft. Stir in mayonnaise, spinach, onion, and lemon pepper. Evenly spread mixture over cooled crust. Sprinkle crab evenly over top. Refrigerate for at least 30 minutes. Cut into 24 pieces.

HINT: Thaw crab by rinsing in a colander under hot water for 1 minute.

Each serving equals:

HE: 1 Bread • 1 Protein • ¼ Vegetable • 5 Optional Calories

153 Calories • 5 gm Fat • 9 gm Protein • 18 gm Carbohydrate • 597 mg Sodium • 89 mg Calcium • 1 gm Fiber

DIABETIC EXCHANGES: 1 Starch • 1 Meat • ½ Fat

CARB CHOICES: 1

Country Club Appetizer Pizza

No, Cliff and I don't belong to a country club—I'm not even sure where the nearest one is, out here in DeWitt. But for me, the words have always meant a certain kind of classic, classy dining that is reserved for special occasions. ☻ Serves 8 (3 pieces each)

> 1 (8-ounce) can Pillsbury Reduced Fat Crescent Rolls
> ½ cup Kraft fat-free mayonnaise
> 1 teaspoon lemon juice
> 1 teaspoon dried basil
> 2 cups finely shredded lettuce
> 1½ cups diced cooked turkey breast
> 1 cup shredded Kraft reduced-fat Cheddar cheese
> 1 cup chopped fresh tomatoes
> ¼ cup Oscar Mayer or Hormel Real Bacon Bits

Preheat oven to 450 degrees. Spray a rimmed 9-by-13-inch baking sheet with olive oil–flavored cooking spray. Unroll crescent rolls and carefully pat into prepared baking sheet, being sure to seal perforations. Bake for 5 to 7 minutes. Place baking sheet on a wire rack and allow to cool completely. In a small bowl, combine mayonnaise, lemon juice, and basil. Evenly spread mixture over cooled crust. Layer shredded lettuce, turkey, Cheddar cheese, and tomato evenly over mayonnaise mixture. Sprinkle bacon bits evenly over top. Cut into 24 pieces.

HINT: If you don't have leftovers, purchase a chunk of cooked turkey breast from your local deli.

Each serving equals:

HE: 1¾ Protein • 1 Bread • ½ Vegetable • 10 Optional Calories

218 Calories • 10 gm Fat • 16 gm Protein • 16 gm Carbohydrate •
488 mg Sodium • 118 mg Calcium • 1 gm Fiber

DIABETIC EXCHANGES: 1½ Meat • 1 Starch • ½ Vegetable • ½ Fat

CARB CHOICES: 1

Pineapple Chicken Salad Appetizers

Having recently returned from a sojourn in Hawaii, I'm ready to put pineapple in and on *everything*! Wait, I'm only kidding—but I do love how this sweet tropical fruit (along with my favorite nut, pecans) transforms plain old chicken salad into a feast.

☻ Serves 8 (3 pieces each)

> 1 (8-ounce) can Pillsbury Reduced Fat Crescent Rolls
> 1 (8-ounce) package Philadelphia fat-free
>   cream cheese
> 1 (8-ounce) can crushed pineapple, packed in
>   fruit juice, drained and 2 tablespoons liquid
>   reserved
> 2 cups finely shredded lettuce
> 2 cups diced cooked chicken breast
> 1 cup finely chopped celery
> 2 tablespoons finely chopped onion
> ¼ cup chopped pecans
> ½ cup Kraft fat-free mayonnaise

Preheat oven to 375 degrees. Spray a rimmed 9-by-13-inch baking sheet with butter-flavored cooking spray. Unroll crescent rolls and carefully pat into prepared baking sheet, being sure to seal perforations. Bake for 8 to 12 minutes or until crust is golden brown. Place baking sheet on a wire rack and allow to cool completely. In a medium bowl, stir cream cheese with a sturdy spoon until soft. Stir in pineapple and reserved 2 tablespoons pineapple juice. Evenly spread mixture over cooled crust. Sprinkle shredded lettuce evenly over cream cheese mixture. In a large bowl, combine chicken, celery, onion, and pecans. Add mayonnaise. Mix well to combine. Evenly sprinkle chicken mixture over lettuce. Refrigerate for at least 15 minutes. Cut into 24 pieces.

HINT: If you don't have leftovers, purchase a chunk of cooked chicken breast from your local deli.

Each serving equals:

HE: 1¾ Protein • 1 Bread • ½ Fat • ½ Vegetable • ¼ Fruit •
10 Optional Calories

245 Calories • 9 gm Fat • 18 gm Protein • 23 gm Carbohydrate •
533 mg Sodium • 101 mg Calcium • 2 gm Fiber

DIABETIC EXCHANGES: 2 Meat • 1½ Starch/Carbohydrate • 1 Fat

CARB CHOICES: 1½

Luau Chicken Appetizer Pizza

People definitely eat out more in Hawaii—I mean, outside! Who wouldn't? The weather is magnificent, and the food simply tastes better in the open air. But on those chilly nights when you don't have any more vacation days to dream about, you can still travel to paradise with these!   ☻   Serves 8 (3 pieces each)

> 1 (8-ounce) can Pillsbury Reduced Fat Crescent Rolls
> 1 (8-ounce) package Philadelphia fat-free cream cheese
> ¼ cup Land O Lakes no-fat sour cream
> ¼ cup Kraft Fat Free Ranch Dressing
> 1 tablespoon dried onion flakes
> 1½ teaspoons dried parsley flakes
> 1½ cups diced cooked chicken breast
> 1 (8-ounce) can pineapple tidbits, packed in fruit juice, drained
> 1 (11-ounce) can mandarin oranges, rinsed and drained
> ½ cup Oscar Mayer or Hormel Real Bacon Bits

Preheat oven to 375 degrees. Spray a rimmed 9-by-13-inch baking sheet with butter-flavored cooking spray. Unroll crescent rolls and carefully pat into prepared baking sheet, being sure to seal perforations. Bake for 8 to 12 minutes or until golden brown. Place baking sheet on a wire rack and allow to cool completely. In a medium bowl, stir cream cheese with a sturdy spoon until soft. Add sour cream, Ranch dressing, onion flakes, and parsley flakes. Mix well to combine. Evenly spread mixture over cooled crust. Sprinkle chicken, pineapple tidbits, and mandarin oranges evenly over cream cheese layer. Sprinkle bacon bits evenly over top. Cut into 24 pieces.

HINTS: 1. If you don't have leftovers, purchase a chunk of cooked chicken breast from your local deli.
2. If you can't find tidbits, use chunk pineapple and coarsely chop.

Each serving equals:

HE: 2 Protein • 1 Bread • ½ Fruit • ¼ Slider

235 Calories • 7 gm Fat • 18 gm Protein • 25 gm Carbohydrate • 618 mg Sodium • 107 mg Calcium • 1 gm Fiber

DIABETIC EXCHANGES: 2 Meat • 1 Starch • ½ Fruit • ½ Fat

CARB CHOICES: 1½

Home for the Holidays
Appetizer Pizza

When you're swamped with holiday preparations, wouldn't it be nice to have this little bit of kitchen magic to prepare for last-minute guests? If you've got the ingredients on hand, you can dazzle whoever walks in the door—even Santa!

● Serves 12 (2 pieces each)

> 1 (4-serving) package Jell-O sugar-free vanilla
>   cook-and-serve pudding mix
> 1 cup unsweetened orange juice
> 2 cups chopped fresh or frozen
>   cranberries
> 1 (8-ounce) package Philadelphia fat-free
>   cream cheese
> 1 (8-ounce) can Pillsbury Reduced Fat
>   Crescent Rolls
> 2 cups diced cooked turkey breast
> ½ cup chopped walnuts

Preheat oven to 425 degrees. Spray a rimmed 9-by-13-inch baking sheet with butter-flavored cooking spray. In a large saucepan, combine dry pudding mix and orange juice. Stir in cranberries. Cook over medium heat until mixture starts to boil and cranberries soften. Remove from heat. Stir in cream cheese. Place pan on a wire rack and allow to cool while preparing crust. Unroll crescent rolls and carefully pat into prepared baking sheet, being sure to seal perforations. Bake for 6 minutes. Evenly spread cranberry mixture over partially baked crust. Sprinkle turkey and walnuts evenly over top. Continue baking for 6 to 8 minutes or until crust is golden brown. Place baking sheet on a wire rack and let set for 5 minutes. Cut into 24 pieces.

HINT: If you don't have leftovers, purchase a chunk of turkey breast from your local deli.

Each serving equals:

HE: 1⅓ Protein • ⅔ Bread • ⅓ Fruit • ⅓ Fat • 7 Optional Calories

166 Calories • 6 gm Fat • 12 gm Protein • 16 gm Carbohydrate • 300 mg Sodium • 64 mg Calcium • 2 gm Fiber

DIABETIC EXCHANGES: 1 Meat • 1 Starch/Carbohydrate • 1 Fat

CARB CHOICES: 1

Grande Party Appetizer Pizza

Whether you're expecting a dozen close friends or many, many more at a harvest season open house, you can serve this and know it'll be a winner with everyone from 7 to 97!

◐ Serves 12 (2 pieces each)

1 (8-ounce) can Pillsbury Reduced Fat Crescent Rolls
1 (8-ounce) package Philadelphia fat-free cream cheese
½ cup chunky salsa (mild, medium, or hot)
2 teaspoons chili seasoning ✩
8 ounces extra-lean ground sirloin beef or turkey breast
½ cup frozen whole-kernel corn, thawed
1 (15-ounce) can Bush's red kidney beans, rinsed and
   drained
2 cups finely shredded lettuce
1 cup finely diced fresh tomatoes
½ cup chopped green bell pepper
½ cup chopped onion
½ cup Kraft Fat Free Catalina Dressing
¾ cup finely shredded Kraft reduced-fat Cheddar cheese

Preheat oven to 375 degrees. Spray a rimmed 9-by-13-inch baking sheet with olive oil–flavored cooking spray. Unroll crescent rolls and carefully pat into prepared baking sheet, being sure to seal perforations. Bake for 8 to 12 minutes or until crust is golden brown. Place baking sheet on a wire rack and allow to cool. In a medium bowl, stir cream cheese with a sturdy spoon until soft. Add salsa and 1 teaspoon chili seasoning. Mix well to combine. Evenly spread mixture over cooled crust. In a large skillet sprayed with olive oil–flavored cooking spray, brown meat. Drain, if necessary. Add corn and kidney beans. Mix well to combine. Place skillet on a wire rack and let set for 10 minutes. Meanwhile, in a large bowl, combine lettuce, tomatoes, green pepper, and onion. Add cooled meat mixture and remaining 1 teaspoon chili seasoning. Mix well to combine. Pour Catalina dressing over top. Toss gently to combine. Evenly spread meat mixture over cream cheese mixture. Sprinkle

Cheddar cheese evenly over top. Refrigerate for at least 30 minutes. Cut into 24 pieces.

Each serving equals:

HE: 1¼ Protein • 1 Bread • ½ Vegetable • 12 Optional Calories

182 Calories • 6 gm Fat • 11 gm Protein • 21 gm Carbohydrate • 455 mg Sodium • 118 mg Calcium • 3 gm Fiber

DIABETIC EXCHANGES: 1½ Meat • 1 Starch • ½ Vegetable

CARB CHOICES: 1½

Mexican Pizza Bites

This just couldn't be easier to fix—why, my truck drivin' man, Cliff, could prepare it for himself if necessary! (Lucky for him, it never is . . .) It's fast, it's flavorful, and oh what fun to munch these while watching your favorite sitcoms.

☕ Serves 4 (2 pieces each)

> 4 ounces extra-lean ground sirloin beef or turkey breast
> ¼ cup chopped onion
> ¼ cup chopped green bell pepper
> ½ cup peeled and finely chopped fresh tomatoes
> 1 teaspoon chili seasoning
> 2 (6-inch) flour tortillas
> ½ cup shredded Kraft reduced-fat Cheddar cheese

Place meat and onion in a microwave-safe colander and place colander in a glass pie plate. Microwave on HIGH (100% power) for 2 minutes or until meat is no longer pink, stirring after 1 minute. Stir in green pepper, tomato, and chili seasoning. Continue to microwave for 2 minutes. Place tortillas in an 8-by-12-inch baking dish. Evenly sprinkle meat mixture over tortillas. Sprinkle Cheddar cheese evenly over top of each. Microwave on HIGH for 2 to 3 minutes or until cheese is melted. Let set for 2 to 3 minutes. Cut each into 4 pieces. Serve at once.

HINT: If microwave plate isn't large enough, process in two batches.

Each serving equals:

HE: 1¼ Protein • ½ Bread • ½ Vegetable

95 Calories • 3 gm Fat • 7 gm Protein • 10 gm Carbohydrate • 32 mg Sodium • 16 mg Calcium • 1 gm Fiber

DIABETIC EXCHANGES: 1 Meat • ½ Starch • ½ Vegetable

CARB CHOICES: 1

Ham and Cheese Appetizers

Invite this "perfect couple" to any party, and you won't be sorry! This classic all-American combo is utterly reliable and yet special in its own way. ☻ Serves 8 (3 pieces each)

> 1 (11-ounce) can Pillsbury refrigerated low-fat French Loaf
> 1 cup Kraft fat-free mayonnaise
> ¼ cup sweet pickle relish
> 1 teaspoon prepared yellow mustard
> 3 full cups diced Dubuque 97% fat-free ham or any extra-
>   lean ham
> 8 (¾-ounce) slices Kraft reduced-fat Swiss cheese, cut into
>   small pieces

Preheat oven to 375 degrees. Spray a rimmed 10-by-15-inch baking sheet with butter-flavored cooking spray. Unroll French loaf and pat into prepared baking sheet and up sides of pan to form a rim. Lightly spray top of crust with butter-flavored cooking spray. Bake for 8 to 10 minutes or until crust is golden brown. Place baking sheet on a wire rack and allow to cool completely. In a small bowl, combine mayonnaise, pickle relish, and mustard. Evenly spread mixture over cooled crust. Sprinkle ham evenly over dressing mixture. Sprinkle Swiss cheese evenly over top. Cut into 24 pieces.

Each serving equals:

HE: 2½ Protein • 1 Bread • ¼ Slider • 7 Optional Calories

257 Calories • 9 gm Fat • 20 gm Protein • 24 gm Carbohydrate • 993 mg Sodium • 233 mg Calcium • 1 gm Fiber

DIABETIC EXCHANGES: 2½ Meat • 1½ Starch

CARB CHOICES: 1½

Ham and Veggie Pizza Appetizers

Here's my version of a sizzling starter—a sort of snack pizza with just about everything you love on top! And, as my tasters commented, "lots of mmm-mmm ham!"

☻ Serves 12 (2 pieces each)

> 1 (11-ounce) can Pillsbury refrigerated low-fat
>   French Loaf
> ½ cup chopped onion
> ½ cup chopped green bell pepper
> 2 full cups finely diced Dubuque 97% fat-free ham or
>   any extra-lean ham
> 1 cup chopped fresh mushrooms
> ¼ cup Kraft fat-free mayonnaise
> 2 tablespoons Grey Poupon Country Style Dijon
>   Mustard
> 1 teaspoon dried parsley flakes
> 8 (¾-ounce) slices Kraft reduced-fat Swiss cheese
> 1½ cups peeled and diced fresh tomatoes

Preheat oven to 375 degrees. Spray a rimmed 10-by-15-inch baking sheet with butter-flavored cooking spray. Unroll French loaf and pat into prepared baking sheet and up sides of pan to form a rim. Lightly spray top of crust with butter-flavored cooking spray. Bake for 6 minutes. Meanwhile, in a large skillet sprayed with butter-flavored cooking spray, sauté onion and green pepper for 3 minutes. Stir in ham and mushrooms. Continue to sauté for 3 minutes. In a small bowl, combine mayonnaise, mustard, and parsley flakes. Spread mayonnaise mixture evenly over partially baked crust. Arrange Swiss cheese slices evenly over mayonnaise mixture. Layer ham mixture over Swiss cheese. Sprinkle tomatoes evenly over top. Continue baking for 8 to 12 minutes or until crust is golden brown and cheese is melted. Place baking sheet on a wire rack and let set for 5 minutes. Cut into 24 pieces.

Each serving equals:

HE: 1⅓ Protein • ⅔ Bread • ½ Vegetable • 3 Optional Calories

161 Calories • 5 gm Fat • 12 gm Protein • 17 gm Carbohydrate •
536 mg Sodium • 155 mg Calcium • 2 gm Fiber

DIABETIC EXCHANGES: 1 Meat • 1 Starch • ½ Vegetable

CARB CHOICES: 1

Reuben Party Pizza

According to the legend, the actress who asked restaurateur Arnold Reuben to make her a combination sandwich (way back in 1914) told him, "I could eat a brick!" She loved the sandwich as much as I bet you will love this "party-on-a-platter."

 Serves 8 (3 pieces each)

> 1 (11-ounce) can Pillsbury refrigerated low-fat French Loaf
> 1 cup Kraft Fat Free Thousand Island Dressing
> 4 (2.5-ounce) packages Carl Buddig 90% lean corned beef, shredded
> 1 (15-ounce) can sauerkraut, very well drained
> ¼ cup finely chopped onion
> 6 (¾-ounce) slices Kraft reduced-fat Swiss cheese, shredded

Preheat oven to 375 degrees. Spray a rimmed 10-by-15-inch baking sheet with butter-flavored cooking spray. Unroll French loaf and pat into prepared baking sheet and up sides of pan to form a rim. Bake for 6 minutes. Evenly spread Thousand Island dressing over partially baked crust. Arrange corned beef, sauerkraut, and onion evenly over dressing. Sprinkle Swiss cheese evenly over top. Bake for 8 to 12 minutes or until crust is golden brown and cheese is melted. Place baking sheet on a wire rack and let set for 5 minutes. Cut into 24 pieces.

HINT: Place sauerkraut in a colander and press juice out with a sturdy spoon.

Each serving equals:

HE: 2 Protein • 1 Bread • ½ Vegetable • ½ Slider • 10 Optional Calories

218 Calories • 6 gm Fat • 12 gm Protein • 29 gm Carbohydrate • 982 mg Sodium • 185 mg Calcium • 3 gm Fiber

DIABETIC EXCHANGES: 2 Meat • 1½ Starch/Carbohydrate • ½ Vegetable

CARB CHOICES: 2

Exciting Entrée

Pizzas

What's perfect about pizza? Let me count the ways! It's colorful, flavorful, and ideal for sharing with loved ones. It's made fresh with good-for-you ingredients, it invites you to eat what you love and vary your meals endlessly. And did I forget to say that it's wonderfully satisfying—from pleasing the eye to warming the tummy to soothing the soul, all at once! Even better, you're getting enough main-dish pizza recipes to dine on this delectable dish every day or night for two whole months!

So don't wait another day to get started on your pizza odyssey. I've topped pizzas with just about anything you can think of—and a few that might never occur to most people! If you love chicken or there's a special at the market, why not put *Chicken Bacon Ranch Pizza* on the menu, or *Chicken Cordon Bleu Pizza*—or one of my recent favorites, *Chicken and Peppers Pizza with Fresh Tomatoes*? If you're a fan of scrumptious suppers from faraway places, I recommend *Hawaiian Luau Pizza*, *Irish Potato Crust Pizza*, or *Italian Spinach Pizza*. But you don't have to stray from the good old U.S.A. when you're planning on pizza—just fix *Coney Island Pizza*, *Chicago-Style Cheese Lover's Pizza*, or *Santa Fe Trail Pizza*!

Fresh Tomato Pizza

Nothing tastes fresher or more "straight from the garden" than tomatoes sliced on top of a crusty pizza! And of course, the tomato's best friend is basil, which brings out all its good qualities.

⊙ Serves 8

> 1 (11-ounce) can Pillsbury refrigerated low-fat French Loaf
> 1 (8-ounce) package Philadelphia fat-free cream cheese
> ½ cup Kraft fat-free mayonnaise
> 2 tablespoons dried basil
> ¼ teaspoon dried minced garlic
> 3 cups peeled and sliced fresh tomatoes
> 1 cup finely chopped onion
> 1 cup finely chopped fresh mushrooms
> 2 cups shredded Kraft reduced-fat mozzarella cheese

Preheat oven to 375 degrees. Spray a rimmed 10-by-15-inch baking sheet with butter-flavored cooking spray. Unroll French loaf and pat into prepared baking sheet and up sides of pan to form a rim. Lightly spray top of crust with butter-flavored cooking spray. Bake for 6 minutes. Meanwhile, in a medium bowl, stir cream cheese with a sturdy spoon until soft. Stir in mayonnaise, basil, and garlic. Spread mixture evenly over partially baked crust. Evenly sprinkle tomatoes, onion, and mushrooms over cream cheese mixture. Sprinkle mozzarella cheese evenly over top. Continue baking for 8 to 10 minutes or until crust is golden brown and cheese is melted. Place baking sheet on a wire rack and let set for 5 minutes. Cut into 8 servings.

Each serving equals:

HE: 1½ Protein • 1¼ Vegetable • 1 Bread • 10 Optional Calories

222 Calories • 6 gm Fat • 14 gm Protein • 28 gm Carbohydrate • 738 mg Sodium • 300 mg Calcium • 3 gm Fiber

DIABETIC EXCHANGES: 1½ Meat • 1 Vegetable • 1 Starch

CARB CHOICES: 2

Pizza Margherita

It's rumored that this delectable classic was named for the Queen of Savoy, who visited Naples, Italy, in 1889. Offered a choice of three specially created pies, she chose the one that featured the colors of the Italian flag: red tomatoes, white mozzarella, and green for the flavorful Italian herbs on top!   ☻   Serves 8

1 (11-ounce) can Pillsbury refrigerated low-fat French Loaf
1 (14.5-ounce) can Hunt's Tomatoes Diced in Sauce
2 tablespoons Splenda Granular
1½ teaspoons pizza or Italian seasoning
2 cups shredded Kraft reduced-fat mozzarella cheese
1 tablespoon + 1 teaspoon olive oil

Preheat oven to 375 degrees. Spray a rimmed 10-by-15-inch baking sheet with olive oil–flavored cooking spray. Unroll French loaf and pat into prepared baking sheet and up sides of pan to form a rim. Lightly spray top of crust with olive oil–flavored cooking spray. Bake for 6 minutes. Meanwhile, in a medium bowl, combine tomato sauce, Splenda, and pizza seasoning. Spread sauce mixture evenly over partially baked crust. Sprinkle mozzarella cheese evenly over sauce. Sprinkle olive oil evenly over top. Bake for 8 to 10 minutes or until crust is golden brown and cheese is melted. Place baking sheet on a wire rack and let set for 5 minutes. Cut into 8 servings.

Each serving equals:

HE: 1 Bread • 1 Protein • ½ Fat • ½ Vegetable • 1 Optional Calorie

200 Calories • 8 gm Fat • 10 gm Protein • 22 gm Carbohydrate • 399 mg Sodium • 194 mg Calcium • 1 gm Fiber

DIABETIC EXCHANGES: 1 Starch • 1 Meat • ½ Fat • ½ Vegetable

CARB CHOICES: 1½

Chicago-Style Cheese Lover's Pizza

If you've never dined on the Windy City's version, let me just say that it's one of the best I've ever tasted! It calls for a deeper crust, lots of filling, and ooh, yes, lots of cheese! ☻ Serves 8

1 (11-ounce) can Pillsbury refrigerated low-fat French Loaf
1 cup finely chopped onion
1 (14.5-ounce) can Hunt's Tomatoes Diced in Sauce
½ teaspoon dried minced garlic
1 tablespoon Splenda Granular
2 teaspoons pizza or Italian seasoning
2 cups chopped fresh mushrooms
½ cup chopped green bell pepper
2 cups shredded Kraft reduced-fat Cheddar cheese
1 cup shredded Kraft reduced-fat mozzarella cheese

Preheat oven to 375 degrees. In a large skillet sprayed with olive oil–flavored cooking spray, sauté onion for 5 minutes. Stir in tomatoes, garlic, Splenda, and pizza seasoning. Bring mixture to a boil. Lower heat and simmer for 6 to 8 minutes, stirring occasionally. Spray a 10-by-15-inch baking sheet with olive oil–flavored cooking spray. Unroll French loaf and pat into prepared baking sheet and up sides of pan to form a rim. Lightly spray top of crust with olive oil–flavored cooking spray. Bake for 6 minutes. Spread sauce mixture evenly over partially baked crust. Evenly sprinkle mushrooms and green pepper over sauce. Sprinkle Cheddar and mozzarella cheeses evenly over top. Bake for 18 to 20 minutes or until crust is golden brown and cheeses are melted. Place baking sheet on a wire rack and let set for 5 minutes. Cut into 8 servings.

Each serving equals:

HE: 1½ Protein • 1 Bread • 1 Vegetable • 1 Optional Calorie

262 Calories • 10 gm Fat • 15 gm Protein • 28 gm Carbohydrate • 482 mg Sodium • 325 mg Calcium • 3 gm Fiber

DIABETIC EXCHANGES: 1½ Meat • 1 Starch • 1 Vegetable

CARB CHOICES: 2

Mediterranean Three-Cheese Pizza

Close your eyes and imagine yourself on a magnificent yacht, sailing the Greek Isles. Suddenly, your tummy rumbles and you wonder, "What's for lunch?" Put this inspired dish on the menu and you'll feel just like Jackie O cruising the romantic seas!

◐ Serves 8

> 1 (11-ounce) can Pillsbury refrigerated low-fat French Loaf
> 1½ teaspoons pizza or Italian seasoning
> 1 tablespoon Splenda Granular
> ¼ cup Kraft Reduced Fat Parmesan Style Grated Topping
> 1 (14.5-ounce) can Hunt's Tomatoes Diced in Sauce
> 2½ cups chopped unpeeled zucchini
> 1 cup crumbled feta cheese
> ¾ cup shredded Kraft reduced-fat mozzarella cheese

Preheat oven to 375 degrees. Spray a rimmed 10-by-15-inch baking sheet with olive oil–flavored cooking spray. Unroll French loaf and pat into prepared baking sheet and up sides of pan to form a rim. Lightly spray top of crust with olive oil–flavored cooking spray. Bake for 6 minutes. Meanwhile, stir pizza seasoning, Splenda, and Parmesan cheese into diced tomatoes. Spread sauce mixture evenly over partially baked crust. Arrange zucchini evenly over sauce. Sprinkle feta and mozzarella cheeses evenly over top. Continue baking for 10 minutes or until crust is golden brown and cheese is melted. Place baking sheet on a wire rack and let set for 5 minutes. Cut into 8 servings.

Each serving equals:

HE: 1¼ Protein • 1 Bread • 1 Vegetable • 1 Optional Calorie

216 Calories • 8 gm Fat • 10 gm Protein • 26 gm Carbohydrate • 559 mg Sodium • 199 mg Calcium • 2 gm Fiber

DIABETIC EXCHANGES: 1 Meat • 1 Starch • 1 Vegetable

CARB CHOICES: 2

Tomato-Basil Pizza

We're so lucky to have a much-improved selection of fresh herbs in the supermarket these days, so even if you don't have a garden or a handy farmer's market, you can enjoy the delicious difference that comes with combining fresh basil and your ripest tomatoes on top of this pizza. ☻ Serves 8

1 (11-ounce) can Pillsbury refrigerated low-fat French Loaf
1 cup Kraft fat-free mayonnaise
¼ cup Kraft Reduced Fat Parmesan Style Grated Topping
1 tablespoon chopped fresh basil
½ teaspoon dried minced garlic
1¾ cups shredded Kraft reduced-fat mozzarella cheese ☆
3 cups peeled and thinly sliced fresh tomatoes

Preheat oven to 375 degrees. Spray a rimmed 10-by-15-inch baking sheet with olive oil–flavored cooking spray. Unroll French loaf and pat into prepared baking sheet and up sides of pan to form a rim. Lightly spray top of crust with olive oil–flavored cooking spray. Bake for 8 minutes. Meanwhile, in a medium bowl, combine mayonnaise, Parmesan cheese, basil, and garlic. Stir in ½ cup mozzarella cheese. Spread mixture evenly over partially baked crust. Arrange tomato slices evenly over mayonnaise mixture. Sprinkle remaining 1¼ cups mozzarella cheese evenly over top. Bake for 14 to 16 minutes or until crust is golden brown and cheese is melted. Place baking sheet on a wire rack and let set for 5 minutes. Cut into 8 servings.

Each serving equals:

HE: 1 Bread • 1 Protein • ¾ Vegetable • ¼ Slider

206 Calories • 6 gm Fat • 11 gm Protein • 27 gm Carbohydrate • 596 mg Sodium • 382 mg Calcium • 2 gm Fiber

DIABETIC EXCHANGES: 1½ Starch/Carbohydrate • 1 Meat • 1 Vegetable

CARB CHOICES: 2

Broccoli-Cheddar Pizza

So many people love the taste of broccoli and Cheddar cheese in a hearty soup, I figured why not try topping a pizza with them? I'm thrilled to say that everyone who tried this really enjoyed it!

◑ Serves 8

1 (11-ounce) can Pillsbury refrigerated low-fat French Loaf
1 (8-ounce) can Hunt's Tomato Sauce
1 tablespoon Splenda Granular
1½ teaspoons pizza seasoning
2 cups finely chopped fresh broccoli
1 cup finely chopped onion
2 cups shredded Kraft reduced-fat Cheddar cheese

Preheat oven to 375 degrees. Spray a rimmed 10-by-15-inch baking sheet with olive oil–flavored cooking spray. Unroll French loaf and pat into prepared baking sheet and up sides of pan to form a rim. Lightly spray top of crust with olive oil–flavored cooking spray. Bake for 6 minutes. Meanwhile, in a small bowl, combine tomato sauce, Splenda, and pizza seasoning. Evenly spread sauce mixture over partially baked crust. Sprinkle broccoli and onion evenly over sauce. Evenly sprinkle Cheddar cheese over top. Continue baking for 6 to 10 minutes or until crust is golden brown and cheese is melted. Place baking sheet on a wire rack and let set for 5 minutes. Cut into 8 servings.

Each serving equals:

HE: 1¼ Vegetable • 1 Bread • 1 Protein • 1 Optional Calorie

220 Calories • 8 gm Fat • 13 gm Protein • 24 gm Carbohydrate • 403 mg Sodium • 245 mg Calcium • 3 gm Fiber

DIABETIC EXCHANGES: 1 Vegetable • 1 Starch • 1 Meat

CARB CHOICES: 1½

Spencer's Easy
Mushroom-Cheese Pizza

What grandma wouldn't enjoy preparing a pizza to appeal to the favorite flavors of a beloved grandchild? I know I had a terrific time fixing this dish for my darling Spencer, who gobbled it up and requested a second piece!　　●　Serves 4 (2 pieces)

¾ cup + 1 tablespoon Bisquick Heart Smart Baking Mix ☆
¼ cup water
1 (8-ounce) can Hunt's Tomato Sauce
1 teaspoon pizza or Italian seasoning
1 (4-ounce) jar sliced mushrooms, drained
¾ cup shredded Kraft reduced-fat mozzarella cheese
¾ cup shredded Kraft reduced-fat Cheddar cheese
¼ cup Kraft Reduced Fat Parmesan Style Grated Topping

Preheat oven to 425 degrees. Spray a 9-inch round pizza pan with butter-flavored cooking spray. In a medium bowl, combine ¾ cup baking mix and water. Sprinkle remaining 1 tablespoon baking mix on counter or cutting board. Knead crust on floured surface for about 1 minute. Roll into a circle about ⅛-inch thick. Place on prepared pizza pan. Turn up edges slightly. Lightly spray top with olive oil–flavored cooking spray. Spread tomato sauce evenly over crust. Sprinkle pizza seasoning over sauce. Evenly layer mushrooms over top. Sprinkle mozzarella and Cheddar cheeses over mushrooms. Top with Parmesan cheese. Bake for 14 to 16 minutes or until crust is golden brown. Place pan on a wire rack and let set for 5 minutes. Cut into 8 servings.

Each serving equals:

HE: 1¾ Protein • 1½ Vegetable • 1 Bread • 8 Optional Calories

258 Calories • 10 gm Fat • 14 gm Protein • 28 gm Carbohydrate • 901 mg Sodium • 385 mg Calcium • 2 gm Fiber

DIABETIC EXCHANGES: 2 Meat • 1 Starch • 1 Vegetable

CARB CHOICES: 2

Italian Spinach Pizza

You might be thinking, cream cheese on top of pizza—how weird does that sound? But when it's blended with the Italian dressing and cheese, you'll be dazzled by how well it works! Now, Mom always said to eat your veggies, so choose this pizza sometime soon.

◐ Serves 8

> 1 (11-ounce) can Pillsbury refrigerated low-fat French Loaf
> 1 (8-ounce) package Philadelphia fat-free cream cheese
> 2 tablespoons Kraft Fat Free Italian Dressing
> ½ cup Kraft Reduced Fat Parmesan Style Grated Topping
> 1 (4-ounce) jar sliced mushrooms, drained
> 2 cups finely shredded fresh spinach
> 1 cup shredded Kraft reduced-fat mozzarella cheese

Preheat oven to 375 degrees. Spray a rimmed 10-by-15-inch baking sheet with olive oil–flavored cooking spray. Unroll French loaf and pat into prepared baking sheet and up sides of pan to form a rim. Lightly spray top of crust with olive oil–flavored cooking spray. Bake for 6 minutes. Meanwhile, in a large bowl, stir cream cheese with a sturdy spoon until soft. Stir in Italian dressing, Parmesan cheese, and mushrooms. Spread mixture evenly over partially baked crust. Arrange spinach evenly over cream cheese mixture. Sprinkle mozzarella cheese evenly over top. Continue baking for 8 to 10 minutes or until crust is golden brown and cheese is melted. Place baking sheet on a wire rack and let set for 5 minutes. Cut into 8 servings.

Each serving equals:

HE: 1¼ Protein • 1 Bread • ½ Vegetable • 2 Optional Calories

189 Calories • 5 gm Fat • 12 gm Protein • 24 gm Carbohydrate • 612 mg Sodium • 210 mg Calcium • 1 gm Fiber

DIABETIC EXCHANGES: 1½ Meat • 1 Starch • ½ Vegetable

CARB CHOICES: 1½

Tomato Florentine Pizza

Here's another great way to add Popeye's favorite food to your dinner menu—and maybe get your kids to give spinach a second look! This is a dish that looks as good as it tastes. ☻ Serves 8

> 1 (11-ounce) can Pillsbury refrigerated low-fat French Loaf
> 1 (8-ounce) package Philadelphia fat-free cream cheese
> ¼ cup Kraft fat-free mayonnaise
> ½ cup Kraft Reduced Fat Parmesan Style Grated Topping
> 1½ teaspoons dried basil
> 3 cups peeled and chopped fresh tomatoes
> 3 cups thinly shredded fresh spinach
> ½ cup finely chopped onion
> 1 cup shredded Kraft reduced-fat mozzarella cheese

Preheat oven to 375 degrees. Spray a rimmed 10-by-15-inch baking sheet with olive oil–flavored cooking spray. Unroll French loaf and pat into prepared baking sheet and up sides of pan to form a rim. Lightly spray top of crust with olive oil–flavored cooking spray. Bake for 6 minutes. Meanwhile, in a medium bowl, stir cream cheese with a sturdy spoon until soft. Add mayonnaise, Parmesan cheese, and basil. Mix well to combine. Spread cream cheese mixture evenly over partially baked crust. Arrange tomatoes, spinach, and onion evenly over cream cheese mixture. Sprinkle mozzarella cheese evenly over top. Continue baking for 10 to 12 minutes or until crust is golden brown and cheese is melted. Place baking sheet on a wire rack and let set for 5 minutes. Cut into 8 servings.

Each serving equals:

HE: 1¼ Protein • 1¼ Vegetable • 1 Bread • 5 Optional Calories

213 Calories • 5 gm Fat • 13 gm Protein • 29 gm Carbohydrate •
642 mg Sodium • 251 mg Calcium • 2 gm Fiber

DIABETIC EXCHANGES: 1½ Starch/Carbohydrate • 1 Meat • 1 Vegetable

CARB CHOICES: 2

Zucchini-Mozzarella Pizza

Zippity doo-dah, here comes that plentiful garden vegetable, the zucchini, looking for a home on top of your next pizza! This combo is a true eye-opener, thanks to some tangy Dijon mustard.

○ Serves 8

> 1 (11-ounce) can Pillsbury refrigerated low-fat French Loaf
> 1 tablespoon Grey Poupon Country Style Dijon Mustard
> ½ cup Kraft Fat Free Italian Dressing
> 4 cups thinly sliced unpeeled zucchini
> 1 cup chopped onion
> 1½ teaspoons pizza or Italian seasoning
> 2 cups shredded Kraft reduced-fat mozzarella cheese

Preheat oven to 375 degrees. Spray a rimmed 10-by-15-inch baking sheet with olive oil–flavored cooking spray. Unroll French loaf and pat into prepared baking sheet and up sides of pan to form a rim. Lightly spray top of crust with olive oil–flavored cooking spray. Bake for 6 minutes. Evenly spread mustard over crust. Meanwhile, heat Italian dressing in a large skillet until hot. Add zucchini, onion, and pizza seasoning. Continue cooking for 5 to 6 minutes or until vegetables are tender, stirring often. Spoon vegetable mixture evenly over partially baked crust. Sprinkle mozzarella cheese evenly over top. Bake for 18 to 20 minutes or until crust is golden brown and cheese is melted. Place baking sheet on a wire rack and let set for 5 minutes. Cut into 8 servings.

Each serving equals:

HE: 1¼ Vegetable • 1 Bread • 1 Protein • 10 Optional Calories

198 Calories • 6 gm Fat • 11 gm Protein • 25 gm Carbohydrate • 639 mg Sodium • 214 mg Calcium • 2 gm Fiber

DIABETIC EXCHANGES: 1 Vegetable • 1 Starch • 1 Meat

CARB CHOICES: 1½

Sunshine State Pizza

When I began listing the ingredients for this pizza, I thought, I could see this becoming the state pizza of Florida! Why? Well, lots of fresh veggies, including those red-gold carrots, and enough cheese to remind you of a sunny afternoon.　　○　Serves 8

1 (11-ounce) can Pillsbury refrigerated low-fat French Loaf
1 cup chopped onion
1 cup chopped unpeeled zucchini
1 cup shredded carrots
1 (8-ounce) can Hunt's Tomato Sauce
2 tablespoons Splenda Granular
1½ teaspoons dried basil
2 cups peeled and chopped fresh tomatoes
½ cup sliced ripe olives
1 cup shredded Kraft reduced-fat Cheddar cheese
1 cup shredded Kraft reduced-fat mozzarella cheese

Preheat oven to 375 degrees. Spray a rimmed 10-by-15-inch baking sheet with olive oil–flavored cooking spray. Unroll French loaf and pat into prepared baking sheet and up sides of pan to form a rim. Lightly spray top of crust with olive oil–flavored cooking spray. Bake for 6 minutes. Meanwhile, in a large skillet sprayed with butter-flavored cooking spray, sauté onion, zucchini, and carrots for 5 to 6 minutes. In a small bowl, combine tomato sauce, Splenda, and basil. Spread sauce mixture evenly over partially baked crust. Evenly arrange tomatoes, olives, and sautéed onion mixture over sauce. Sprinkle Cheddar and mozzarella cheeses evenly over top. Continue baking for 8 to 12 minutes or until crust is golden brown and cheese is melted. Place baking sheet on a wire rack and let set for 5 minutes. Cut into 8 servings.

Each serving equals:

HE: 1¾ Vegetable • 1 Bread • 1 Protein • ¼ Fat • 1 Optional Calorie

215 Calories • 7 gm Fat • 11 gm Protein • 27 gm Carbohydrate • 543 mg Sodium • 234 mg Calcium • 3 gm Fiber

DIABETIC EXCHANGES: 1½ Vegetable • 1 Starch • 1 Meat • ½ Fat

CARB CHOICES: 2

Tuscan Pizza

This gorgeous farm region of Italy is renowned for irresistible food, and I think this pizza would be right at home in any of the locale's historic villas! Tuscan food often includes hearty beans along with other veggies, so this should fit in perfectly. ☻   Serves 8

1 (11-ounce) can Pillsbury refrigerated low-fat French Loaf
¼ cup Kraft Fat Free Italian Dressing
¼ cup Kraft fat-free mayonnaise
¼ cup Kraft Reduced Fat Parmesan Style Grated Topping
2 tablespoons chopped fresh parsley or 2 teaspoons dried
    parsley flakes
1½ cups chopped fresh tomatoes
½ cup chopped onion
1 (15-ounce) can Bush's great northern beans, rinsed and
    drained
1½ cups shredded Kraft reduced-fat mozzarella cheese

Preheat oven to 375 degrees. Spray a rimmed 10-by-15-inch baking sheet with olive oil–flavored cooking spray. Unroll French loaf and pat into prepared baking sheet and up sides of pan to form a rim. Lightly spray top of crust with olive oil–flavored cooking spray. Bake for 6 minutes. Meanwhile, in a large bowl, combine Italian dressing, mayonnaise, Parmesan cheese, and parsley. Add tomatoes, onion, and great northern beans. Mix well to combine. Spread mixture evenly over partially baked crust. Sprinkle mozzarella cheese evenly over top. Continue baking for 10 to 14 minutes or until crust is golden brown and cheese is melted. Place baking sheet on a wire rack and let set for 5 minutes. Cut into 8 servings.

Each serving equals:

HE: 1¼ Bread • 1¼ Protein • ½ Vegetable • 11 Optional Calories

205 Calories • 5 gm Fat • 11 gm Protein • 29 gm Carbohydrate •
598 mg Sodium • 362 mg Calcium • 3 gm Fiber

DIABETIC EXCHANGES: 1½ Starch • 1 Meat • ½ Vegetable

CARB CHOICES: 2

Mexican Black-Bean Pizza

Beans are such an amazing source of protein and fiber, they're just great for topping a vegetarian pizza like this one! When I make it for Cliff and me, I add some of his hotter-than-hot salsa on one side while using the milder stuff for me. Peace under one roof, and plenty of festive flavor. ☺ Serves 8

> 1 (11-ounce) can Pillsbury refrigerated low-fat French Loaf
> 1 (15-ounce) can black beans, rinsed and drained
> 2 tablespoons chopped fresh cilantro or parsley
> 1 cup chunky salsa (mild, medium, or hot) ☆
> 1½ cups shredded Kraft reduced-fat Cheddar cheese
> ½ cup Land O Lakes no-fat sour cream

Preheat oven to 375 degrees. Spray a rimmed 10-by-15-inch baking sheet with butter-flavored cooking spray. Unroll French loaf and pat into prepared baking sheet and up sides of pan to form a rim. Lightly spray top of crust with butter-flavored cooking spray. Bake for 6 minutes. Meanwhile, in a blender container, combine black beans, cilantro, and ¼ cup salsa. Cover and process on BLEND for 30 to 40 seconds or until mixture is smooth. Evenly spread bean mixture over partially baked crust. Carefully drop ½ cup salsa by spoonfuls over bean mixture. Sprinkle Cheddar cheese evenly over top. Continue baking for 8 to 10 minutes or until crust is golden brown and cheese is melted. Place baking sheet on a wire rack and let set for 5 minutes. In a small bowl, combine sour cream and remaining ¼ cup salsa. Cut into 8 servings. When serving, top each piece with 1 tablespoon sour cream mixture.

Each serving equals:

HE: 1¼ Bread • 1¼ Protein • ¼ Vegetable • 15 Optional Calories

---

230 Calories • 6 gm Fat • 13 gm Protein • 31 gm Carbohydrate • 603 mg Sodium • 200 mg Calcium • 4 gm Fiber

---

DIABETIC EXCHANGES: 2 Starch/Carbohydrate • 1 Meat

CARB CHOICES: 2

Tamale Olé Pizza

If you're unfamiliar with tamales, they're a Mexican delicacy that involves blending meat or beans with a special cornmeal *(masa)* and spices, and then steaming it inside a corn husk. (It's a lot of work but very tasty!) Here, I've tried to take some of those fabulous flavors and create a fun pizza topping. ☺ Serves 8

1 (11-ounce) can Pillsbury refrigerated low-fat French Loaf
2 (15-ounce) cans Bush's pinto beans, rinsed and drained
1 cup chunky salsa (mild, medium, or hot)
1 cup fresh or frozen whole-kernel corn, thawed
1 cup shredded Kraft reduced-fat Cheddar cheese
1 cup peeled and coarsely chopped fresh tomatoes
1 cup crushed Doritos Baked Corn Chips

Preheat oven to 375 degrees. Spray a rimmed 10-by-15-inch baking sheet with olive oil–flavored cooking spray. Unroll French loaf and pat into prepared baking sheet and up sides of pan to form a rim. Lightly spray top of crust with olive oil–flavored cooking spray. Bake for 6 minutes. Meanwhile, in a large bowl, mash pinto beans with a fork. Stir in salsa. Spread bean mixture evenly over partially baked crust. Evenly sprinkle corn, Cheddar cheese, and tomatoes over bean mixture. Sprinkle crushed corn chips evenly over top. Continue baking for 10 to 12 minutes or until crust is golden brown and cheese is melted. Place baking sheet on a wire rack and let set for 5 minutes. Cut into 8 servings.

HINT: Thaw corn by rinsing in a colander under hot water for 1 minute.

Each serving equals:

HE: 2 Protein • 1½ Bread • ½ Vegetable

282 Calories • 6 gm Fat • 15 gm Protein • 42 gm Carbohydrate • 496 mg Sodium • 144 mg Calcium • 6 gm Fiber

DIABETIC EXCHANGES: 2 Starch/Carbohydrate • 1 Meat • ½ Vegetable

CARB CHOICES: 2½

Rosemary Chicken Pizza

There are several herbs that go beautifully with chicken, and one of those is rosemary. It's got a sort of woodsy flavor, and a little goes a long way. I hope you agree that this pizza makes an elegant statement and tastes scrumptious.   ◑   Serves 8

1 (11-ounce) can Pillsbury refrigerated low-fat French Loaf
1 (8-ounce) can Hunt's Tomato Sauce
1 (15-ounce) can diced tomatoes, very well drained
2 tablespoons Splenda Granular
1 teaspoon dried rosemary
2 cups diced cooked chicken breast
1 cup finely chopped red onion
1 cup chopped green bell pepper
1½ cups shredded Kraft reduced-fat mozzarella cheese

Preheat oven to 375 degrees. Spray a rimmed 10-by-15-inch baking sheet with olive oil–flavored cooking spray. Unroll French loaf and pat into prepared baking sheet and up sides of pan to form a rim. Lightly spray top of crust with olive oil–flavored cooking spray. Bake for 6 minutes. Meanwhile, in a medium bowl, combine tomato sauce, tomatoes, Splenda, and rosemary. Spread sauce mixture evenly over partially baked crust. Top with chicken, onion, and green pepper. Sprinkle mozzarella cheese evenly over top. Continue baking for 8 to 10 minutes or until crust is golden brown and cheese is melted. Place baking sheet on a wire rack and let set for 5 minutes. Cut into 8 servings.

HINT: If you don't have leftovers, purchase a chunk of cooked chicken breast from your local deli.

Each serving equals:

HE: 2 Protein • 1½ Vegetable • 1 Bread • 1 Optional Calorie

225 Calories • 5 gm Fat • 21 gm Protein • 24 gm Carbohydrate • 617 mg Sodium • 170 mg Calcium • 2 gm Fiber

DIABETIC EXCHANGES: 2 Meat • 1 Vegetable • 1 Starch

CARB CHOICES: 1½

Tuscany Chicken Pizza

Dreaming of a summer spent *Under the Tuscan Sun*? If you remember the movie, Diane Lane's character bought a villa on an impulse and proceeded to build a new life there, with great meals prepared for friends (and the workmen doing her renovations!). This is a lovely pizza that will make you long for a visit. ☻   Serves 8

> 1 (11-ounce) can Pillsbury refrigerated low-fat French Loaf
> 2 cups diced cooked chicken breast
> 1 cup finely chopped red onion
> 1 cup chopped fresh mushrooms
> 1 (8-ounce) can Hunt's Tomato Sauce
> 1½ teaspoons Italian seasoning
> 1 tablespoon Splenda Granular
> ½ cup sliced ripe olives
> 2 cups chopped fresh tomatoes
> 1½ cups shredded Kraft reduced-fat mozzarella cheese

Preheat oven to 375 degrees. Spray a rimmed 10-by-15-inch baking sheet with olive oil–flavored cooking spray. Unroll French loaf and pat into prepared baking sheet and up sides of pan to form a rim. Lightly spray top of crust with olive oil–flavored cooking spray. Bake for 6 minutes. Meanwhile, in a large skillet sprayed with olive oil–flavored cooking spray, sauté chicken, onion, and mushrooms for 5 minutes. Set aside. In a medium bowl, combine tomato sauce, Italian seasoning, and Splenda. Spread sauce mixture evenly over partially baked crust. Evenly sprinkle chicken mixture, olives, and tomatoes over sauce. Sprinkle mozzarella cheese evenly over top. Continue baking for 8 to 10 minutes or until crust is golden brown and cheese is melted. Place baking sheet on a wire rack and let set for 5 minutes. Cut into 8 servings.

HINT: If you don't have leftovers, purchase a chunk of cooked chicken breast from your local deli.

Each serving equals:

HE: 2 Protein • 1½ Vegetable • 1 Bread • ¼ Fat • 1 Optional Calorie

243 Calories • 7 gm Fat • 21 gm Protein • 24 gm Carbohydrate •
649 mg Sodium • 173 mg Calcium • 2 gm Fiber

DIABETIC EXCHANGES: 2 Meat • 1½ Vegetable • 1 Starch

CARB CHOICES: 1½

Chicken Cordon Bleu Pizza

Okay, so pizza is not a native French dish, and the French authorities might quibble a bit with this recipe, purists that they often are. But—I don't see any reason why we can't be inspired by their classic chicken stuffed with ham and cheese, and top a pizza with it!

◐ Serves 8

1 (11-ounce) can Pillsbury refrigerated low-fat
   French Loaf
½ cup Kraft Fat Free Ranch Dressing
2 tablespoons Kraft fat-free mayonnaise
½ teaspoon dried minced garlic
¼ cup Oscar Mayer or Hormel Real Bacon Bits
1½ cups diced cooked chicken breast
1 full cup diced Dubuque 97% fat-free ham or any
   extra-lean ham
¼ cup finely chopped green onion
¾ cup shredded Kraft reduced-fat mozzarella
   cheese
4 (¾-ounce) slices Kraft reduced-fat Swiss cheese,
   shredded

Preheat oven to 375 degrees. Spray a rimmed 10-by-15-inch baking sheet with butter-flavored cooking spray. Unroll French loaf and pat into prepared baking sheet and up sides of pan to form a rim. Lightly spray top of crust with butter-flavored cooking spray. Bake for 6 minutes. Meanwhile, in a medium bowl, combine Ranch dressing, mayonnaise, garlic, and bacon bits. Spread dressing mixture evenly over partially baked crust. Evenly sprinkle chicken, ham, and green onion over dressing mixture. Sprinkle mozzarella cheese and Swiss cheese evenly over top. Continue baking for 8 to 12 minutes or until crust is golden brown and cheese is melted. Place baking sheet on a wire rack and let set for 5 minutes. Cut into 8 servings.

HINT: If you don't have leftovers, purchase a chunk of cooked chicken breast from your local deli.

Each serving equals:

HE: 2⅔ Protein • 1 Bread • ¼ Slider • 7 Optional Calories

260 Calories • 8 gm Fat • 23 gm Protein • 24 gm Carbohydrate •
854 mg Sodium • 198 mg Calcium • 1 gm Fiber

DIABETIC EXCHANGES: 2½ Meat • 1½ Starch

CARB CHOICES: 1½

Grande Chicken Pizza

It's saucy, it's spicy, and it's a great way to dine while watching soccer on TV! If you enjoy the glorious tastes of our neighbor to the south, you might just love this pizza enough to hear a mariachi band in your head. ☻ Serves 8

1 (11-ounce) can Pillsbury refrigerated low-fat
    French Loaf
1 (10¾-ounce) can Healthy Request Cream of Chicken
    Soup
2 tablespoons Land O Lakes no-fat sour cream
2 cups diced cooked chicken breast
½ cup sliced ripe olives
1 cup chunky salsa (mild, medium, or hot)
1 (8-ounce) can Hunt's Tomato Sauce
1 tablespoon Splenda Granular
1 teaspoon taco seasoning
1½ cups shredded Kraft reduced-fat
    Cheddar cheese

Preheat oven to 375 degrees. Spray a rimmed 10-by-15-inch baking sheet with butter-flavored cooking spray. Unroll French loaf and pat into prepared baking sheet and up sides of pan to form a rim. Lightly spray top of crust with butter-flavored cooking spray. Bake for 6 minutes. Meanwhile, in a small bowl, combine chicken soup and sour cream. Evenly spread soup mixture over partially baked crust. Sprinkle chicken and olives evenly over soup mixture. In a medium bowl, combine salsa, tomato sauce, Splenda, and taco seasoning. Spoon mixture evenly over chicken. Sprinkle Cheddar cheese evenly over top. Continue baking for 8 to 10 minutes or until crust is golden brown and cheese is melted. Place baking sheet on a wire rack and let set for 5 minutes. Cut into 8 servings.

HINT: If you don't have leftovers, purchase a chunk of cooked chicken breast from your local deli.

Each serving equals:

HE: 2 Protein • 1 Bread • ¾ Vegetable • ¼ Fat • ¼ Slider • 7 Optional Calories

295 Calories • 9 gm Fat • 24 gm Protein • 27 gm Carbohydrate • 969 mg Sodium • 172 mg Calcium • 2 gm Fiber

DIABETIC EXCHANGES: 2 Meat • 1½ Starch • 1 Vegetable

CARB CHOICES: 2

Chicken and Peppers Pizza with Fresh Tomatoes

There's something so magnificent about displays of fresh peppers in the market, I always find myself buying more than I can use right away! My friend Barbara has been known to buy five pounds of red peppers when they're on sale—and she only cooks for one. But with a recipe like this one, you can eat peppers more often—and with all the vitamins they contain, that's good news!

◐ Serves 8

1 cup chopped green bell pepper
1 cup chopped red bell pepper
2 cups diced cooked chicken breast
1 (11-ounce) can Pillsbury refrigerated low-fat
    French Loaf
2 cups peeled and chopped fresh tomatoes
1 teaspoon dried basil
1½ cups shredded Kraft reduced-fat
    mozzarella cheese

Preheat oven to 375 degrees. In a large skillet sprayed with olive oil–flavored cooking spray, sauté green and red peppers for 5 to 6 minutes. Stir in chicken. Continue sautéing for 2 to 3 minutes. Spray a rimmed 10-by-15-inch baking sheet with olive oil–flavored cooking spray. Unroll French loaf and pat into prepared baking sheet and up sides of pan to form a rim. Lightly spray top of crust with olive oil–flavored cooking spray. Bake for 6 minutes. Spoon chicken mixture evenly over partially baked crust. Arrange tomatoes over chicken mixture. Sprinkle basil evenly over tomatoes. Sprinkle mozzarella cheese evenly over top. Continue to bake for 12 to 16 minutes or until crust is golden brown and cheese is melted. Place baking sheet on a wire rack and let set for 5 minutes. Cut into 8 servings.

HINT: If you don't have leftovers, purchase a chunk of cooked chicken breast from your local deli.

Each serving equals:

HE: 2 Protein • 1 Bread • 1 Vegetable

213 Calories • 5 gm Fat • 20 gm Protein • 22 gm Carbohydrate • 404 mg Sodium • 315 mg Calcium • 2 gm Fiber

DIABETIC EXCHANGES: 2 Meat • 1 Starch • 1 Vegetable

CARB CHOICES: 1½

L.A. Chicken Pizza

Lots of our most exciting culinary ideas have come from California, including the sunset-colored dressing named for a beautiful island off the coast near Los Angeles. Knowing how those Hollywood types are always watching their weight, I figure they'll love knowing they can eat pizza without feeling guilty!   ☺   Serves 8

1 (11-ounce) can Pillsbury refrigerated low-fat French Loaf
16 ounces skinned and boned uncooked chicken breast, cut
    into bite-size pieces
¾ cup chopped onion
¾ cup chopped green bell pepper
½ cup Kraft Fat Free Catalina Dressing
2 teaspoons chili seasoning
1½ cups chopped fresh tomatoes
1 cup shredded Kraft reduced-fat Cheddar cheese

Preheat oven to 375 degrees. Spray a rimmed 10-by-15-inch baking sheet with olive oil–flavored cooking spray. Unroll French loaf and pat into prepared baking sheet and up sides of pan to form a rim. Lightly spray top of crust with olive oil–flavored cooking spray. Bake for 6 minutes. Meanwhile, in a large skillet sprayed with olive oil–flavored cooking spray, cook chicken pieces, onion, and green pepper for 5 to 6 minutes or until chicken is browned and vegetables are tender. Stir in Catalina dressing and chili seasoning. Spread chicken mixture evenly over partially baked crust. Sprinkle tomatoes and Cheddar cheese evenly over top. Continue baking for 16 to 20 minutes or until crust is browned and cheese is melted. Place baking sheet on a wire rack and let set for 5 minutes. Cut into 8 servings.

Each serving equals:

HE: 2 Protein • 1 Bread • ¾ Vegetable • ¼ Slider • 5 Optional Calories

234 Calories • 6 gm Fat • 19 gm Protein • 26 mg Carbohydrate •
429 mg Sodium • 123 mg Calcium • 2 gm Fiber

DIABETIC EXCHANGES: 2 Meat • 1½ Starch/Carbohydrate • ½ Vegetable

CARB CHOICES: 2

Chicken Bacon Ranch Pizza

Think of this as a classic chicken club sandwich made even better with the addition of Ranch dressing—then toss away the bread and substitute a crispy pizza crust. I know you'll agree that's a recipe for pleasure in every bite!   ☺   Serves 8

> 1 (11-ounce) can Pillsbury refrigerated low-fat French Loaf
> ¾ cup Kraft Fat Free Ranch Dressing
> ½ cup Kraft fat-free mayonnaise
> 2 teaspoons dried parsley flakes
> 2 teaspoons dried onion flakes
> 2 cups diced cooked chicken breast
> ¾ cup Oscar Mayer or Hormel Real Bacon Bits
> 1½ cups finely chopped fresh tomatoes
> ½ cup finely chopped red onion

Preheat oven to 375 degrees. Spray a rimmed 10-by-15-inch baking sheet with butter-flavored cooking spray. Unroll French loaf and pat into prepared baking sheet and up sides of pan to form a rim. Lightly spray top of crust with butter-flavored cooking spray. Bake for 8 to 12 minutes or until crust is golden brown. Meanwhile, in a medium bowl, combine Ranch dressing, mayonnaise, parsley flakes, and onion flakes. Spread sauce mixture evenly over baked crust. Sprinkle chicken, bacon bits, tomatoes, and onion evenly over sauce. Cut into 8 servings.

HINT: If you don't have leftovers, purchase a chunk of cooked chicken breast from your local deli.

Each serving equals:

HE: 2 Protein • 1 Bread • ½ Vegetable • ½ Slider • 7 Optional Calories

241 Calories • 5 gm Fat • 18 gm Protein • 31 gm Carbohydrate • 925 mg Sodium • 25 mg Calcium • 2 gm Fiber

DIABETIC EXCHANGES: 2 Meat • 1½ Starch/Carbohydrate • ½ Vegetable

CARB CHOICES: 2

Chicken Chow Mein Pizza

I know that China has grown very Westernized in recent years, but I wonder if they've developed a passion for pizza just like the American public! (With all its millions of people, that could mean *a lot* of pizza . . .) I thought stirring up an Asian-inspired pizza would be fun—and hurray, it tastes yummy, too.   ☯   Serves 8

1 (11-ounce) can Pillsbury refrigerated low-fat French Loaf
1½ cups sliced celery
1 cup finely chopped carrots
1 cup chopped red bell pepper
½ cup chopped green onion
1 (10¾-ounce) can Healthy Request Cream of Chicken Soup
2 tablespoons reduced-sodium soy sauce
½ teaspoon dried minced garlic
⅛ teaspoon black pepper
2 cups diced cooked chicken breast
2 cups fresh snow peas
1 cup shredded Kraft reduced-fat mozzarella cheese

Preheat oven to 375 degrees. Spray a rimmed 10-by-15-inch baking sheet with butter-flavored cooking spray. Unroll French loaf and pat into prepared baking sheet and up sides of pan to form a rim. Lightly spray top of crust with butter-flavored cooking spray. Bake for 6 minutes. Meanwhile, in a large skillet sprayed with butter-flavored cooking spray, sauté celery, carrots, red pepper, and green onion for 5 minutes. Remove from heat. In a medium bowl, combine chicken soup, soy sauce, garlic, and black pepper. Spread soup mixture evenly over partially baked crust. Evenly sprinkle chicken, sautéed vegetables, and snow peas over soup mixture. Sprinkle mozzarella cheese evenly over top. Continue baking for 10 to 12 minutes or until crust is golden brown and cheese is melted. Place baking sheet on a wire rack and let set for 5 minutes. Cut into 8 servings.

HINT: If you don't have leftovers, purchase a chunk of cooked chicken breast from your local deli.

Each serving equals:

HE: 1¾ Protein • 1¼ Vegetable • 1 Bread • ¼ Slider • 2 Optional Calories

233 Calories • 5 gm Fat • 19 gm Protein • 28 gm Carbohydrate •
499 mg Sodium • 138 mg Calcium • 3 gm Fiber

DIABETIC EXCHANGES: 2 Meat • 1½ Starch • 1 Vegetable

CARB CHOICES: 2

Chicken Caesar Pizza

It might just be the most popular main dish salad in the country these days—the twenty-first century's answer to the classic chef's salad of yesteryear! Topping a pizza with this Italian classic's ingredients made sense to my taste buds—how about yours?

◐ Serves 8

> 1 (11-ounce) can Pillsbury refrigerated low-fat
>   French Loaf
> 1 (8-ounce) package Philadelphia fat-free
>   cream cheese
> ¾ cup Kraft Light Done Right! Golden Caesar
>   Dressing ☆
> ¼ cup Kraft fat-free mayonnaise
> ½ cup Kraft Reduced Fat Parmesan Style
>   Grated Topping ☆
> 2 cups torn romaine lettuce
> 2 cups diced cooked chicken breast
> 1½ cups garlic-flavored croutons

Preheat oven to 375 degrees. Spray a rimmed 10-by-15-inch baking sheet with butter-flavored cooking spray. Unroll French loaf and pat into prepared baking sheet and up sides of pan to form a rim. Lightly spray top of crust with butter-flavored cooking spray. Bake for 8 to 12 minutes or until crust is golden brown. Place baking sheet on a wire rack and let set for 5 minutes. Meanwhile, in a medium bowl, stir cream cheese with a sturdy spoon until soft. Add ¼ cup Caesar dressing, mayonnaise, and ¼ cup Parmesan cheese. Mix well to combine. Spread cream cheese mixture evenly over cooled crust. Sprinkle lettuce, chicken, remaining ¼ cup Parmesan cheese, and croutons evenly over cream cheese layer. Drizzle remaining ½ cup Caesar dressing evenly over top. Cut into 8 servings. Serve at once.

HINT: If you don't have leftovers, purchase a chunk of cooked chicken breast from your local deli.

Each serving equals:

HE: 2 Protein • 1¼ Bread • ¼ Vegetable • ½ Slider • 10 Optional Calories

281 Calories • 9 gm Fat • 20 gm Protein • 30 gm Carbohydrate • 845 mg Sodium • 140 mg Calcium • 1 gm Fiber

DIABETIC EXCHANGES: 2 Meat • 2 Starch/Carbohydrate • 1 Fat

CARB CHOICES: 2

Chicken Gyro Pizza

Now for a taste of something really different—a pizza that should be served to Greek bouzouki music, rich with feta cheese and tangy olives! Pizza is a proud member of the family of "good food served up fast," just like the famous gyro sandwich sold in street markets around the globe.   ○   Serves 8

> 1 (11-ounce) can Pillsbury refrigerated low-fat French Loaf
> ½ teaspoon dried oregano
> 1½ cups diced cooked chicken breast
> ½ cup sliced ripe olives
> ½ cup crumbled feta cheese
> 1½ cups shredded Kraft reduced-fat mozzarella cheese
> 1 cup chopped unpeeled fresh tomatoes
> 1 cup chopped unpeeled cucumber
> ½ cup Dannon plain fat-free yogurt or Land O Lakes no-fat
>   sour cream

Preheat oven to 375 degrees. Spray a rimmed 10-by-15-inch baking sheet with butter-flavored cooking spray. Unroll French loaf and pat into prepared baking sheet and up sides of pan to form a rim. Sprinkle oregano evenly over top. Lightly spray top of crust with butter-flavored cooking spray. Bake for 6 minutes. Evenly sprinkle chicken, olives, feta cheese, and mozzarella cheese over partially baked crust. Continue baking for 10 to 12 minutes or until crust is golden brown and cheese is melted. Place baking sheet on a wire rack. Top with tomatoes and cucumber. Cut into 8 servings. When serving, top each piece with 1 tablespoon yogurt or sour cream.

HINT: If you don't have leftovers, purchase a chunk of cooked chicken breast from your local deli.

Each serving equals:

HE: 2 Protein • 1 Bread • ½ Vegetable • ¼ Fat • 6 Optional Calories

232 Calories • 8 gm Fat • 18 gm Protein • 22 gm Carbohydrate • 558 mg Sodium • 224 mg Calcium • 1 gm Fiber

DIABETIC EXCHANGES: 2 Meat • 1 Starch • ½ Vegetable • ½ Fat

CARB CHOICES: 1½

Barbeque Chicken Pizza

Hmm, was I watching a barbecue cook-off on the Food Network when I created this pizza? No, I wasn't, but I love the idea of tangy-sauced chicken on top of a pizza so much, it makes me want to enter next year's championship! ☻   Serves 6

> 1 (7.5-ounce) can Pillsbury refrigerated buttermilk biscuits
> 1 cup finely chopped onion
> 1½ cups diced cooked chicken breast
> 1 (8-ounce) can Hunt's Tomato Sauce
> 3 tablespoons Splenda Granular
> 2 tablespoons white distilled vinegar
> 2 teaspoons dried parsley flakes
> 1 cup shredded Kraft reduced-fat Cheddar cheese

Preheat oven to 425 degrees. Spray a 12-inch round pizza pan with butter-flavored cooking spray. Separate and flatten biscuits and pat each onto prepared pizza pan, being sure to press together to cover pan and forming an edge around the outside. In a large skillet sprayed with butter-flavored cooking spray, sauté onion for 5 minutes. Stir in chicken. Add tomato sauce, Splenda, vinegar, and parsley flakes. Mix well to combine. Spread chicken mixture evenly over crust. Sprinkle Cheddar cheese evenly over top. Bake for 12 to 15 minutes or until crust is golden brown and cheese is melted. Place pan on a wire rack and let set for 3 minutes. Cut into 6 servings.

HINT: If you don't have leftovers, purchase a chunk of cooked chicken breast from your local deli.

Each serving equals:

HE: 2 Protein • 1¼ Bread • 1 Vegetable • 2 Optional Calories

226 Calories • 6 gm Fat • 20 gm Protein • 23 gm Carbohydrate • 530 mg Sodium • 161 mg Calcium • 1 gm Fiber

DIABETIC EXCHANGES: 2 Meat • 1 Starch • 1 Vegetable

CARB CHOICES: 1½

Chicken Fajita Pizza

You might just shout "Olé!" at the first bite of this piquant, Tex-Mex inspired pizza—it's that good! And here's a piece of advice to keep things interesting: Try a new brand of salsa every so often, something lively from a specialty shop or ordered online. Take your taste buds on vacation, even if you can't get away. ☻ Serves 4

> ½ cup Cheez Whiz Light ☆
> 4 (6-inch) flour tortillas
> 1 cup finely diced cooked chicken breast
> ½ cup chunky salsa (mild, medium, or hot)
> ½ cup chopped fresh tomatoes
> ¼ cup sliced ripe olives

Preheat oven to 375 degrees. Spray a baking sheet with olive oil–flavored cooking spray. Spread 1 tablespoon Cheez Whiz Light on each tortilla. In a small bowl, combine chicken, salsa, tomatoes, and olives. Spread about ½ cup chicken mixture over each tortilla. Evenly arrange pizzas on prepared baking sheet. Drizzle 1 tablespoon Cheez Whiz over top of each. Bake for 6 to 8 minutes. Serve at once.

HINT: If you don't have leftovers, purchase a chunk of cooked chicken breast from your local deli.

Each serving equals:

HE: 1¾ Protein • 1 Bread • ½ Vegetable • ¼ Fat

225 Calories • 9 gm Fat • 16 gm Protein • 20 gm Carbohydrate • 686 mg Sodium • 96 mg Calcium • 1 gm Fiber

DIABETIC EXCHANGES: 2 Meat • 1 Starch • 1 Fat

CARB CHOICES: 1

Turkey Club Pizza

The turkey club was a favorite sandwich of the Duke and Duchess of Windsor. (Remember, he gave up his crown for the woman—and the sandwich—he loved!) Probably invented by the chef at a snobby country club, this combo is one of the most popular ever made, so it's perfect for a pizza. ❂ Serves 8

1 (11-ounce) can Pillsbury refrigerated low-fat French Loaf
1 cup Kraft fat-free mayonnaise
½ cup Oscar Mayer or Hormel Real Bacon Bits
2 cups finely shredded lettuce
2 full cups diced cooked turkey breast
1 cup chopped fresh tomatoes
4 slices reduced-calorie white bread, toasted, and cut into
    very small pieces

Preheat oven to 375 degrees. Spray a rimmed 10-by-15-inch baking sheet with butter-flavored cooking spray. Unroll French loaf and pat into prepared baking sheet and up sides of pan to form a rim. Lightly spray top of crust with butter-flavored cooking spray. Bake for 8 to 12 minutes or until crust is golden brown. Place baking sheet on a wire rack and let set for 5 minutes. Meanwhile, in a small bowl, combine mayonnaise and bacon bits. Spread mayonnaise mixture evenly over cooled crust. Layer lettuce, turkey, and tomatoes evenly over mayonnaise mixture. Evenly sprinkle toast pieces over top. Cut into 8 servings. Serve at once.

HINT: If you don't have leftovers, purchase a chunk of cooked turkey breast from your local deli.

Each serving equals:

HE: 2 Protein • 1¼ Bread • ½ Vegetable • ¼ Slider • 1 Optional Calorie

224 Calories • 4 gm Fat • 20 gm Protein • 27 gm Carbohydrate •
786 mg Sodium • 22 mg Calcium • 3 gm Fiber

DIABETIC EXCHANGES: 2 Meat • 1½ Starch • ½ Vegetable

CARB CHOICES: 2

West Coast Turkey Pizza

New Jersey may be called the Garden State, but these days we get so much of our beautiful produce from the Golden State (California), it seemed only right to name this pizza after their passion for colorful salads. With its three cheeses and calcium-rich sauce, it just might be worthy of a golden statue, too!   ☺   Serves 8

1 (11-ounce) can Pillsbury refrigerated low-fat French Loaf
1 (12-fluid-ounce) can Carnation Evaporated Fat Free Milk
3 tablespoons all-purpose flour
⅓ cup Carnation Nonfat Dry Milk Powder
½ cup water
½ cup Kraft Reduced Fat Parmesan Style Grated Topping
½ teaspoon dried minced garlic
1 tablespoon chopped fresh basil or 1 teaspoon dried basil
1½ cups frozen whole-kernel corn, thawed
½ cup chopped red onion
2 cups diced cooked turkey breast
½ cup grated carrots
1 cup chopped red bell pepper
¾ cup shredded Kraft reduced-fat Cheddar cheese
¾ cup shredded Kraft reduced-fat mozzarella cheese

Preheat oven to 375 degrees. Spray a rimmed 10-by-15-inch baking sheet with butter-flavored cooking spray. Unroll French loaf and pat into prepared baking sheet and up sides of pan to form a rim. Lightly spray top of crust with butter-flavored cooking spray. Bake for 6 minutes. Meanwhile, in a covered jar, combine evaporated milk, flour, dry milk powder, and water. Shake well to blend. Pour mixture into a medium saucepan sprayed with butter-flavored cooking spray. Stir in Parmesan cheese, garlic, and basil. Cook over medium heat for 5 minutes or until mixture thickens, stirring often. Spread hot mixture evenly over partially baked crust. Sprinkle corn, onion, turkey, carrots, and red pepper evenly over sauce mixture. Sprinkle Cheddar and mozzarella cheeses evenly over top. Continue baking for 8 to 10 minutes or until crust is golden brown and cheeses are melted. Place baking pan on a wire rack and let set for 3 minutes. Cut into 8 servings.

HINTS:
1. Thaw corn by rinsing in a colander under hot water for 1 minute.
2. If you don't have leftovers, purchase a chunk of cooked turkey breast from your local deli.

Each serving equals:

HE: 2¼ Protein • 1½ Bread • ½ Fat Free Milk • ½ Vegetable

303 Calories • 7 gm Fat • 25 gm Protein • 35 gm Carbohydrate • 477 mg Sodium • 331 mg Calcium • 2 gm Fiber

DIABETIC EXCHANGES: 2½ Meat • 1½ Starch • ½ Fat Free Milk

CARB CHOICES: 2

Turkey Divan Pizza

This much-loved dish hit its heyday in the 1950s, when house-wives everywhere served it to their hubbys—at least, those who agreed to eat broccoli (unlike my husband, Cliff!). With its creamy, cheesy sauce, it's a lip-smacking addition to your pizza repertoire.

☻ Serves 8

1 (11-ounce) can Pillsbury refrigerated low-fat French Loaf
½ cup Land O Lakes no-fat sour cream
½ cup Kraft fat-free mayonnaise
½ cup Kraft Reduced Fat Parmesan Style Grated Topping
2 cups diced cooked turkey breast
2 cups frozen chopped broccoli, thawed
1¼ cups shredded Kraft reduced-fat mozzarella cheese

Preheat oven to 375 degrees. Spray a rimmed 10-by-15-inch baking sheet with butter-flavored cooking spray. Unroll French loaf and pat into prepared baking sheet and up sides of pan to form a rim. Lightly spray top of crust with butter-flavored cooking spray. Bake for 6 minutes. Meanwhile, in a medium bowl, combine sour cream, mayonnaise, and Parmesan cheese. Spread sour cream mixture evenly over partially baked crust. Sprinkle turkey and broccoli evenly over sour cream layer. Evenly sprinkle mozzarella cheese over top. Continue baking for 10 to 12 minutes or until crust is golden brown and cheese is melted. Place baking sheet on a wire rack and let set for 5 minutes. Cut into 8 servings.

HINT: If you don't have leftovers, purchase a chunk of cooked turkey breast from your local deli.

Each serving equals:

HE: 2 Protein • 1 Bread • ½ Vegetable

246 Calories • 6 gm Fat • 20 gm Protein • 28 gm Carbohydrate • 632 mg Sodium • 195 mg Calcium • 2 gm Fiber

DIABETIC EXCHANGES: 2 Meat • 1½ Starch/Carbohydrate • ½ Vegetable

CARB CHOICES: 2

Bacon and Tomato Pizzas

Individual pizzas seem to please children even more than the regular kind, probably because they're just so *cute!* These are super-easy and super-fast to prepare, but they make no excuses when it comes to flavor—probably because they call for fresh tomatoes and real bacon. ☻ Serves 4

¼ cup Kraft fat-free mayonnaise
2 teaspoon dried basil
2 English muffins, halved and toasted
1 cup peeled and chopped fresh tomatoes
¼ cup Oscar Mayer or Hormel Real Bacon Bits
4 (¾-ounce) slices Kraft reduced-fat American cheese

In a small bowl, combine mayonnaise and basil. Spread about 1 tablespoon mayonnaise mixture over each English muffin half. Sprinkle ¼ cup tomato and 1 tablespoon bacon bits over each. Evenly arrange 1 slice American cheese over top of each. Place muffin halves on a microwave-safe plate. Microwave on MEDIUM (50% power) for 2 to 3 minutes. Serve at once.

Each serving equals:

HE: 1½ Protein • 1 Bread • ½ Vegetable • 10 Optional Calories

165 Calories • 5 gm Fat • 11 gm Protein • 19 gm Carbohydrate • 753 mg Sodium • 221 mg Calcium • 2 gm Fiber

DIABETIC EXCHANGES: 1½ Meat • 1 Starch • ½ Vegetable

CARB CHOICES: 1

Spinach and Bacon Pizza

This is my pizza "hymm" to the great spinach salad, a restaurant staple that just never loses its charm! Make sure you rinse your spinach before using it, but dry it well afterward.

● Serves 8

1 (11-ounce) can Pillsbury refrigerated low-fat French Loaf
1 (8-ounce) can Hunt's Tomato Sauce
2 tablespoons Splenda Granular
1½ teaspoons pizza or Italian seasoning
1¾ cups shredded Kraft reduced-fat mozzarella cheese ☆
2 cups shredded fresh spinach leaves
½ cup Oscar Mayer or Hormel Real Bacon Bits
2 cups peeled and chopped fresh tomatoes
¼ cup Kraft Reduced Fat Parmesan Style Grated Topping

Preheat oven to 375 degrees. Spray a rimmed 10-by-15-inch baking sheet with butter-flavored cooking spray. Unroll French loaf and pat into prepared baking sheet and up sides of pan to form a rim. Lightly spray top of crust with butter-flavored cooking spray. Bake for 6 minutes. Meanwhile, in a small bowl, combine tomato sauce, Splenda, and pizza seasoning. Spread sauce mixture evenly over partially baked crust. Sprinkle ¾ cup mozzarella cheese, spinach, bacon bits, and tomatoes over sauce. Evenly sprinkle Parmesan cheese and remaining 1 cup mozzarella cheese over top. Bake for 10 to 12 minutes or until topping is hot and bubbly and crust is golden brown. Place baking sheet on a wire rack and let set for 5 minutes. Cut into 8 servings.

Each serving equals:

HE: 1½ Protein • 1¼ Vegetable • 1 Bread • 2 Optional Calories

211 Calories • 7 gm Fat • 12 gm Protein • 25 gm Carbohydrate •
806 mg Sodium • 209 mg Calcium • 2 gm Fiber

DIABETIC EXCHANGES: 1½ Meat • 1 Vegetable • 1 Starch

CARB CHOICES: 1½

BLT Pizza Supreme

I don't believe in settling for just okay in any recipe, so I decided to raise my original idea for a BLT pizza "another notch," to borrow a phrase from a beloved TV chef. In addition to the big three basics (bacon, lettuce, and tomatoes), I've stirred in some cream cheese and Thousand Island dressing for a taste that is truly "supreme."

○ Serves 8

1 (11-ounce) can Pillsbury refrigerated low-fat French Loaf
1 (8-ounce) package Philadelphia fat-free cream cheese
¼ cup Kraft fat-free mayonnaise
½ cup Kraft Fat Free Thousand Island Dressing
3 cups finely shredded lettuce
2½ cups finely chopped fresh tomatoes
½ cup Oscar Mayer or Hormel Real Bacon Bits

Preheat oven to 375 degrees. Spray a rimmed 10-by-15-inch baking sheet with butter-flavored cooking spray. Unroll French loaf and pat into prepared baking sheet and up sides of pan to form a rim. Lightly spray top of crust with butter-flavored cooking spray. Bake for 8 to 12 minutes or until crust is golden brown. Place baking sheet on a wire rack and allow to cool completely. In a medium bowl, stir cream cheese with a sturdy spoon until soft. Add mayonnaise and Thousand Island dressing. Mix well to combine. Spread mixture evenly over cooled crust. In a large bowl, combine lettuce, tomatoes, and bacon bits. Sprinkle lettuce mixture evenly over cream cheese mixture. Refrigerate for at least 30 minutes. Cut into 8 servings.

Each serving equals:

HE: 1 Bread • ¾ Vegetable • ½ Protein • ½ Slider • 10 Optional Calories

188 Calories • 4 gm Fat • 11 gm Protein • 27 gm Carbohydrate •
814 mg Sodium • 88 mg Calcium • 2 gm Fiber

DIABETIC EXCHANGES: 1½ Starch/Carbohydrate • 1 Meat • 1 Vegetable

CARB CHOICES: 2

Bacon Cheeseburger Pizza

Why go out for the same old, same old, fast food meal when you can dine on your favorite flavors right at home? For all of you (including my sons, James and Tom) who like to order their cheeseburgers topped with bacon, here's a sensational pizza that always gets applause. ☻ Serves 8

> 1 (11-ounce) can Pillsbury refrigerated low-fat French Loaf
> 16 ounces extra-lean ground sirloin beef or turkey breast
> 1 cup chopped onion
> 1 (15-ounce) can Hunt's Tomato Sauce
> 1½ teaspoons pizza or Italian seasoning
> 1 tablespoon Splenda Granular
> 1 (15-ounce) can diced tomatoes, very well drained
> ¾ cup Oscar Mayer or Hormel Real Bacon Bits
> 1½ cups shredded Kraft reduced-fat Cheddar cheese

Preheat oven to 375 degrees. Spray a rimmed 10-by-15-inch baking sheet with olive oil–flavored cooking spray. Unroll French loaf and pat into prepared baking sheet and up sides of pan to form a rim. Lightly spray top of crust with olive oil–flavored cooking spray. Bake for 6 minutes. Meanwhile, in a large skillet sprayed with olive oil–flavored cooking spray, brown meat and onion. In a small bowl, combine tomato sauce, pizza seasoning, and Splenda. Spread sauce mixture evenly over partially baked crust. Spoon meat mixture evenly over sauce. Sprinkle tomatoes, bacon bits, and Cheddar cheese evenly over top. Continue baking for 8 to 10 minutes or until crust is golden brown and cheese is melted. Place baking sheet on a wire rack and let set for 2 to 3 minutes. Cut into 8 servings.

Each serving equals:

HE: 2½ Protein • 1½ Vegetable • 1 Bread • ¼ Slider • 18 Optional Calories

294 Calories • 10 gm Fat • 25 gm Protein • 26 gm Carbohydrate • 903 mg Sodium • 186 mg Calcium • 2 gm Fiber

DIABETIC EXCHANGES: 3 Meat • 1½ Vegetable • 1 Starch

CARB CHOICES: 2

Cliff's Classic Pizza

As he crosses the country in his big rig, Cliff admits that he thinks about what he's going to be eating for lunch or supper—what driver doesn't? I know what he loves best when it comes to pizza—a meaty, cheesy combo on a golden crust. What better welcome home could I offer than his very own pizza! **●** Serves 8

16 ounces extra-lean ground sirloin beef or turkey breast
1 cup finely chopped onion
1 (11-ounce) can Pillsbury refrigerated low-fat French Loaf
1 (14.5-ounce) can Hunt's Tomatoes Diced in Sauce
1 tablespoon Splenda Granular
1½ teaspoons pizza or Italian seasoning
½ cup sliced ripe olives
1 (2.5-ounce) jar sliced mushrooms, drained
¾ cup shredded Kraft reduced-fat Cheddar cheese
¾ cup shredded Kraft reduced-fat mozzarella cheese

Preheat oven to 375 degrees. In a large skillet sprayed with olive oil–flavored cooking spray, brown meat and onion. Meanwhile, spray a rimmed 10-by-15-inch baking sheet with olive oil–flavored cooking spray. Unroll French loaf and pat into prepared baking sheet and up sides of pan to form a rim. Lightly spray top of crust with olive oil–flavored cooking spray. Bake for 6 minutes. Stir Splenda and pizza seasoning into tomato sauce. Spread tomato sauce evenly over partially baked crust. Layer browned meat mixture, olives, and mushrooms over sauce. Sprinkle Cheddar and mozzarella cheeses evenly over top. Bake for 20 to 25 minutes or until crust is golden brown and cheeses are melted. Place baking sheet on a wire rack and let set for 5 minutes. Cut into 8 servings.

Each serving equals:

HE: 2¼ Protein • 1 Bread • 1 Vegetable • ¼ Fat • 1 Optional Calorie

252 Calories • 8 gm Fat • 20 gm Protein • 25 gm Carbohydrate • 442 mg Sodium • 169 mg Calcium • 2 gm Fiber

DIABETIC EXCHANGES: 2 Meat • 1 Starch • 1 Vegetable • ½ Fat

CARB CHOICES: 1½

Spinach Supreme Pizza

Here's a hearty blend of meat and veggies that is a tasty and thrifty way to serve a crowd! When was the last time you made a pound of ground beef serve eight people, right? This is so good, it might just serve four *ravenous* friends.   ☯   Serves 8

1 (11-ounce) can Pillsbury refrigerated low-fat
    French Loaf
16 ounces extra-lean ground sirloin beef or
    turkey breast
1 cup chopped onion
1 (10-ounce) package frozen chopped spinach,
    thawed and well drained
1 (4-ounce) can sliced mushrooms, drained
1 (2-ounce) jar chopped pimiento, drained
½ teaspoon dried minced garlic
1 (15-ounce) can Hunt's Tomato Sauce
1½ teaspoons pizza or Italian seasoning
1 tablespoon Splenda Granular
1½ cups shredded Kraft reduced-fat mozzarella cheese

Preheat oven to 375 degrees. Spray a rimmed 10-by-15-inch baking sheet with olive oil–flavored cooking spray. Unroll French loaf and pat into prepared baking sheet and up sides of pan to form a rim. Lightly spray top of crust with olive oil–flavored cooking spray. Bake for 6 minutes. Meanwhile, in a large skillet sprayed with olive oil–flavored cooking spray, brown meat and onion. Stir in spinach, mushrooms, pimiento, and garlic. Remove from heat. In a small bowl, combine tomato sauce, pizza seasoning, and Splenda. Spread sauce mixture evenly over partially baked crust. Evenly sprinkle meat mixture over sauce mixture. Sprinkle mozzarella cheese evenly over top. Continue baking for 7 to 9 minutes or until crust is golden brown and cheese is melted. Place baking sheet on a wire rack and let set for 2 to 3 minutes. Cut into 8 servings.

HINT: Thaw spinach by rinsing in a colander under hot water for 1 minute.

Each serving equals:

HE: 2¼ Protein • 1½ Vegetable • 1 Bread • 1 Optional Calorie

243 Calories • 7 gm Fat • 22 gm Protein • 23 gm Carbohydrate • 692 mg Sodium • 233 mg Calcium • 3 gm Fiber

DIABETIC EXCHANGES: 2½ Meat • 1½ Vegetable • 1 Starch

CARB CHOICES: 1½

Runza Pizza

If you've never eaten a runza, you've been missing out—until now. This meat-and-cabbage blend in a luscious, saucy gravy is a Midwestern specialty, but I don't think it's ever taken a starring role on top of a pizza! Yum, yum. ☺ Serves 8

1 (11-ounce) can Pillsbury refrigerated low-fat French Loaf
16 ounces extra-lean ground sirloin beef or turkey breast
4 cups purchased coleslaw mix
1 cup chopped onion
1½ teaspoons meat seasoning
1 (10¾-ounce) can Healthy Request Cream of Mushroom
    Soup
1½ cups shredded Kraft reduced-fat Cheddar cheese

Preheat oven to 375 degrees. In a large skillet sprayed with butter-flavored cooling spray, brown meat, coleslaw mix, and onion for 6 to 8 minutes. Stir in meat seasoning and mushroom soup. Meanwhile, spray a rimmed 10-by-15-inch baking sheet with butter-flavored cooking spray. Unroll French loaf and pat into prepared baking sheet and up sides of pan to form a rim. Lightly spray top of crust with butter-flavored cooking spray. Bake for 6 minutes. Spread meat mixture evenly over partially baked crust. Sprinkle Cheddar cheese evenly over top. Continue baking for 8 to 10 minutes or until crust is golden brown and cheese is melted. Place baking sheet on a wire rack and let set for 5 minutes. Cut into 8 servings.

HINT: 3½ cups shredded cabbage and ½ cup shredded carrots may be used in place of purchased coleslaw mix.

Each serving equals:

HE: 2¼ Protein • 1 Bread • ¾ Vegetable • ¼ Slider • 1 Optional Calorie

269 Calories • 9 gm Fat • 21 gm Protein • 26 gm Carbohydrate •
435 mg Sodium • 211 mg Calcium • 1 gm Fiber

DIABETIC EXCHANGES: 2½ Meat • 1½ Starch • ½ Vegetable

CARB CHOICES: 2

Meat Lover's Chunky Pizza

If you've got a hungry family hoping for a truly hearty meal, why not fix this meaty classic with two kinds of cheese and plenty of chunky veggies (including canned diced tomatoes!) along with plenty of meat to love? ☻ Serves 8

16 ounces extra-lean ground sirloin beef or turkey breast
½ cup chopped onion
½ cup chopped green bell pepper
1 (11-ounce) can Pillsbury refrigerated low-fat French Loaf
1 (14.5-ounce) can Hunt's Tomatoes Diced in Sauce
1 teaspoon Italian seasoning
½ cup sliced ripe olives
1 (2.5-ounce) jar sliced mushrooms, drained
¾ cup shredded Kraft reduced-fat Cheddar cheese
¾ cup shredded Kraft reduced-fat mozzarella cheese

Preheat oven to 375 degrees. In a large skillet sprayed with olive oil–flavored cooking spray, brown meat, onion, and green pepper. Meanwhile, spray a rimmed 10-by-15-inch baking sheet with olive oil–flavored cooking spray. Unroll French loaf and pat into prepared baking sheet and up sides of pan to form a rim. Lightly spray top of crust with olive oil–flavored cooking spray. Bake for 6 minutes. Evenly spread tomato sauce over partially baked crust. Sprinkle Italian seasoning over sauce. Layer browned meat mixture, olives, and mushrooms over sauce. Sprinkle Cheddar and mozzarella cheeses evenly over top. Bake for 20 to 24 minutes or until crust is golden brown and cheeses are melted. Place baking sheet on a wire rack and let set for 5 minutes. Cut into 8 servings.

Each serving equals:

HE: 2¼ Protein • 1 Bread • 1 Vegetable • ¼ Fat

257 Calories • 9 gm Fat • 20 gm Protein • 24 gm Carbohydrate • 442 mg Sodium • 168 mg Calcium • 2 gm Fiber

DIABETIC EXCHANGES: 2 Meat • 1 Starch • 1 Vegetable • ½ Fat

CARB CHOICES: 1½

Homemade Deep-Dish Pizza

It's true, it's true, now you don't have to go out to dine on a DEEP-dish pizza! I'm happy to share with you my secrets for making a really good one without a lot of fuss. It serves a big crowd, so plan a party and preheat the oven!   ◑   Serves 12

16 ounces extra-lean ground sirloin beef or
    turkey breast
½ cup chopped onion
1 teaspoon dried parsley flakes
¼ teaspoon dried minced garlic
1½ cups + 3 tablespoons Bisquick Heart Smart
    Baking Mix ☆
6 tablespoons water
1 (14.5-ounce) can Hunt's Tomatoes Diced in Sauce
1½ teaspoons pizza or Italian seasoning
1 tablespoon Splenda Granular
1 (4-ounce) can sliced mushrooms, drained
1 cup chopped green bell pepper
¾ cup shredded Kraft reduced-fat Cheddar cheese
1½ cups shredded Kraft reduced-fat mozzarella
    cheese

Preheat oven to 425 degrees. In a large skillet sprayed with olive oil–flavored cooking spray, brown meat and onion. Add parsley flakes and garlic. Spray an 11-by-16-inch jelly-roll pan with olive oil–flavored cooking spray. In a large bowl, combine 1½ cups baking mix and water until a soft ball is formed. Sprinkle remaining 3 tablespoons baking mix on counter or large piece of waxed paper. Knead crust on prepared surface for about 1 minute. Pat dough in bottom of prepared pan and up sides to form a crust. Bake for 5 minutes. In a small bowl, combine tomato sauce, pizza seasoning, and Splenda. Spread sauce mixture over partially baked crust. Spoon meat mixture over sauce. Arrange mushrooms and green pepper over meat mixture. Top with Cheddar and mozzarella cheeses. Bake for 15 to 17 minutes or until crust is golden brown and cheeses are melted. Cut into 12 servings.

Each serving equals:

HE: 1¾ Protein • 1 Vegetable • ¾ Bread

162 Calories • 6 gm Fat • 14 gm Protein • 13 gm Carbohydrate • 296 mg Sodium • 167 mg Calcium • 1 gm Fiber

DIABETIC EXCHANGES: 2 Meat • 1 Starch • ½ Vegetable

CARB CHOICES: 1

Santa Fe Trail Pizza

Have you ever driven the Santa Fe Trail? It's a wonderful sight-seeing experience if you've got the time (and a terrific driver, as I had in my husband, Cliff). It's also a great route for eating the flavorful food of the great Southwest. Here's a pizza that I hope you'll agree deserves the name! ☻ Serves 8

1 (11-ounce) can Pillsbury refrigerated low-fat
     French Loaf
2 teaspoons cornmeal
8 ounces extra-lean ground sirloin beef or turkey
     breast
1 (15-ounce) can diced tomatoes, drained
1 cup frozen whole-kernel corn, thawed
¼ cup chunky salsa (mild, medium, or hot)
1 (15-ounce) can Bush's red kidney beans, rinsed and
     drained
2 tablespoons reduced-sodium ketchup
1 tablespoon chili seasoning
¾ cup shredded Kraft reduced-fat Cheddar cheese

Preheat oven to 375 degrees. Spray a rimmed 10-by-15-inch baking sheet with butter-flavored cooking spray. Unroll French loaf and pat into prepared baking sheet and up sides of pan to form a rim. Lightly spray top of crust with butter-flavored cooking spray and sprinkle dry cornmeal evenly over top. Bake for 6 minutes. Meanwhile, brown meat in a large skillet sprayed with butter-flavored cooking spray. Add tomatoes, corn, salsa, and kidney beans. Mix well to combine. Stir in ketchup and chili seasoning. Spoon meat mixture evenly over partially baked crust. Sprinkle Cheddar cheese evenly over top. Bake for 10 to 12 minutes or until crust is golden brown and cheese is melted. Place baking sheet on a wire rack and let set for 5 minutes. Cut into 8 servings.

HINT: Thaw corn by rinsing in a colander under hot water for 1 minute.

Each serving equals:

HE: 1½ Bread • 1¼ Protein • ½ Vegetable • 5 Optional Calories

229 Calories • 5 gm Fat • 14 gm Protein • 32 gm Carbohydrate • 463 mg Sodium • 103 mg Calcium • 4 gm Fiber

DIABETIC EXCHANGES: 2 Starch • 1½ Meat • ½ Vegetable

CARB CHOICES: 2

Easy Taco Pizza

Some of my most successful recipes involve blending two culinary traditions—in this case, an Italian-style crust with a Mexican-inspired topping that delivers the best of both worlds! It's a true bonus of living—and eating—the bounty of the American melting pot. ☻ Serves 8

> 1 (11-ounce) can Pillsbury refrigerated low-fat
>   French Loaf
> 16 ounces extra-lean ground sirloin beef or
>   turkey breast
> 1 cup chopped onion
> 1 (8-ounce) can Hunt's Tomato Sauce
> ½ cup chopped ripe olives
> 1 tablespoon taco seasoning
> 1½ cups shredded Kraft reduced-fat
>   Cheddar cheese
> 2 cups finely shredded lettuce
> 2 cups chopped fresh tomatoes
> ¾ cup crushed Baked! Doritos Nacho Cheese
>   Tortilla Chips or Baked! Tostitos Tortilla Chips
> 1 cup Land O Lakes no-fat sour cream

Preheat oven to 375 degrees. Spray a rimmed 10-by-15-inch baking sheet with butter-flavored cooking spray. Unroll French loaf and pat into prepared baking sheet and up sides of pan to form a rim. Lightly spray top of crust with butter-flavored cooking spray. Bake for 6 minutes. Meanwhile, in a large skillet sprayed with butter-flavored cooking spray, brown meat and onion. Stir in tomato sauce, olives, and taco seasoning. Spread meat mixture evenly over partially baked crust. Sprinkle Cheddar cheese evenly over top. Continue baking for 8 to 10 minutes or until crust is golden brown and cheese is melted. Place baking sheet on a wire rack. Top with lettuce, tomatoes, and tortilla chips. Cut into 8 servings. When serving, top each piece with 2 tablespoons sour cream.

Each serving equals:

HE: 2¼ Protein • 1½ Vegetable • 1¼ Bread • ¼ Fat • ¼ Slider •
10 Optional Calories

305 Calories • 9 gm Fat • 22 gm Protein • 34 gm Carbohydrate •
606 mg Sodium • 235 mg Calcium • 3 gm Fiber

DIBETIC EXCHANGES: 2½ Meat • 1½ Vegetable • 1½ Starch/Carbohydrate

CARB CHOICES: 2

Tex-Mex Chili Pizza

When Cliff comes home for the weekend, he gets to taste-test all my chili-themed recipes, since his motto is, "The hotter, the better"! He called this pizza dish "impressive" for its blend of savory ingredients. ☻ Serves 8

1 (11-ounce) can Pillsbury refrigerated low-fat
    French Loaf
16 ounces extra-lean ground sirloin beef or
    turkey breast
½ cup chopped onion
½ cup chopped green bell pepper
1 cup frozen whole-kernel corn, thawed
1 (8-ounce) can red kidney beans, rinsed and
    drained
1 (8-ounce) can Hunt's Tomato Sauce
1 cup chunky salsa (mild, medium, or hot)
2 tablespoons Splenda Granular
1 teaspoon taco seasoning
1 cup shredded Kraft reduced-fat Cheddar cheese

Preheat oven to 375 degrees. Spray a rimmed 10-by-15-inch baking sheet with butter-flavored cooking spray. Unroll French loaf and pat into prepared baking sheet and up sides of pan to form a rim. Lightly spray top of crust with butter-flavored cooking spray. Bake for 6 minutes. Meanwhile, in a large skillet sprayed with butter-flavored cooking spray, brown meat, onion, and green pepper. Stir in corn and kidney beans. In a small bowl, combine tomato sauce, salsa, Splenda, and taco seasoning. Reserve ½ cup sauce mixture. Evenly spread remaining sauce mixture over partially baked crust. Sprinkle meat mixture evenly over sauce mixture. Drizzle remaining ½ cup sauce mixture over meat mixture. Sprinkle Cheddar cheese evenly over top. Continue baking for 8 to 10 minutes or until crust is golden brown and cheese is melted. Place baking sheet on a wire rack and let set for 5 minutes. Cut into 8 servings.

Each serving equals:

HE: 2½ Protein • 1¼ Bread • ¾ Vegetable • 9 Optional Calories

288 Calories • 8 gm Fat • 22 gm Protein • 32 gm Carbohydrate • 709 mg Sodium • 143 mg Calcium • 4 gm Fiber

DIABETIC EXCHANGES: 2½ Meat • 1½ Starch • 1 Vegetable

CARB CHOICES: 2

Southwestern Pizza

For years, cilantro (Italian parsley) was one of those "gourmet" ingredients that rarely made it to my small-town supermarket, but oh, how things have changed. Nowadays, I love adding its unique touch to many of my recipes—and I bet you will, too.

☺ Serves 8

> 1 (11-ounce) can Pillsbury refrigerated low-fat French Loaf
> 16 ounces extra-lean ground sirloin beef or turkey breast
> 1 cup chunky salsa (mild, medium, or hot)
> 1 tablespoon chopped fresh cilantro or parsley
> 1 cup frozen whole-kernel corn, thawed
> ½ cup sliced ripe olives
> 1½ cups shredded Kraft reduced-fat Cheddar cheese

Preheat oven to 375 degrees. Spray a rimmed 10-by-15-inch baking sheet with butter-flavored cooking spray. Unroll French loaf and pat into prepared baking sheet and up sides of pan to form a rim. Lightly spray top of crust with butter-flavored cooking spray. Bake for 6 minutes. Meanwhile, in a large skillet sprayed with butter-flavored cooking spray, brown meat. Stir in salsa and cilantro. Spoon meat mixture evenly over partially baked crust. Sprinkle corn, olives, and Cheddar cheese evenly over top. Continue baking for 8 to 10 minutes or until crust is golden brown and cheese is melted. Place baking sheet on a wire rack and let set for 5 minutes. Cut into 8 servings.

HINT: Thaw corn by rinsing in a colander under hot water for 1 minute.

Each serving equals:

HE: 2¼ Protein • 1¼ Bread • ¼ Fat • ¼ Vegetable

265 Calories • 9 gm Fat • 21 gm Protein • 25 gm Carbohydrate • 559 mg Sodium • 170 mg Calcium • 2 gm Fiber

DIABETIC EXCHANGES: 2½ Meat • 1½ Starch

CARB CHOICES: 1½

Individual Grande Pizzas

For a speedy snack or kid-pleasing lunch, these are an appealing choice—and so full of flavor! It's just another case of mixing two cuisines to make one terrific dish that is fresh and fun to eat.

☻ Serves 2

> 4 ounces extra-lean ground sirloin beef or turkey breast
> ½ teaspoon chili seasoning
> 2 (6-inch) flour tortillas
> 2 tablespoons reduced-sodium ketchup
> ¼ cup peeled and chopped fresh tomatoes
> ¼ cup chopped green bell pepper
> ¼ cup shredded Kraft reduced-fat Cheddar cheese

Preheat oven to 375 degrees. In a medium skillet sprayed with olive oil–flavored cooking spray, brown meat. Stir in chili seasoning. Spray a baking sheet with olive oil–flavored cooking spray. Place tortillas on prepared baking sheet and spread 1 tablespoon ketchup over each. Evenly arrange browned meat mixture over ketchup on each tortilla. Sprinkle 2 tablespoons tomato, 2 tablespoons green pepper, and 2 tablespoons Cheddar cheese over each. Bake for 10 minutes.

HINT: Purchase a 16-ounce package of lean meat, divide by 4 and freeze 3 portions for future use. Don't forget to date and mark the packages.

Each serving equals:

HE: 2 Protein • 1 Bread • ½ Vegetable • 15 Optional Calories

229 Calories • 9 gm Fat • 17 gm Protein • 20 gm Carbohydrate • 52 mg Sodium • 106 mg Calcium • 1 gm Fiber

DIABETIC EXCHANGES: 2 Meat • 1 Starch • ½ Vegetable

CARB CHOICES: 1

Pepper Steak Pizza

Talk about a true "meat lover's" meal, and you must mean this superb and surprising recipe! The sauce is mouthwatering, the aroma irresistible, so bring a big appetite, and race for the table.

◐ Serves 8

> 16 ounces lean tenderized round steak, cut into
>   bite-size pieces
> 1 (11-ounce) can Pillsbury refrigerated low-fat
>   French Loaf
> 1 cup chopped green bell pepper
> 1 cup chopped red bell pepper
> 1 cup chopped onion
> ½ cup Kraft Fat Free Italian Dressing
> 2 tablespoons reduced-sodium ketchup
> ½ teaspoon dried minced garlic
> 1 cup chopped fresh tomatoes
> 1 (8-ounce) can Hunt's Tomato Sauce
> 1 cup shredded Kraft reduced-fat mozzarella
>   cheese

Preheat oven to 375 degrees. In a large skillet sprayed with butter-flavored cooking spray, sauté meat for 8 to 10 minutes. Meanwhile, spray a rimmed 10-by-15-inch baking sheet with olive oil–flavored cooking spray. Unroll French loaf and pat into prepared baking sheet and up sides of pan to form a rim. Light spray top of crust with olive oil–flavored cooking spray. Bake for 6 minutes. Meanwhile, add green pepper, red pepper, and onion to partially cooked meat and continue sautéing for 6 minutes. Stir in Italian dressing, ketchup, and garlic. Remove from heat. Add tomatoes. Mix gently to combine. Evenly sprinkle meat mixture over partially baked crust. Drizzle tomato sauce evenly over meat mixture. Sprinkle mozzarella cheese evenly over top. Continue baking for 8 to 10 minutes or until crust is golden brown and cheese is melted. Place baking sheet on a wire rack and let set for 5 minutes. Cut into 8 servings.

Each serving equals:

HE: 2 Protein • 1½ Vegetable • 1 Bread • 8 Optional Calories

233 Calories • 5 gm Fat • 20 gm Protein • 27 gm Carbohydrate • 719 mg Sodium • 109 mg Calcium • 2 gm Fiber

DIABETIC EXCHANGES: 2 Meat • 1½ Vegetable • 1 Starch

CARB CHOICES: 2

Fajita Supreme Pizza

If you can't decide whether to order chicken or beef fajitas, you're in luck. This spectacular dish features both (both!) as well as plenty of sautéed onions and peppers! If too much of a good thing can be wonderful, as the saying goes, this is it!　　🌑　Serves 8

> 8 ounces lean round steak, cut into bite-size pieces
> 8 ounces skinned and boned uncooked chicken breast,
>   cut into bite-size pieces
> 2 cups chopped onion
> 1 cup chopped red bell pepper
> 1 cup chopped green bell pepper
> 1 (11-ounce) can Pillsbury refrigerated low-fat
>   French Loaf
> 2 cups chunky salsa (mild, medium, or hot)
> ½ cup Land O Lakes no-fat sour cream
> 1 cup chopped fresh tomatoes
> ½ cup sliced ripe olives
> 1 cup shredded Kraft reduced-fat Cheddar cheese

Preheat oven to 375 degrees. In a large skillet sprayed with butter-flavored cooking spray, sauté steak and chicken pieces or 6 to 8 minutes. In another large skillet sprayed with butter-flavored cooking spray, sauté onion, red pepper, and green pepper for 5 to 6 minutes. Meanwhile, spray a rimmed 10-by-15-inch baking sheet with butter-flavored cooking spray. Unroll French loaf and pat into prepared baking sheet and up sides of pan to form a rim. Lightly spray top of crust with butter-flavored cooking spray. Bake for 6 minutes. Meanwhile, in a medium bowl, combine salsa and sour cream. Evenly spread salsa mixture over partially baked crust. Sprinkle meat and vegetable mixtures evenly over salsa mixture. Evenly sprinkle tomatoes and olives over vegetable mixture. Top with Cheddar cheese. Continue baking for 8 to 10 minutes or until crust is golden brown and cheese is melted. Place baking sheet on a wire rack and let set for 5 minutes. Cut into 8 servings.

Each serving equals:

HE: 2 Protein • 1¾ Vegetable • 1 Bread • ¼ Fat • 15 Optional Calories

274 Calories • 6 gm Fat • 22 gm Protein • 33 gm Carbohydrate •
765 mg Sodium • 126 mg Calcium • 4 gm Fiber

DIABETIC EXCHANGES: 2 Meat • 2 Vegetable • 1½ Starch

CARB CHOICES: 2

Philly Cheese Steak Pizza

If it's good on a roll in the City of Brotherly Love, it's got to be good on a pizza crust! When you watch those cheeses melt and mix with succulent beef, you might just find yourself sighing over having to wait until your pizza's ready. ☉ Serves 8

> 16 ounces lean tenderized round steak, cut into bite-size
>   pieces
> 2 cups chopped onion
> 1 cup chopped green bell pepper
> 1 (11-ounce) can Pillsbury refrigerated low-fat French Loaf
> ¼ cup reduced-sodium ketchup
> ⅛ teaspoon black pepper
> ¾ cup shredded Kraft reduced-fat Cheddar cheese
> ¾ cup shredded Kraft reduced-fat mozzarella cheese

Preheat oven to 375 degrees. In a large skillet sprayed with butter-flavored cooking spray, brown meat, onion, and green pepper for 8 to 10 minutes. Meanwhile, spray a rimmed 10-by-15-inch baking sheet with butter-flavored cooking spray. Unroll French loaf and pat into prepared baking sheet and up sides of pan to form a rim. Lightly spray top of crust with butter-flavored cooking spray. Bake for 6 minutes. Stir ketchup and black pepper into meat mixture. Evenly spread meat mixture over partially baked crust. Sprinkle Cheddar and mozzarella cheeses evenly over top. Continue baking for 8 to 10 minutes or until crust is golden brown and cheeses are melted. Place baking sheet on a wire rack and let set for 5 minutes. Cut into 8 servings.

Each serving equals:

HE: 2¼ Protein • 1 Bread • ¾ Vegetable • 4 Optional Calories

243 Calories • 7 gm Fat • 22 gm Protein • 23 gm Carbohydrate •
343 mg Sodium • 181 mg Calcium • 2 gm Fiber

DIABETIC EXCHANGES: 2½ Meat • 1 Starch • 1 Vegetable

CARB CHOICES: 1½

Chef Salad Pizza

I've heard people express disbelief when they first saw fresh salad ingredients on top of a pizza, but I like to keep an open mind—and offer something for everyone in my cookbooks. Here's an inventive way to eat this classic salad with its ham, turkey, and egg, and have your pizza, too! ☺ Serves 8

> 1 (11-ounce) can Pillsbury refrigerated low-fat French Loaf
> 1 cup Kraft fat-free mayonnaise
> 1 teaspoon dried parsley flakes
> 2 cups finely shredded lettuce
> 1½ cups diced Dubuque 97% fat-free ham or any extra-lean ham
> 1 cup diced cooked turkey breast
> 1 cup chopped fresh tomatoes
> ¾ cup shredded Kraft reduced-fat Cheddar cheese
> 2 hard-boiled eggs, chopped
> ½ cup Kraft Fat Free Thousand Island Dressing

Preheat oven to 425 degrees. Spray a rimmed 10-by-15-inch baking sheet with butter-flavored cooking spray. Unroll French loaf and pat into prepared baking sheet and up sides of pan to form a rim. Lightly spray top of crust with butter-flavored cooking spray. Bake for 8 to 10 minutes or until golden brown. Place baking sheet on a wire rack and allow to cool. In a small bowl, combine mayonnaise and parsley flakes. Spread mayonnaise mixture evenly over cooled crust. Layer lettuce, ham, turkey, tomatoes, Cheddar cheese, and chopped eggs evenly over mayonnaise mixture. Evenly drizzle Thousand Island dressing over top. Cut into 8 servings.

HINT: If you don't have leftovers, purchase a chunk of cooked turkey breast from your local deli.

Each serving equals:

HE: 2 Protein • 1 Bread • ½ Vegetable • ½ Slider • 2 Optional Calories

251 Calories • 7 gm Fat • 19 gm Protein • 28 gm Carbohydrate • 905 mg Sodium • 95 mg Calcium • 2 gm Fiber

DIABETIC EXCHANGES: 2 Meat • 1½ Starch/Carbohydrate • ½ Vegetable

CARB CHOICES: 2

Sub Sandwich Pizza

Here's a great suggestion for anyone who adores pizza but hates to skip his or her favorite ham-and-cheese sandwich: Top one with the other! Ham is often partnered with pineapple in some takeout pizza places, but I'm intrigued by this blend of crunchy and tangy, creamy and warm. It's a pizza—no, it's a sandwich—no, it's a pizza sandwich, or is it sandwich pizza? ☻ Serves 8

1 (11-ounce) can Pillsbury refrigerated low-fat French
    Loaf
1 (8-ounce) package Philadelphia fat-free cream cheese
½ cup Kraft fat-free mayonnaise
1 tablespoon prepared yellow mustard
2 cups finely shredded lettuce
2 (2.5-ounce) packages Carl Buddig 90% lean ham,
    shredded
¾ cup shredded Kraft reduced-fat Cheddar cheese
4 (¾-ounce) slices Kraft reduced-fat Swiss cheese,
    shredded
½ cup sliced ripe olives
½ cup finely diced onion
1½ cups finely chopped fresh tomatoes
¼ cup Kraft Fat Free Italian Dressing

Preheat oven to 425 degrees. Spray a rimmed 10-by-15-inch baking sheet with olive oil–flavored cooking spray. Unroll French loaf and pat into prepared baking sheet and up sides of pan to form a rim. Lightly spray top of crust with olive oil–flavored cooking spray. Bake for 8 to 10 minutes or until crust is golden brown. Place baking sheet on a wire rack and allow to cool. In a small bowl, stir cream cheese with a sturdy spoon until soft. Add mayonnaise and mustard. Mix well to combine. Spread cream cheese mixture evenly over cooled crust. In a large bowl, combine lettuce, ham, Cheddar cheese, Swiss cheese, olives, onion, and tomatoes. Add Italian dressing. Mix gently to coat. Arrange lettuce mixture evenly over cream cheese mixture. Refrigerate for at least 30 minutes. Cut into 8 servings.

HINT: 1 (5-ounce) package Hillshire Farm Deli Select Pastrami can be used instead of Carl Buddig.

Each serving equals:

HE: 1½ Protein • 1 Bread • ½ Vegetable • ¼ Fat • 16 Optional Calories

258 Calories • 10 gm Fat • 16 gm Protein • 26 gm Carbohydrate • 895 mg Sodium • 266 mg Calcium • 2 gm Fiber

DIABETIC EXCHANGES: 1½ Meat • 1 Starch • ½ Vegetable • ½ Fat

CARB CHOICES: 2

Ham and Pineapple Pizza

Fruit on a pizza that isn't for dessert? Why yes, of course, try it and see if you don't agree it's one of the tastiest and most enjoyable pizzas you've ever eaten! ◓ Serves 8

1 (11-ounce) can Pillsbury refrigerated low-fat French Loaf
1 (8-ounce) can Hunt's Tomato Sauce
2 tablespoons Splenda Granular
1½ teaspoons Italian or pizza seasoning
1 cup chopped green bell pepper
2 (8-ounce) cans pineapple tidbits, packed in fruit juice, drained
1½ cups diced Dubuque 97% fat-free ham or any extra-lean ham
1½ cups shredded Kraft reduced-fat mozzarella cheese

Preheat oven to 375 degrees. Spray a rimmed 10-by-15-inch baking sheet with butter-flavored cooking spray. Unroll French loaf and pat into prepared baking sheet and up sides of pan to form a rim. Lightly spray top of crust with butter-flavored cooking spray. Bake for 6 minutes. Meanwhile, in a small bowl, combine tomato sauce, Splenda, and Italian seasoning. Spread sauce mixture evenly over partially baked crust. Evenly sprinkle green pepper, pineapple, and ham over sauce mixture. Sprinkle mozzarella cheese evenly over top. Continue baking for 8 to 10 minutes or until crust is golden brown and cheese is melted. Place baking sheet on a wire rack and let set for 5 minutes. Cut into 8 servings.

Each serving equals:

HE: 1½ Protein • 1 Bread • ¾ Vegetable • ½ Fruit • 2 Optional Calories

230 Calories • 6 gm Fat • 15 gm Protein • 29 gm Carbohydrate • 794 mg Sodium • 177 mg Calcium • 2 gm Fiber

DIABETIC EXCHANGES: 1½ Meat • 1 Starch • ½ Vegetable • ½ Fruit

CARB CHOICES: 2

Hawaiian Luau Pizza

I've nicknamed this recipe "Take Me Back to Maui"—if only it could! This is a kind of luau on a plate, with ham instead of suckling pig and lush pineapple that shimmers with Hawaiian sunshine. When the day is cold and dreary, dine on this and dream of warmer climes. ☉ Serves 8

> 1 (11-ounce) can Pillsbury refrigerated low-fat French Loaf
> 2 (8-ounce) cans pineapple tidbits, packed in fruit juice, drained
> 1 cup chopped green bell pepper
> 1 cup chopped onion
> 2 cups diced Dubuque 97% fat-free ham or any extra-lean ham
> 2 cups shredded Kraft reduced-fat Cheddar cheese

Preheat oven to 375 degrees. Spray a rimmed 10-by-15-inch baking sheet with butter-flavored cooking spray. Unroll French loaf and pat into prepared baking sheet and up sides of pan to form a rim. Lightly spray top of crust with butter-flavored cooking spray. Bake for 6 minutes. Evenly sprinkle pineapple, green pepper, onion, and ham over crust. Sprinkle Cheddar cheese evenly over top. Bake for 8 to 10 minutes or until crust is golden brown and cheese is melted. Place baking sheet on a wire rack and let set for 5 minutes. Cut into 8 servings.

Each serving equals:

HE: 2 Protein • 1 Bread • ½ Fruit • ½ Vegetable

246 Calories • 6 gm Fat • 18 gm Protein • 30 gm Carbohydrate • 665 mg Sodium • 406 mg Calcium • 2 gm Fiber

DIABETIC EXCHANGES: 2 Meat • 1 Starch • ½ Fruit • ½ Vegetable

CARB CHOICES: 2

Ham Alfredo Pizza

The "marriage" of ham and creamy, cheesy Alfredo sauce might not be predictable, but it's remarkably right. The cheese really blends beautifully with the ham, and I think you'll love the addition of the fresh mushrooms. ☻ Serves 8

> 1 (11-ounce) can Pillsbury refrigerated low-fat
>   French Loaf
> 2 full cups diced Dubuque 97% fat-free ham or any
>   extra-lean ham
> 1 cup finely chopped onion
> 2 cups finely chopped fresh mushrooms
> 1 (12-fluid-ounce) can Carnation Evaporated
>   Fat Free Milk
> 3 tablespoons all-purpose flour
> ½ cup Kraft Reduced Fat Parmesan Style Grated
>   Topping
> 1 cup shredded Kraft reduced-fat mozzarella cheese

Preheat oven to 375 degrees. Spray a rimmed 10-by-15-inch baking sheet with butter-flavored cooking spray. Unroll French loaf and pat into prepared baking sheet and up sides of pan to form a rim. Lightly spray top of crust with butter-flavored cooking spray. Bake for 6 minutes. Meanwhile, in a large skillet sprayed with butter-flavored cooking spray, sauté ham, onion, and mushrooms for 6 minutes. Drain, if necessary, and evenly sprinkle ham mixture over partially baked crust. In a covered jar, combine evaporated milk and flour. Shake well to blend. Pour milk mixture into a medium saucepan sprayed with butter-flavored cooking spray. Stir in Parmesan cheese. Cook over medium heat for 5 to 6 minutes or until mixture thickens, stirring often. Drizzle hot Parmesan sauce evenly over ham mixture. Sprinkle mozzarella cheese evenly over top. Bake for 8 to 10 minutes or until crust is golden brown and cheese is melted. Place baking sheet on a wire rack and let set for 5 minutes. Cut into 8 servings.

Each serving equals:

HE: 1¾ Protein • 1 Bread • ½ Vegetable • ⅓ Fat Free Milk •
11 Optional Calories

254 Calories • 6 gm Fat • 18 gm Protein • 32 gm Carbohydrate •
975 mg Sodium • 269 mg Calcium • 2 gm Fiber

DIABETIC EXCHANGES: 2 Meat • 1½ Starch/Carbohydrate • ½ Vegetable

CARB CHOICES: 2

Jambalaya Pizza

The joyful wildness of New Orleans cuisine can't be over-shadowed by the tough times the city has experienced since Hurricane Katrina, and this pizza is my way of encouraging everyone to keep the spirit of the Big Easy alive. True jambalaya is a magnificent mélange of flavors, so enjoy this dish's delightful variety.

☉ Serves 8

> 1 (11-ounce) can Pillsbury refrigerated low-fat
>   French Loaf
> 8 ounces Healthy Choice 97% lean kielbasa sausage,
>   cut into ½-inch pieces
> 1 full cup diced Dubuque 97% fat-free ham or any
>   extra-lean ham
> ¾ cup chopped green bell pepper
> ¾ cup chopped onion
> ½ cup finely diced celery
> 1 (15-ounce) can diced tomatoes, very well drained
> 1 (5-ounce) package frozen cooked shrimp,
>   thawed
> 1 teaspoon dried thyme
> 1 teaspoon Tabasco sauce
> 1 (8-ounce) can Hunt's Tomato Sauce

Preheat oven to 375 degrees. Spray a rimmed 10-by-15-inch baking sheet with olive oil–flavored cooking spray. Unroll French loaf and pat into prepared baking sheet and up sides of pan to form a rim. Lightly spray top of crust with olive oil–flavored cooking spray. Bake for 6 minutes. Meanwhile, in a large skillet sprayed with olive oil–flavored cooking spray, sauté sausage, ham, green pepper, onion, and celery for 5 minutes. Stir in tomatoes, shrimp, thyme, and Tabasco sauce. Continue cooking for 2 to 3 minutes, stirring often. Evenly spread tomato sauce over partially baked crust. Spoon ham mixture evenly over top. Continue baking for 8 to 10 minutes or until crust is golden brown. Place baking sheet on a wire rack and let set for 5 minutes. Cut into 8 servings.

Each serving equals:

HE: 1¾ Protein • 1½ Vegetable • 1 Bread

208 Calories • 4 gm Fat • 16 gm Protein • 27 gm Carbohydrate • 936 mg Sodium • 41 mg Calcium • 3 gm Fiber

DIABETIC EXCHANGES: 2 Meat • 1½ Vegetable • 1 Starch

CARB CHOICES: 2

Asparagus and Ham Pizza

For an elegant, even sumptuous pizza topping, just perfect for a ladies' lunch, this dish is designed to impress! I used frozen asparagus (available all year), but if you've got the fresh kind, blanch it first (drop in boiling water for just a bit, then rinse in cool water).

● Serves 8

1 (11-ounce) can Pillsbury refrigerated low-fat French Loaf
1 cup Kraft fat-free mayonnaise
½ teaspoon prepared yellow mustard
¼ cup Kraft Reduced Fat Parmesan Style Grated Topping
2 cups frozen cut asparagus, thawed and finely chopped
1½ cups diced Dubuque 97% fat-free ham or any extra-lean ham
¾ cup shredded Kraft reduced-fat Cheddar cheese
¾ cup shredded Kraft reduced-fat mozzarella cheese

Preheat oven to 375 degrees. Spray a rimmed 10-by-15-inch baking sheet with butter-flavored cooking spray. Unroll French loaf and pat into prepared baking sheet and up sides of pan to form a rim. Lightly spray top of crust with butter-flavored cooking spray. Bake for 6 minutes. Meanwhile, in a medium bowl, combine mayonnaise, mustard, and Parmesan cheese. Spread mayonnaise mixture evenly over partially baked crust. Arrange asparagus pieces and ham evenly over mayonnaise mixture. Sprinkle Cheddar and mozzarella cheeses evenly over top. Continue baking for 8 to 10 minutes or until crust is golden brown and cheeses are melted. Place baking sheet on a wire rack and let set for 5 minutes. Cut into 8 servings.

HINT: Thaw asparagus by rinsing in a colander under hot water for 1 minute.

Each serving equals:

HE: 1¾ Protein • 1 Bread • ½ Vegetable • ¼ Slider • 7 Optional Calories

232 Calories • 8 gm Fat • 16 gm Protein • 24 gm Carbohydrate • 854 mg Sodium • 195 mg Calcium • 2 gm Fiber

DIABETIC EXCHANGES: 1½ Meat • 1½ Starch/Carbohydrate • ½ Vegetable

CARB CHOICES: 1½

Coney Island Pizza

It has a splendid history as a playground for New Yorkers who love to have fun and eat, especially classic hot dogs under the summer sun! Now you can share the magic with this pizza named for the home of the famed roller coaster, the Cyclone! ☻ Serves 8

1 (11-ounce) can Pillsbury refrigerated low-fat French Loaf
8 ounces extra-lean ground sirloin beef or turkey breast
1 (16-ounce) package Oscar Mayer or Healthy Choice
    reduced-fat frankfurters, cut into ¼-inch pieces
1 cup finely chopped onion
1 (15-ounce) can diced tomatoes, very well drained
1 tablespoon Splenda Granular
1 (8-ounce) can Hunt's Tomato Sauce
¾ cup shredded Kraft reduced-fat Cheddar cheese

Preheat oven to 375 degrees. Spray a rimmed 10-by-15-inch baking sheet with butter-flavored cooking spray. Unroll French loaf and pat into prepared baking sheet and up sides of pan to form a rim. Lightly spray top of crust with butter-flavored cooking spray. Bake for 6 minutes. Meanwhile, in a large skillet sprayed with butter-flavored cooking spray, brown meat, frankfurters, and onion for 5 minutes. Stir in tomatoes and Splenda. Evenly spread tomato sauce over partially baked crust. Spoon meat mixture evenly over sauce. Sprinkle Cheddar cheese evenly over top. Continue baking for 8 to 10 minutes or until crust is golden brown and cheese is melted. Place baking sheet on a wire rack and let set for 5 minutes. Cut into 8 servings.

Each serving equals:

HE: 2 Protein • 1¼ Vegetable • 1 Bread • 1 Optional Calorie

276 Calories • 8 gm Fat • 19 gm Protein • 32 gm Carbohydrate • 893 mg Sodium • 98 mg Calcium • 2 gm Fiber

DIABETIC EXCHANGES: 2 Meat • 1 Vegetable • 1 Starch

CARB CHOICES: 2

Jo's Canadian Bacon and Kraut Pizza

Canadian bacon is a great protein source, considered healthier than regular bacon. It goes great with one of my favorite foods, the tangy sauerkraut that comes with caraway seeds included. For a lively lunch before a football game in the fall, serve this—and come home a winner! ☻ Serves 8

> 1 (11-ounce) can Pillsbury refrigerated low-fat
>   French Loaf
> 1 (8-ounce) can Hunt's Tomato Sauce
> 1 teaspoon pizza seasoning
> 1 (15-ounce) can Frank's Bavarian Style sauerkraut,
>   very well drained
> ½ cup finely chopped onion
> 1 (6-ounce) package Hormel Canadian Bacon, diced
> ¾ cup shredded Kraft reduced-fat mozzarella cheese

Preheat oven to 375 degrees. Spray a rimmed 10-by-15-inch baking sheet with butter-flavored cooking spray. Unroll French loaf and pat into prepared baking sheet and up sides of pan to form a rim. Lightly spray top of crust with butter-flavored cooking spray. Bake for 6 minutes. Meanwhile, in a medium bowl, combine tomato sauce and pizza seasoning. Spread sauce mixture evenly over partially baked crust. Arrange sauerkraut, onion, and Canadian bacon evenly over sauce mixture. Sprinkle mozzarella cheese evenly over top. Continue baking for 8 to 10 minutes or until crust is golden brown and cheese is melted. Place baking sheet on a wire rack and let set for 5 minutes. Cut into 8 servings.

HINTS: 1. If you can't find Bavarian sauerkraut, use regular sauerkraut, ½ teaspoon caraway seeds, and 1 teaspoon Brown Sugar Twin.
2. Place sauerkraut in a colander and press juice out with a sturdy spoon.

Each serving equals:

HE: 1¼ Protein • 1 Bread • 1 Vegetable

188 Calories • 4 gm Fat • 10 gm Protein • 28 gm Carbohydrate • 982 mg Sodium • 93 mg Calcium • 1 gm Fiber

DIABETIC EXCHANGES: 1 Meat • 1 Starch • 1 Vegetable

CARB CHOICES: 2

Frankfurter Pizza

For a festive entrée for a children's party, why not serve their two favorites rolled into one? This yummy treat is a birthday wish come true. ☻ Serves 8

1 (11-ounce) can Pillsbury refrigerated low-fat French Loaf
2 tablespoons prepared yellow mustard
1 (16-ounce) package Oscar Mayer or Healthy Choice
    reduced-fat frankfurters, cut into bite-size pieces
¾ cup chopped onion
¾ cup chopped green bell pepper
1 cup diced fresh tomato
1 cup chopped fresh mushrooms
1½ cups shredded Kraft reduced-fat Cheddar cheese

Preheat oven to 375 degrees. Spray a rimmed 10-by-15-inch baking sheet with butter-flavored cooking spray. Unroll French loaf and pat into prepared baking sheet and up sides of pan to form a rim. Lightly spray top of crust with butter-flavored cooking spray. Bake for 6 minutes. Spread mustard evenly over partially baked crust using a rubber spatula. Layer frankfurter pieces, onion, green pepper, tomato, and mushrooms over mustard. Sprinkle Cheddar cheese evenly over top. Continue baking for 8 to 10 minutes or until crust is golden brown and cheese is melted. Place baking sheet on a wire rack and let set for 5 minutes. Cut into 8 servings.

Each serving equals:

HE: 2 Protein • 1 Bread • ¾ Vegetable

243 Calories • 7 gm Fat • 17 gm Protein • 28 gm Carbohydrate •
926 mg Sodium • 173 mg Calcium • 2 gm Fiber

DIABETIC EXCHANGES: 2 Meat • 1 Starch • 1 Vegetable

CARB CHOICES: 2

Emerald Isle Pizza

I wonder if pizza topped with corned beef is a new idea with me, or whether Irish fans of this popular pie have been enjoying it for years. (Write and let me know, if you know . . .) My taste-testers called it a mouthwatering treat. Thanks, guys! ☻ Serves 8

> 1 (11-ounce) can Pillsbury refrigerated low-fat French Loaf
> 2 (2.5-ounce) packages Carl Buddig 90% lean corned beef, shredded
> ½ cup chopped onion
> 2½ cups purchased coleslaw mix
> 1 (8-ounce) can Hunt's Tomato Sauce
> 1 tablespoon Splenda Granular
> 1 (8-ounce) package Philadelphia fat-free cream cheese
> ⅓ cup Kraft Fat Free Thousand Island Dressing
> ¾ cup shredded Kraft reduced-fat Cheddar cheese

Preheat oven to 425 degrees. Spray a rimmed 10-by-15-inch baking sheet with butter-flavored cooking spray. Unroll French loaf and pat into prepared baking sheet and up sides of pan to form a rim. Lightly spray top of crust with butter-flavored cooking spray. Bake for 8 to 10 minutes or until crust is golden brown. Place baking sheet on a wire rack and allow to cool. Meanwhile, in a large skillet sprayed with butter-flavored cooking spray, sauté corned beef, onion, and coleslaw mix for 5 to 7 minutes or until cabbage is tender. Remove from heat. Stir in tomato sauce and Splenda. Simmer for 5 minutes. In a medium bowl, stir cream cheese with a sturdy spoon until soft. Add Thousand Island dressing. Mix well to combine. Spread cream cheese mixture over cooled crust. Layer cabbage mixture over cream cheese layer. Sprinkle Cheddar cheese evenly over top. Cut into 8 servings.

Each serving equals:

HE: 1½ Protein • 1 Bread • 1 Vegetable • 14 Optional Calories

213 Calories • 5 gm Fat • 14 gm Protein • 28 gm Carbohydrate • 763 mg Sodium • 171 mg Calcium • 2 gm Fiber

DIABETIC EXCHANGES: 1½ Meat • 1 Starch • 1 Vegetable

CARB CHOICES: 2

Deli Pastrami Pizza

Well, if you can put ham on a pizza, why not pastrami? I asked myself that question, and here's my answer, starring the "darling of the delicatessen," served hot and savory, anytime you crave it!

◐ Serves 8

1 (11-ounce) can Pillsbury refrigerated low-fat
   French Loaf
½ cup Kraft Fat Free Thousand Island Dressing
2 tablespoons Kraft fat-free mayonnaise
2 tablespoons Land O Lakes no-fat sour cream
3 (¾-ounce) slices Kraft reduced-fat Swiss cheese, shredded
2 (2.5-ounce) packages Carl Buddig lean pastrami, shredded
1 (15-ounce) can Frank's Bavarian Style sauerkraut, well
   drained
¾ cup shredded Kraft reduced-fat mozzarella cheese

Preheat oven to 375 degrees. Spray a rimmed 10-by-15-inch baking sheet with butter-flavored cooking spray. Unroll French loaf and pat into prepared baking sheet and up sides of pan to form a rim. Lightly spray top of crust with butter-flavored cooking spray. Bake for 6 minutes. Meanwhile, in a small bowl, combine Thousand Island dressing, mayonnaise, and sour cream. Spread dressing mixture evenly over partially baked crust. Layer Swiss cheese, pastrami, sauerkraut, and mozzarella cheese over top. Continue baking for 8 to 10 minutes or until crust is golden brown and cheese is melted. Place baking sheet on a wire rack and let set for 5 minutes. Cut into 8 servings.

HINTS: 1. If you can't find Bavarian sauerkraut, use regular sauerkraut, ½ teaspoon caraway seeds, and 1 teaspoon Brown Sugar Twin.
2. Place sauerkraut in a colander and press juice out with a sturdy spoon.
3. 1 (5-ounce) package Hillshire Farm Deli Select Pastrami can be used instead of Carl Buddig.

Each serving equals:

HE: 1½ Protein • 1 Bread • ½ Vegetable • ¼ Slider • 7 Optional Calories

218 Calories • 6 gm Fat • 11 gm Protein • 30 gm Carbohydrate •
910 mg Sodium • 150 mg Calcium • 1 gm Fiber

DIABETIC EXCHANGES: 1½ Meat • 1½ Starch/Carbohydrate • ½ Vegetable

CARB CHOICES: 2

Octoberfest Pizza

Sausage-topped pizza is one of the most popular orders in takeout shops around the country, so I had to offer a version I'd serve to all you sausage lovers out there! You'll notice I settled on Cheddar instead of mozzarella for this recipe. Why? I think it goes better with sausage—and maybe a few sips of beer, if that's your drink.

○ Serves 8

> 1 (11-ounce) can Pillsbury refrigerated low-fat
>   French Loaf
> 16 ounces Healthy Choice or Hillshire Farm lean kielbasa
>   sausage, cut into bite-size pieces
> ½ cup chopped onion
> 1 (14½-ounce) can Frank's Bavarian-style sauerkraut,
>   well drained
> 1 (14.5-ounce) can Hunt's Tomatoes Diced in Sauce
> 1½ cups shredded Kraft reduced-fat Cheddar cheese

Preheat oven to 375 degrees. Spray a rimmed 10-by-15-inch baking sheet with butter-flavored cooking spray. Unroll French loaf and pat into prepared baking sheet and up sides of pan to form a rim. Lightly spray top of crust with butter-flavored cooking spray. Bake for 6 minutes. Meanwhile, in a large skillet sprayed with butter-flavored cooking spray, sauté sausage and onion for 5 minutes. Stir in sauerkraut. Spread tomato sauce evenly over partially baked crust. Evenly sprinkle sausage mixture over sauce. Sprinkle Cheddar cheese evenly over top. Continue baking for 12 to 14 minutes or until crust is golden brown and cheese is melted. Place baking sheet on a wire rack and let set for 5 minutes. Cut into 8 servings.

HINTS: 1. If you can't find Bavarian sauerkraut, use regular sauerkraut, ½ teaspoon caraway seeds, and 1 teaspoon Brown Sugar Twin.
2. Place sauerkraut in a colander and press juice out with a sturdy spoon.

Each serving equals:

HE: 2¼ Protein • 1½ Vegetable • 1 Bread

290 Calories • 10 gm Fat • 18 gm Protein • 32 gm Carbohydrate •
921 mg Sodium • 168 mg Calcium • 1 gm Fiber

DIABETIC EXCHANGES: 2 Meat • 1½ Vegetable • 1 Starch

CARB CHOICES: 2

Irish Potato Crust Pizza

My Irish roots—and trip to Ireland not so long ago—probably inspired me to cook up a new kind of pizza crust featuring the ever-loving potato! If you're one of those potato lovers who could eat those spuds at every meal, this one's for you!   ☉   Serves 6

1 (12-fluid-ounce) can Carnation Evaporated Fat Free Milk
½ cup water
2 cups instant potato flakes
1 teaspoon prepared horseradish sauce
1 teaspoon dried parsley flakes
1 egg, or equivalent in egg substitute
1 (2.5-ounce) jar sliced mushrooms, drained
¾ cup shredded Kraft reduced-fat Cheddar cheese ☆
2 (2.5-ounce) packages Carl Buddig 90% lean corned beef or
      any lean corned beef, shredded
2 cups purchased coleslaw mix
½ cup chopped onion

Preheat oven to 375 degrees. Spray a 12-inch round pizza pan with butter-flavored cooking spray. In a medium saucepan, combine evaporated milk and water. Cook over medium heat until hot, but not boiling, stirring often. Remove from heat. Add potato flakes, horseradish, and parsley flakes. Mix well to combine. Stir in egg, mushrooms, and ¼ cup Cheddar cheese. Pat mixture onto prepared pizza pan using a sturdy spoon sprayed with butter-flavored cooking spray. Bake for 5 minutes. Sprinkle corned beef, coleslaw, and onion evenly over partially baked potato crust. Top with remaining ½ cup Cheddar cheese. Bake for 24 to 26 minutes. Place pan on a wire rack and let set for 5 minutes. Cut into 6 servings.

Each serving equals:

HE: 1½ Protein • 1 Bread • ¾ Vegetable • ½ Fat Free Milk •
3 Optional Calories

210 Calories • 6 gm Fat • 15 gm Protein • 24 gm Carbohydrate •
496 mg Sodium • 295 mg Calcium • 2 gm Fiber

DIABETIC EXCHANGES: 1½ Meat • 1 Starch • ½ Vegetable • ½ Fat Free Milk

CARB CHOICES: 1½

Dazzling Dessert

Pizzas

You don't need a special occasion to bring a gloriously sweet pizza to the table after a hearty meal—but you'll soon discover that any time you give pizza the job of grand finale, it's a time to celebrate! It's just a festive way to end an everyday dinner, a relaxing weekend lunch, or an impromptu supper with your neighbors. Everyone feels more special when you serve a crusty treat topped with luscious fruit, rich chocolate, and other tasty delights—make these and see!

As a woman with her own orchard, I'm often inclined to design my desserts as the fruit is picked off the trees. But even if you buy your apples, pears, peaches, and berries from the farmer's market, you'll find lots of great choices in this chapter. Start with *Heavenly Strawberry Pizza* when the rosy gems are at their sweetest, or try *Peach Melba Dessert Pizza* when peaches are super juicy. But don't stop there—after all, I've got pizzas created with decadent desserts in mind, fabulous finales like *Caramel Apple Pizza Pie*, *Banana Split Dessert Pizza*, and *Strawberry Shortcake Pizza*. There is just so much "yummy" in this collection of goodies, it's going to be hard to choose what to make first. My grandkids tasted lots of these, and they especially loved *Strawberry Chocolate Cream Dessert Pizza* and *Ultimate Chocolate Dessert Pizza,* so take it from them!

Cupid's Cherry Dessert Pizza

If you're ready to start looking for love in all the *right* places, why not start by serving your prospective beau this luscious dessert? Never forget the old saying about the way to a man's (or woman's) heart—and offer your beloved the nearest fork.

❤ Serves 12

1 Pillsbury refrigerated unbaked 9-inch pie crust
2 (8-ounce) packages Philadelphia fat-free cream cheese
2 tablespoons Splenda Granular
2 eggs, or equivalent in egg substitute
½ cup slivered almonds ☆
1 teaspoon almond extract
1 (20-ounce) can Lucky Leaf No Sugar Added Cherry Pie
   Filling
¾ cup Cool Whip Lite

Preheat oven to 425 degrees. Let pie crust warm to room temperature. Spray a 12-inch round pizza pan with butter-flavored cooking spray. Gently pat pie crust into prepared pizza pan. Evenly prick bottom of crust with tines of a fork. Bake for 5 minutes or until crust is light golden brown. Meanwhile, in a medium bowl, stir cream cheese with a sturdy spoon until soft. Add Splenda and eggs. Mix well to combine. Stir in ¼ cup almonds and almond extract. Evenly spread mixture over partially baked crust. Bake for an additional 12 to 14 minutes. Place pan on a wire rack and allow to cool completely. When cooled, evenly spread cherry pie filling over cream cheese mixture. Drop Cool Whip Lite by tablespoonful to form 12 mounds. Sprinkle remaining ¼ cup almonds evenly over top. Cut into 12 servings.

Each serving equals:

HE: 1 Protein • ⅔ Bread • ⅔ Fat • ⅓ Fruit • 14 Optional Calories

172 Calories • 8 gm Fat • 7 gm Protein • 18 gm Carbohydrate •
270 mg Sodium • 122 mg Calcium • 1 gm Fiber

DIABETIC EXCHANGES: 1½ Fat • 1 Meat • 1 Starch/Carbohydrate • ½ Fruit

CARB CHOICES: 1

Pretty in Pink Brownie Dessert Pizza

Sweet and inviting for a young girl's birthday party, this lovely treat is chocolatey, creamy, and yes, PINK. Enjoy! 🌙   Serves 8

> ¾ cup Bisquick Heart Smart Baking Mix
> ¼ cup unsweetened cocoa powder
> ½ cup Splenda Granular
> ½ cup fat-free milk
> 2 tablespoons Land O Lakes no-fat sour cream
> 1½ teaspoons vanilla extract
> 1 (4-serving) package Jell-O sugar-free instant chocolate
>   pudding mix
> ⅔ cup Carnation Nonfat Dry Milk Powder
> 1 cup water
> 1 (20-ounce) can Lucky Leaf No Sugar Added Cherry Pie
>   Filling
> ¾ cup Cool Whip Free
> ½ teaspoon brandy extract
> 2 tablespoons chopped walnuts
> 2 tablespoons mini chocolate chips

Preheat oven to 375 degrees. Spray a 12-inch round pizza pan with butter-flavored cooking spray. In a large bowl, combine baking mix, cocoa powder, and Splenda. Add milk, sour cream, and vanilla extract. Mix gently to combine using a wire whisk. Evenly spread batter into prepared pizza pan. Bake for 10 to 14 minutes or until crust tests done in center. Place pizza pan on a wire rack and allow crust to cool completely. In a medium bowl, combine dry pudding mix, dry milk powder, and water. Mix well using a wire whisk. Spread pudding mixture evenly over cooled crust. In a medium bowl, combine cherry pie filling, Cool Whip Free, and brandy extract. Spread cherry mixture evenly over set chocolate mixture. Evenly sprinkle walnuts and chocolate chips over top. Refrigerate for at least 1 hour. Cut into 8 wedges.

Each serving equals:

HE: ½ Bread • ½ Fruit • ¼ Fat Free Milk • ¾ Slider • 14 Optional Calories

167 Calories • 3 gm Fat • 5 gm Protein • 30 gm Carbohydrate •
351 mg Sodium • 116 mg Calcium • 2 gm Fiber

DIABETIC EXCHANGES: 1½ Starch/Carbohydrate • ½ Fruit

CARB CHOICES: 2

Refreshing Rhubarb Pizza Dessert

Crusty and creamy, this juicy and delicious delight is a wonderful choice all year-round—but it's especially good during fresh rhubarb season, which comes to Iowa in the merry month of May!

◐ Serves 12

    1 (8-ounce) can Pillsbury Reduced Fat Crescent Rolls
    1 (8-ounce) package Philadelphia fat-free cream cheese
    2 tablespoons Splenda Granular
    1 tablespoon Land O Lakes Fat Free Half & Half
    2½ cups water ☆
    1 (4-serving) package Jell-O sugar-free strawberry gelatin
    4 cups finely chopped fresh or frozen rhubarb, thawed
    2 (4-serving) packages Jell-O sugar-free instant vanilla
        pudding mix
    1⅓ cups Carnation Nonfat Dry Milk Powder
    ¾ cup Cool Whip Free
    1 teaspoon vanilla extract
    3 tablespoons chopped pecans

Preheat oven to 375 degrees. Spray a rimmed 9-by-13-inch baking sheet with butter-flavored cooking spray. Unroll crescent rolls and carefully pat into prepared baking sheet, being sure to seal perforations. Bake for 8 to 10 minutes or until crust is golden brown. Place baking sheet on a wire rack and allow crust to cool completely. In a medium bowl, stir cream cheese with a sturdy spoon until soft. Add Splenda and half & half. Mix gently to combine. Evenly spread cream cheese mixture over cooled crust. In a large saucepan, combine ½ cup water and dry gelatin. Stir in rhubarb. Cook over medium heat for 8 to 10 minutes or until rhubarb becomes soft, stirring often. Remove from heat. Place saucepan on a wire rack and let set for 15 minutes. Evenly spoon cooled rhubarb mixture over cream cheese mixture. In a medium bowl, combine dry pudding mix, dry milk powder, and remaining 2 cups water. Mix well using a wire whisk. Blend in Cool Whip Free and vanilla extract. Evenly spread pudding mixture over rhubarb mixture. Sprinkle pecans evenly over top. Refrigerate for at least 1 hour. Cut into 12 servings.

Each serving equals:

HE: ⅔ Bread • ⅓ Fat Free Milk • ⅓ Protein • ⅓ Vegetable • ¼ Fat • ¼ Slider • 8 Optional Calories

156 Calories • 4 gm Fat • 8 gm Protein • 22 gm Carbohydrate • 534 mg Sodium • 191 mg Calcium • 1 gm Fiber

DIABETIC EXCHANGES: 1½ Starch/Carbohydrate • ½ Fat

CARB CHOICES: 1½

Rhubarb-Coconut Pizza Dessert

Now here's a combination you don't find very often—rhubarb and coconut—but now that I've discovered how good it is, I know I'll want to taste it again and again! By layering the coconut flavor with an extract, I can bring the taste of the tropics home.

◐ Serves 12

1 Pillsbury refrigerated unbaked 9-inch pie crust
2½ cups water ☆
1 (4-serving) package Jell-O sugar-free strawberry gelatin
4 cups finely chopped fresh or frozen rhubarb, thawed
1 (8-ounce) package Philadelphia fat-free cream cheese
2 tablespoons Splenda Granular
2 teaspoons coconut extract ☆
2 (4-serving) packages Jell-O sugar-free instant vanilla
   pudding mix
1⅓ cups Carnation Nonfat Dry Milk Powder
1 cup Cool Whip Lite
3 tablespoons flaked coconut

Preheat oven to 425 degrees. Let pie crust warm to room temperature. Spray a 12-inch round pizza pan with butter-flavored cooking spray. Gently pat pie crust into prepared pizza pan. Evenly prick bottom of crust with tines of a fork. Bake for 8 to 10 minutes or until crust is golden brown. Place pizza pan on a wire rack and allow to cool completely. Meanwhile, in a large saucepan, combine ½ cup water and dry gelatin. Stir in rhubarb. Cover and cook over medium heat for 10 minutes or until rhubarb becomes soft, stirring often. Remove from heat. Add cream cheese, Splenda, and 1 teaspoon coconut extract. Mix well using a wire whisk until cream cheese is blended. Reserve ¾ cup rhubarb mixture. Spread remaining rhubarb mixture evenly over cooled crust. Refrigerate for at least 30 minutes. In a large bowl, combine dry pudding mix, dry milk powder, and remaining 2 cups water. Mix well using a wire whisk. Blend in Cool Whip Lite and remaining 1 teaspoon coconut extract. Evenly spread pudding mixture over rhubarb mixture. Drop reserved rhubarb mixture by tablespoonful over Cool Whip

Lite to form 12 mounds. Sprinkle coconut evenly over top. Refrigerate for at least 1 hour. Cut into 12 servings.

Each serving equals:

HE: ⅔ Bread • ½ Vegetable • ⅓ Fat Free Milk • ⅓ Protein • ⅓ Fat • ¼ Slider • 6 Optional Calories

166 Calories • 6 gm Fat • 6 gm Protein • 22 gm Carbohydrate • 442 mg Sodium • 189 mg Calcium • 1 gm Fiber

DIABETIC EXCHANGES: 1½ Starch/Carbohydrate • 1 Fat

CARB CHOICES: 1½

Ruby Rhubarb-Raspberry Pizza Dessert

If I could only roll my "R"s as some wonderful actors do, I would have such fun saying the name of this r-r-r-recipe over and over! Still, I'm satisfied to r-r-r-revel in the r-r-r-rich flavors of this full-of-fruit finale. It's r-r-r-really a wonderful way to end a meal!

● Serves 12

> 1 (8-ounce) can Pillsbury Reduced Fat Crescent Rolls
> 1 (4-serving) package Jell-O sugar-free vanilla cook-and-serve pudding mix
> 1 (4-serving) package Jell-O sugar-free raspberry gelatin
> 1 cup water
> 3 cups finely chopped fresh or frozen rhubarb, thawed
> 1 (8-ounce) package Philadelphia fat-free cream cheese
> 2¼ cups fresh or frozen raspberries
> ¾ cup Cool Whip Lite

Preheat oven to 375 degrees. Spray a rimmed 9-by-13-inch baking sheet with butter-flavored cooking spray. Unroll crescent rolls and carefully pat into prepared baking sheet, being sure to seal perforations. Bake for 8 to 10 minutes or until crust is golden brown. Place baking sheet on a wire rack and allow crust to cool completely. In a medium saucepan, combine dry pudding mix, dry gelatin, and water. Stir in rhubarb. Cook over medium heat for 8 to 10 minutes or until mixture thickens and rhubarb becomes soft, stirring constantly. Remove from heat. Add cream cheese. Mix well using a wire whisk until cream cheese is blended. Reserve 12 raspberries for garnish. Gently fold remaining raspberries into rhubarb mixture. Evenly spread raspberry mixture over cooled crust. Refrigerate for at least 1 hour. Drop Cool Whip Lite by tablespoons to form 12 mounds. Place a reserved raspberry on top of each mound. Cut into 12 servings.

Each serving equals:

HE: ⅔ Bread • ⅓ Protein • ¼ Fruit • ¼ Vegetable

120 Calories • 4 gm Fat • 5 gm Protein • 16 gm Carbohydrate •
306 mg Sodium • 74 mg Calcium • 2 gm Fiber

DIABETIC EXCHANGES: 1 Starch/Carbohydrate • ½ Fat

CARB CHOICES: 1

Stellar Raspberry-Chocolate Dessert Pizza

If you're looking to offer guests a superstar dish at meal's end, this partnership between chocolate and raspberry is worthy—and extraordinary! ◗ Serves 12

1½ cups + 2 teaspoons Bisquick Heart Smart Baking Mix ☆
1¼ cups Splenda Granular ☆
⅔ cup fat-free milk
1 egg, or equivalent in egg substitute
2 tablespoons + 2 teaspoons I Can't Believe It's Not Butter!
    Light Margarine
1½ teaspoons vanilla extract
6 tablespoons mini chocolate chips ☆
1 (8-ounce) package Philadelphia fat-free cream cheese
¼ cup Land O Lakes Fat Free Half & Half
1 teaspoon coconut extract
3 cups fresh or frozen unsweetened raspberries
1 (4-serving) package Jell-O sugar-free vanilla cook-and-
    serve pudding mix
1 (4-serving) package Jell-O sugar-free raspberry gelatin
1¾ cups water
3 tablespoons flaked coconut

Preheat oven to 375 degrees. Spray a rimmed 9-by-13-inch baking sheet with butter-flavored cooking spray. Sprinkle 2 teaspoons baking mix onto prepared baking sheet. Gently pat pan to coat. In a large bowl, combine remaining 1½ cups baking mix and ¾ cup Splenda. Add milk, egg, margarine, and vanilla extract. Mix gently just to combine using a sturdy spoon. Stir in ¼ cup chocolate chips. Evenly spread batter into prepared baking sheet. Bake for 10 to 12 minutes or until crust tests done in center. Place baking sheet on a wire rack and allow crust to cool completely. In a medium bowl, stir cream cheese with a sturdy spoon until soft. Add half & half, remaining ½ cup Splenda, and coconut extract. Mix well to combine. Carefully spread cream cheese mixture over cooled crust. Sprinkle raspberries evenly over cream cheese mixture. In a medium saucepan, combine dry pudding mix, dry gelatin, and water. Cook over medium heat until mixture thickens and starts to boil, stirring constantly using a wire whisk. Drizzle hot mixture evenly over raspberries. Refrigerate for at least 1 hour. In a small bowl, combine coconut and remaining chocolate chips. Sprinkle mixture evenly over top. Cut into 12 servings.

Each serving equals:

HE: ⅔ Bread • ½ Protein • ⅓ Fruit • ⅓ Fat • ¾ Slider • 1 Optional Calorie

169 Calories • 5 gm Fat • 6 gm Protein • 25 gm Carbohydrate • 379 mg Sodium • 102 mg Calcium • 2 gm Fiber

DIABETIC EXCHANGES: 1½ Starch/Carbohydrate • ½ Meat • ½ Fat

CARB CHOICES: 1½

Raspberry-Almond Pizza

It's wonderfully refreshing and just a little bit glamorous, this rosy-hued dessert that is both moist and crunchy. I've used a lot of almond extract in this recipe, so if you prefer to use a bit less, feel free. ☻ Serves 8

> 1 (8-ounce) can Pillsbury Reduced Fat Crescent
>   Rolls
> 1 (8-ounce) package Philadelphia fat-free
>   cream cheese
> 1½ teaspoons almond extract ☆
> ¼ cup Splenda Granular ☆
> 1 (4-serving) package Jell-O sugar-free vanilla
>   cook-and-serve pudding mix
> 1 (4-serving) package Jell-O sugar-free raspberry
>   gelatin
> 1 cup water
> 1½ cups frozen unsweetened red raspberries
> 2 cups Cool Whip Free
> ¼ cup slivered almonds

Preheat oven to 375 degrees. Spray a rimmed 9-by-13-inch baking sheet with butter-flavored cooking spray. Unroll crescent rolls and carefully pat into prepared baking sheet, being sure to seal perforations. Bake for 8 to 10 minutes or until crust is golden brown. Place baking sheet on a wire rack and allow to cool completely. In a medium bowl, stir cream cheese with a sturdy spoon until soft. Stir in 1 teaspoon almond extract and 2 teaspoons Splenda. Evenly spread cream cheese mixture over cooled crust. In a medium saucepan, combine dry pudding mix, dry gelatin, and water. Cook over medium heat until mixture thickens and starts to boil, stirring constantly. Remove from heat. Place saucepan on a wire rack and let set for 10 minutes. Add remaining ½ teaspoon almond extract and raspberries. Mix gently just to combine. Evenly spread raspberry mixture over cream cheese mixture. Sprinkle almonds evenly over top. Refrigerate for at least 1 hour. Cut into 8 servings.

Each serving equals:

HE: 1 Bread • ⅔ Protein • ¼ Fruit • ¼ Fat • ½ Slider • 8 Optional Calories

203 Calories • 7 gm Fat • 8 gm Protein • 27 gm Carbohydrate •
468 mg Sodium • 96 mg Calcium • 2 gm Fiber

DIABETIC EXCHANGES: 1½ Starch/Carbohydrate • 1 Fat • ½ Meat

CARB CHOICES: 2

Black Forest Dessert Pizza

Many dessert lovers who have never been to Germany may not make the connection between a chocolate-cherry treat and that country's famed forests. But you don't have to be a world traveler to appreciate how scrumptious every bite of this pie is!

◑ Serves 8

> ¼ cup I Can't Believe It's Not Butter! Light Margarine
> 1 egg, or equivalent in egg substitute
> ½ cup fat-free milk
> ¾ cup cake flour
> ½ cup Splenda Granular
> ¼ cup unsweetened cocoa powder
> 1 teaspoon baking powder
> ½ teaspoon baking soda
> 2 (20-ounce) cans Lucky Leaf No Sugar Added Cherry Pie
>   Filling
> 2 tablespoons mini chocolate chips
> ¼ cup chopped walnuts
> ¾ cup Cool Whip Lite

Preheat oven to 375 degrees. Spray a 12-inch round pizza pan with butter-flavored cooking spray. In a large bowl, combine margarine and egg. Stir in milk. Add flour, Splenda, cocoa powder, baking powder, and baking soda. Mix gently just to combine using a sturdy spoon. Evenly spread batter into prepared pizza pan. Bake for 13 to 15 minutes or until crust tests done in center. Place pan on a wire rack and allow crust to cool completely. Evenly spread cherry pie filling over cooled crust. Sprinkle chocolate chips and walnuts evenly over top. Drop Cool Whip Lite by large spoonfuls to form 8 mounds. Refrigerate for at least 30 minutes. Cut into 8 wedges.

Each serving equals:

HE: 1 Fruit • 1 Fat • ½ Bread • ¼ Protein • ½ Slider • 5 Optional Calories

174 Calories • 6 gm Fat • 3 gm Protein • 27 gm Carbohydrate •
205 mg Sodium • 44 mg Calcium • 3 gm Fiber

DIABETIC EXCHANGES: 1 Fruit • 1 Fat • 1 Starch/Carbohydrate

CARB CHOICES: 2

Strawberry Shortcake Pizza

I've always said that it's one of my favorite desserts, and that hasn't changed. I consider strawberries the most precious gems of the fruit "world," and no other dessert shows them off better. Now I've had the pleasure of presenting them on a new "canvas," a work of art that you can eat and enjoy.   ☻   Serves 16

> 1 cup Splenda Granular
> ⅓ cup I Can't Believe It's Not Butter! Light Margarine
> 1 (12-fluid-ounce) can Carnation Evaporated Fat Free Milk
> 2 eggs, or equivalent in egg substitute
> 2 teaspoons vanilla extract
> 2¼ cups Bisquick Heart Smart Baking Mix
> 3 cups Cool Whip Lite
> 8 cups chopped fresh strawberries

Preheat oven to 375 degrees. Spray a rimmed 10-by-15-inch baking sheet with butter-flavored cooking spray. In a large bowl, combine Splenda and margarine using a wire whisk. Stir in evaporated milk, eggs, and vanilla extract. Add baking mix. Mix gently just to combine using a sturdy spoon. Evenly spread batter into prepared baking sheet. Bake for 13 to 15 minutes or until crust tests done in center. Do not overbake. Place baking sheet on a wire rack and allow to cool completely. Evenly spread Cool Whip Lite over cooled crust. Sprinkle strawberries evenly over Cool Whip Lite. Refrigerate for at least 30 minutes. Cut into 16 servings.

Each serving equals:

HE: ¾ Bread • ½ Fruit • ½ Fat • ½ Slider • 9 Optional Calories

165 Calories • 5 gm Fat • 4 gm Protein • 26 gm Carbohydrate • 279 mg Sodium • 91 mg Calcium • 2 gm Fiber

DIABETIC EXCHANGES: 1½ Starch/Carbohydrate • ½ Fruit • ½ Fat

CARB CHOICES: 1½

Heavenly Strawberry Pizza

As enchanting as a fairy tale, as refreshing as a breath of fresh air, this dessert pizza is a new classic, a dish to serve your dearest friends and most beloved family members. Choose the very best strawberries you can find—and bring your appetite to the table!

● Serves 12

1 (8-ounce) can Pillsbury Reduced Fat Crescent Rolls
1 (8-ounce) package Philadelphia fat-free cream cheese
½ cup Land O Lakes no-fat sour cream
2 tablespoons Splenda Granular
4 to 6 drops red food coloring (optional)
4 cups fresh strawberries, quartered
1 (4-serving) package Jell-O sugar-free vanilla cook-and-serve pudding mix
1 (4-serving) package Jell-O sugar-free strawberry gelatin
1¾ cups water
½ teaspoon almond extract
¼ cup slivered almonds

Preheat oven to 375 degrees. Spray a rimmed 9-by-13-inch baking sheet with butter-flavored cooking spray. Unroll crescent rolls and carefully pat into prepared baking sheet, being sure to seal perforations. Bake for 8 to 10 minutes or until crust is golden brown. Place baking sheet on a wire rack and allow crust to cool completely. In a medium bowl, stir cream cheese with a sturdy spoon until soft. Add sour cream and Splenda. Mix well to combine. Stir in red food coloring. Spread cream cheese mixture evenly over cooled crust. Evenly arrange strawberries over cream cheese mixture. In a medium saucepan, combine dry pudding mix, dry gelatin, and water. Cook over medium heat until mixture thickens and starts to boil, stirring constantly using a wire whisk. Remove from heat. Stir in almond extract. Drizzle hot mixture evenly over strawberries. Refrigerate for at least 1 hour. Just before serving, sprinkle almonds evenly over top. Cut into 12 servings.

Each serving equals:

HE: ⅔ Bread • ½ Protein • ⅓ Fruit • ¼ Slider • 11 Optional Calories

128 Calories • 4 gm Fat • 5 gm Protein • 18 gm Carbohydrate •
319 mg Sodium • 81 mg Calcium • 1 gm Fiber

DIABETIC EXCHANGES: 1 Starch/Carbohydrate • ½ Fat • ½ Meat

CARB CHOICES: 1

Chocolate-Strawberry
Pizza Dessert

Are you one of those "kids" who can never decide between chocolate and strawberry when asked to state your favorite flavor? Well,
now you don't have to, because I'm giving you both in one deliri-
ously good dessert. Three cheers for the makers of sugar-free
chocolate syrup; you can't taste the difference.

◐ Serves 12

 1 Pillsbury refrigerated unbaked 9-inch pie crust
 1 (8-ounce) package Philadelphia fat-free
    cream cheese
 ¼ cup Hershey's Sugar Free Chocolate Syrup
 ¾ cup Cool Whip Free
 4 cups diced fresh strawberries
 6 tablespoons strawberry spreadable fruit
 1 teaspoon almond extract
 2 tablespoons slivered almonds
 2 tablespoons mini chocolate chips

Preheat oven to 425 degrees. Let pie crust warm to room
temperature. Spray a 12-inch round pizza pan with butter-
flavored cooking spray. Gently pat pie crust into prepared pizza
pan. Evenly prick bottom of crust with tines of a fork. Bake for 8
to 10 minutes or until crust is golden brown. Place pizza pan on a
wire rack and allow crust to cool completely. Meanwhile, in a
large bowl, stir cream cheese with a sturdy spoon until soft. Add
chocolate syrup and Cool Whip Free. Mix gently to combine.
Evenly spread cream cheese mixture over cooled crust. Sprinkle
strawberries evenly over cream cheese mixture. In a small bowl,
combine spreadable fruit and almond extract. Microwave on
HIGH (100% power) for 15 seconds. Drizzle hot fruit spread
evenly over strawberries. Refrigerate for at least 30 minutes.
Sprinkle almonds and chocolate chips evenly over top. Cut into
12 servings.

Each serving equals:

HE: ⅔ Bread • ⅔ Fruit • ½ Fat • ⅓ Protein • ¼ Slider • 1 Optional Calorie

158 Calories • 6 gm Fat • 3 gm Protein • 23 gm Carbohydrate •
179 mg Sodium • 65 mg Calcium • 2 gm Fiber

DIABETIC EXCHANGES: 1½ Starch/Carbohydrate • ½ Fruit • ½ Fat

CARB CHOICES: 1½

Strawberry-Chocolate Cream Dessert Pizza

Do your best to find the chocolate fudge pudding mix, not just the regular chocolate—it really does make a difference! If your store manager doesn't stock the flavors you love, ask him or her to get them, and then buy plenty. ◑ Serves 12

1 (8-ounce) can Pillsbury Reduced Fat Crescent Rolls
1 (8-ounce) package Philadelphia fat-free cream cheese
2 tablespoons Splenda Granular
1½ teaspoons vanilla extract ☆
2 (4-serving) packages Jell-O sugar-free instant chocolate
    fudge pudding mix
1 cup Carnation Nonfat Dry Milk Powder
¾ cup Land O Lakes no-fat sour cream
1¼ cups water
1 cup Cool Whip Free
4 cups fresh whole strawberries
¼ cup Hershey's Sugar Free Chocolate Syrup

Preheat oven to 375 degrees. Spray a rimmed 9-by-13-inch baking sheet with butter-flavored cooking spray. Unroll crescent rolls and carefully pat into prepared baking sheet, being sure to seal perforations. Bake for 8 to 10 minutes or until crust is golden brown. Place baking sheet on a wire rack and allow to cool completely. In a medium bowl, stir cream cheese with a sturdy spoon until soft. Add Splenda and ½ teaspoon vanilla extract. Mix well to combine. Evenly spread mixture over cooled crust. In a large bowl, combine dry pudding mix and dry milk powder. Add sour cream and water. Mix well using a wire whisk. Fold in remaining 1 teaspoon vanilla extract and Cool Whip Free. Evenly spread chocolate mixture over cream cheese mixture. Cut strawberries in half lengthwise. Attractively place strawberries, cut-side down, in chocolate mixture. Drizzle chocolate syrup evenly over strawberries. Refrigerate for at least 1 hour. Cut into 12 servings.

Each serving equals:

HE: ⅔ Bread • ⅓ Protein • ⅓ Fruit • ¼ Fat Free Milk • ½ Slider •
9 Optional Calories

167 Calories • 3 gm Fat • 7 gm Protein • 28 gm Carbohydrate •
524 mg Sodium • 158 mg Calcium • 1 gm Fiber

DIABETIC EXCHANGES: 2 Starch/Carbohydrate

CARB CHOICES: 2

Strawberry Brownie Pizza

The aroma of good cocoa powder is so sensational, you might succumb to temptation and taste it—and go, *"yecch!"* Remember, it's unsweetened and will taste very bitter without the sweet support of Splenda. ☻ Serves 8

¾ cup Bisquick Heart Smart Baking Mix
¼ cup unsweetened cocoa powder
1 teaspoon baking powder
½ teaspoon baking soda
½ cup Splenda Granular
⅓ cup Land O Lakes no-fat sour cream
¼ cup Land O Lakes Fat Free Half & Half
1 teaspoon vanilla extract
2 cups water ☆
1 (8-ounce) package Philadelphia fat-free cream cheese
½ cup Cool Whip Free
1 teaspoon coconut extract
2 cups sliced fresh strawberries
1 (4-serving) package Jell-O sugar-free vanilla cook-and-
     serve pudding mix
1 (4-serving) package Jell-O sugar-free strawberry gelatin
2 tablespoons mini chocolate chips
2 tablespoons flaked coconut

Preheat oven to 375 degrees. Spray a 12-inch round pizza pan with butter-flavored cooking spray. In a large bowl, combine baking mix, cocoa powder, baking powder, baking soda, and Splenda. In a small bowl, combine sour cream, half & half, vanilla extract, and ½ cup water. Add sour cream mixture to baking mix mixture. Mix gently to combine using a sturdy spoon. Evenly spread mixture into prepared pizza pan. Bake for 10 to 14 minutes or until crust tests done in center. Place pan on a wire rack and allow crust to cool completely. In a medium bowl, stir cream cheese with a sturdy spoon until soft. Stir in Cool Whip Free and coconut extract. Spread cream cheese mixture evenly over cooled crust. Arrange strawberries evenly over cream cheese mixture. In a medium saucepan, combine dry pudding mix, dry gelatin, and remaining 1½ cups water. Cook over medium heat until mixture thickens and starts to boil, stirring often using a wire whisk. Drizzle hot mixture evenly over strawberries. Refrigerate for 1 hour. Sprinkle chocolate chips and coconut evenly over top. Cut into 8 wedges.

Each serving equals:

HE: ½ Bread • ½ Protein • ¼ Fruit • ¾ Slider • 4 Optional Calories

142 Calories • 2 gm Fat • 7 gm Protein • 24 gm Carbohydrate • 512 mg Sodium • 153 mg Calcium • 2 gm Fiber

DIABETIC EXCHANGES: 1½ Starch/Carbohydrate • ½ Meat

CARB CHOICES: 1½

Strawberry Peach Dessert Pizza

If you're new to my cookbooks, you might be surprised that I "cook" with Diet Mountain Dew. Don't be—it's an easy and fun way to introduce lemony flavor into my recipes, and you may be more likely to have it on hand than fresh lemon juice or a few lemons.

◐ Serves 12

1 (8-ounce) can Pillsbury Reduced Fat Crescent Rolls
3 cups whole fresh strawberries
1¾ cups Diet Mountain Dew ☆
½ cup Splenda Granular
3 to 5 drops red food coloring
2 (8-ounce) packages Philadelphia fat-free cream cheese
2½ cups (5 medium) chopped fresh peaches
1 (4-serving) package Jell-O sugar-free vanilla cook-and-
    serve pudding mix
1 (4-serving) package Jell-O sugar-free strawberry gelatin
1½ cups Cool Whip Lite

Preheat oven to 375 degrees. Spray a rimmed 9-by-13-inch baking sheet with butter-flavored cooking spray. Unroll crescent rolls and carefully pat into prepared pan, being sure to seal perforations. Bake for 8 to 10 minutes or until crust is golden brown. Place baking sheet on a wire rack and allow crust to cool completely. Reserve 12 strawberries for garnish. In a medium saucepan, combine remaining strawberries and ¼ cup Diet Mountain Dew. Cover and cook over medium-low heat for 6 to 8 minutes or until strawberries soften, stirring occasionally. Remove from heat. Stir in Splenda and red food coloring. Place saucepan on a wire rack. Meanwhile, in a large bowl, stir cream cheese with a sturdy spoon until soft. Add partially cooled strawberry mixture. Mix well to combine. Evenly spread mixture over cooled crust. Refrigerate for 10 minutes. Sprinkle peaches evenly over top of partially cooled strawberry mixture. In a medium saucepan, combine dry pudding mix, dry gelatin, and remaining 1½ cups Diet Mountain Dew. Cook over medium heat until mixture thickens and starts to boil, stirring constantly using a wire whisk. Drizzle hot mixture evenly over peaches. Refrigerate for at least 1 hour. Cut into 12 servings. When serving, top each piece with 2 tablespoons Cool Whip Lite and garnish with 1 strawberry.

Each serving equals:

HE: ⅔ Bread • ⅔ Protein • ⅔ Fruit • ¼ Slider • 14 Optional Calories

156 Calories • 4 gm Fat • 7 gm Protein • 23 gm Carbohydrate •
402 mg Sodium • 115 mg Calcium • 2 gm Fiber

DIABETIC EXCHANGES: 1 Starch/Carbohydrate • 1 Meat • 1 Fruit

CARB CHOICES: 1½

Peach Melba Dessert Pizza

There is almost no experience like it, the luscious sensation of biting into a perfectly ripe peach. The velvety skin, the juicy flesh, the incredible sweetness, all combine to send you into a dreamworld of delight. ◐ Serves 8

> 1 (8-ounce) can Pillsbury Reduced Fat Crescent
>   Rolls
> 1 (8-ounce) package Philadelphia fat-free
>   cream cheese
> 1 teaspoon vanilla extract
> ¼ cup Splenda Granular
> 3 cups (6 medium) peeled and finely chopped
>   fresh peaches
> 1½ cups fresh red raspberries
> 2 (4-serving) packages Jell-O sugar-free vanilla
>   cook-and-serve pudding mix
> 1 (4-serving) package Jell-O sugar-free raspberry gelatin
> 2½ cups Diet Mountain Dew

Preheat oven to 375 degrees. Spray a rimmed 9-by-13-inch baking sheet with butter-flavored cooking spray. Unroll crescent rolls and carefully pat into prepared baking sheet, being sure to seal perforations. Bake for 8 to 10 minutes or until crust is golden brown. Place baking sheet on a wire rack and allow crust to cool completely. In a medium bowl, stir cream cheese with a sturdy spoon until soft. Stir in vanilla extract and Splenda. Spread cream cheese mixture evenly over cooled crust. Arrange peaches and raspberries evenly over cream cheese. In a medium saucepan, combine dry pudding mixes, dry gelatin, and Diet Mountain Dew. Cook over medium heat for 6 to 8 minutes or until mixture thickens and starts to boil, stirring constantly using a wire whisk. Drizzle hot mixture evenly over fruit. Refrigerate for at least 1 hour. Cut into 8 servings.

HINT: Frozen unsweetened peaches and raspberries, thawed, well drained, and chopped may be used instead of fresh.

Each serving equals:

HE: 1 Bread • 1 Fruit • ½ Protein • ½ Slider • 6 Optional Calories

169 Calories • 5 gm Fat • 7 gm Protein • 24 gm Carbohydrate • 413 mg Sodium • 89 mg Calcium • 3 gm Fiber

DIABETIC EXCHANGES: 1 Starch • 1 Fruit • ½ Meat • ½ Fat

CARB CHOICES: 1½

Peach Pecan Dessert Pizza

Have you ever eaten a fresh peach that's been sitting in the sun? It's amazingly sweet and warm, and you can't help but think that this must be what the ancients called nectar, the drink of the gods.

❂ Serves 8

1 (8-ounce) can Pillsbury Reduced Fat Crescent Rolls
1 (8-ounce) package Philadelphia fat-free cream cheese
3 tablespoons peach spreadable fruit
4 cups peeled and chopped fresh peaches
1 (4-serving) package Jell-O sugar-free vanilla cook-and-
    serve pudding mix
1 (4-serving) package Jell-O sugar-free orange gelatin
1¾ cups water
¼ cup chopped pecans

Preheat oven to 375 degrees. Spray a rimmed 9-by-13-inch baking sheet with butter-flavored cooking spray. Unroll crescent rolls and carefully pat into prepared baking sheet, being sure to seal perforations. Bake for 8 to 10 minutes or until crust is golden brown. Place baking sheet on a wire rack and allow crust to cool completely. In a medium bowl, stir cream cheese with a sturdy spoon until soft. Stir in spreadable fruit. Spread cream cheese mixture evenly over cooled crust. Evenly arrange peaches over cream cheese layer. In a medium saucepan, combine dry pudding mix, dry gelatin, and water. Cook over medium heat until mixture thickens and starts to boil, stirring constantly using a wire whisk. Drizzle hot mixture evenly over peaches. Sprinkle pecans evenly over top. Refrigerate for at least 1 hour. Cut into 8 servings.

Each serving equals:

HE: 1¼ Fruit • 1 Bread • ½ Protein • ½ Fat • 15 Optional Calories

195 Calories • 7 gm Fat • 7 gm Protein • 26 gm Carbohydrate •
416 mg Sodium • 86 mg Calcium • 2 gm Fiber

DIABETIC EXCHANGES: 1 Fruit • 1 Starch • ½ Meat • ½ Fat

CARB CHOICES: 2

Pears Helene Dessert Pizza

Inspired by a famous dessert that invites chocolate and pears to join their equally scrumptious flavors, this sweetly succulent delight is a showstopper! ☻ Serves 12

> 1 Pillsbury refrigerated unbaked 9-inch pie crust
> 1 (8-ounce) package Philadelphia fat-free cream cheese
> ¾ cup Cool Whip Lite
> 2 (4-serving) packages Jell-O sugar-free instant chocolate pudding mix
> 1⅓ cups Carnation Nonfat Dry Milk Powder
> 2 (15-ounce) cans pears, packed in fruit juice, drained, finely chopped, and ½ cup liquid reserved
> 2 cups water
> ½ cup chopped walnuts

Preheat oven to 425 degrees. Let pie crust warm to room temperature. Spray a 12-inch round pizza pan with butter-flavored cooking spray. Gently pat pie crust into prepared pizza pan. Evenly prick bottom of crust with tines of a fork. Bake for 8 to 10 minutes or until crust is golden brown. Place pizza pan on a wire rack and allow crust to cool completely. In a medium bowl, stir cream cheese with a sturdy spoon until soft. Stir in Cool Whip Lite. Spread cream cheese mixture evenly over cooled crust. In a large bowl, combine dry pudding mixes, dry milk powder, reserved pear juice, and water. Mix well using a wire whisk. Evenly spread chocolate pudding mixture over cream cheese mixture. Arrange chopped pears evenly over pudding mixture. Sprinkle walnuts evenly over top. Refrigerate for at least 30 minutes. Cut into 12 servings.

Each serving equals:

HE: ¾ Fat • ⅔ Bread • ⅔ Fruit • ½ Protein • ⅓ Fat Free Milk • ¼ Slider • 1 Optional Calorie

232 Calories • 8 gm Fat • 7 gm Protein • 33 gm Carbohydrate • 428 mg Sodium • 159 mg Calcium • 2 gm Fiber

DIABETIC EXCHANGES: 1½ Starch/Carbohydrate • 1 Fat • ½ Fruit • ½ Meat

CARB CHOICES: 2

Apricot Nectar Dessert Pizza

I thought of making this recipe with fresh apricots, but they're often harder to find in season than peaches. Besides, the canned ones are packed at the height of their sweetness and are available anytime at all. Take your time when you eat this special dessert—it will be a truly sensuous experience! ◑ Serves 12

  1 (8-ounce) can Pillsbury Reduced Fat Crescent
     Rolls
  1 (8-ounce) package Philadelphia fat-free
     cream cheese
  6 tablespoons apricot spreadable fruit
  2 tablespoons Splenda Granular
  1 teaspoon coconut extract
  2 (15-ounce) cans apricot halves, packed in fruit juice,
     drained and chopped
  1 (4-serving) package Jell-O sugar-free vanilla
     cook-and-serve pudding mix
  1 (4-serving) package Jell-O sugar-free lemon gelatin
  1½ cups water
  3 tablespoons chopped pecans
  3 tablespoons flaked coconut

Preheat oven to 375 degrees. Spray a rimmed 9-by-13-inch baking sheet with butter-flavored cooking spray. Unroll crescent rolls and carefully pat into prepared pan, being sure to seal perforations. Bake for 8 to 10 minutes or until crust is golden brown. Place baking sheet on a wire rack and allow crust to cool completely. In a medium bowl, stir cream cheese with a sturdy spoon until soft. Stir in spreadable fruit, Splenda, and coconut extract. Evenly spread mixture over cooled crust. Arrange apricots evenly over cream cheese mixture. In a medium saucepan, combine dry pudding mix, dry gelatin, and water. Cook over medium heat until mixture thickens and starts to boil, stirring constantly using a wire whisk. Drizzle hot mixture evenly over apricots. Refrigerate for at least 1 hour. In a small bowl, combine pecans and coconut. Sprinkle mixture evenly over top. Cut into 12 servings.

Each serving equals:

HE: 1 Fruit • ⅔ Bread • ⅓ Protein • ¼ Fat • 13 Optional Calories

169 Calories • 5 gm Fat • 5 gm Protein • 26 gm Carbohydrate •
308 mg Sodium • 63 mg Calcium • 1 gm Fiber

DIABETIC EXCHANGES: 1 Fruit • 1 Starch/Carbohydrate • ½ Fat

CARB CHOICES: 1½

Blueberry Hill Dessert Pizza

Did Fats Domino know of a real place called Blueberry Hill, a special spot where a person might experience a kind of thrill never before known? I suppose it's possible, and I like to think that this is the kind of dessert that would be served in such a place.

☾ Serves 8

> 1 (8-ounce) can Pillsbury Reduced Fat Crescent
>   Rolls
> 1 (8-ounce) package Philadelphia fat-free
>   cream cheese
> ½ cup Cool Whip Free
> 1 teaspoon vanilla extract
> 1 (4-serving) package Jell-O sugar-free vanilla
>   cook-and-serve pudding mix
> 1 (4-serving) package Jell-O sugar-free lemon
>   gelatin
> 1 cup Diet Mountain Dew
> 3 cups fresh or frozen unsweetened blueberries
> ¼ cup chopped pecans

Preheat oven to 375 degrees. Spray a rimmed 9-by-13-inch baking sheet with butter-flavored cooking spray. Unroll crescent rolls and carefully pat into prepared baking sheet, being sure to seal perforations. Bake for 8 to 10 minutes or until crust is golden brown. Place baking sheet on a wire rack and allow crust to cool completely. In a medium bowl, stir cream cheese with a sturdy spoon until soft. Stir in Cool Whip Free and vanilla extract. Evenly spread mixture over cooled crust. In a medium saucepan, combine dry pudding mix, dry gelatin, and Diet Mountain Dew. Cook over medium heat until mixture thickens and starts to boil, stirring often using a wire whisk. Remove from heat. Gently stir in blueberries. Place saucepan on a wire rack and let set for 5 minutes, stirring occasionally. Spoon blueberry mixture evenly over cream cheese mixture. Refrigerate for at least 1 hour. Just before serving, sprinkle pecans evenly over top. Cut into 8 servings.

Each serving equals:

HE: 1 Bread • ½ Protein • ½ Fruit • ½ Fat • ¼ Slider • 2 Optional Calories

195 Calories • 7 gm Fat • 7 gm Protein • 26 gm Carbohydrate •
463 mg Sodium • 85 mg Calcium • 2 gm Fiber

DIABETIC EXCHANGES: 1½ Starch/Carbohydrate • ½ Meat • ½ Fruit • ½ Fat

CARB CHOICES: 1½

Diamond Head Blueberry Pizza Dessert

As the morning sun rises over this famed Hawaiian landmark, you can't help but ooh and aah—it's just that magnificent, as is this mouthwatering dessert! I've tried it with fresh and frozen blueberries and liked both versions, so you'll have to decide which you prefer.   ☻   Serves 12

> 1 Pillsbury refrigerated unbaked 9-inch pie crust
> 1 (4-serving) package Jell-O sugar-free vanilla cook-and-
>   serve pudding mix
> 1 (4-serving) package Jell-O sugar-free lemon gelatin
> ½ cup Diet Mountain Dew
> 3 cups fresh or frozen unsweetened blueberries
> 1 (8-ounce) package Philadelphia fat-free cream cheese
> ¼ cup Splenda Granular
> 1 (8-ounce) can crushed pineapple, packed in fruit juice,
>   drained, and ¼ cup liquid reserved
> 1 (8-ounce) can pineapple tidbits, packed in fruit juice,
>   drained, and ¼ cup liquid reserved
> ½ cup Cool Whip Lite
> 1 teaspoon coconut extract
> 2 tablespoons flaked coconut

Preheat oven to 425 degrees. Let pie crust warm to room temperature. Spray a 12-inch round pizza pan with butter-flavored cooking spray. Gently pat pie crust into prepared pizza pan. Evenly prick bottom of crust with tines of a fork. Bake for 8 to 10 minutes or until golden brown. Place pizza pan on a wire rack and allow crust to cool completely. In a medium saucepan, combine dry pudding mix, dry gelatin, Diet Mountain Dew, and reserved pineapple liquid. Cook over medium heat until mixture thickens and starts to boil, stirring constantly using a wire whisk. Stir in blueberries. Place saucepan on a wire rack and allow to cool, stirring occasionally. In a medium bowl, stir cream cheese with a sturdy spoon until soft. Blend in Splenda and crushed pineapple. Add Cool Whip Lite and coconut extract. Mix gently to combine. Refrigerate until crust and blueberry filling have cooled. Spread cream cheese mixture evenly over cooled crust. Evenly spoon cooled blueberry mixture over cream cheese mixture. Sprinkle pineapple tidbits and coconut evenly over top. Refrigerate for at least 1 hour. Cut into 12 servings.

HINT: If you can't find tidbits, use pineapple chunks and coarsely chop.

Each serving equals:

HE: ⅔ Bread • ⅔ Fruit • ⅓ Protein • ⅓ Fat • ¼ Slider • 1 Optional Calorie

161 Calories • 5 gm Fat • 4 gm Protein • 25 gm Carbohydrate • 218 mg Sodium • 61 mg Calcium • 2 gm Fiber

DIABETIC EXCHANGES: 1 Starch/Carbohydrate • 1 Fat • ½ Fruit

CARB CHOICES: 1½

Pineapple-Chocolate Dessert Pizza

Imagine taking chunks of juicy pineapple and dipping them in chocolate fondue—that's sort of the inspiration for this spirited dessert! It's a luscious contrast, and I think it works really well.

◐ Serves 12

1 Pillsbury refrigerated unbaked 9-inch pie crust
1 (4-serving) package Jell-O sugar-free chocolate cook-and-serve pudding mix
⅔ cup Carnation Nonfat Dry Milk Powder
1 cup fat-free milk
2 (8-ounce) cans pineapple tidbits, packed in fruit juice, drained, and 2 tablespoons liquid reserved
1 (8-ounce) package Philadelphia fat-free cream cheese
1 teaspoon coconut extract
3 tablespoons flaked coconut
2 tablespoons mini chocolate chips

Preheat oven to 425 degrees. Let pie crust warm to room temperature. Spray a 12-inch round pizza pan with butter-flavored cooking spray. Gently pat pie crust into prepared pizza pan. Evenly prick bottom of crust with tines of a fork. Bake for 8 to 10 minutes or until crust is golden brown. Place pizza pan on a wire rack and allow crust to cool completely. In a medium saucepan, combine dry pudding mix, dry milk powder, milk, and reserved pineapple liquid. Cook over medium heat until mixture thickens and starts to boil, stirring constantly using a wire whisk. Remove from heat. Stir in cream cheese and coconut extract. Mix well until cream cheese is blended. Spread mixture evenly over cooled crust. Refrigerate for at least 30 minutes. Evenly sprinkle pineapple tidbits over chocolate mixture. Sprinkle coconut and chocolate chips evenly over top. Refrigerate for at least 1 hour. Cut into 12 servings.

HINT: If you can't find tidbits, use pineapple chunks and coarsely chop.

Each serving equals:

HE: ²⁄₃ Bread • ⅓ Protein • ⅓ Fruit • ⅓ Fat • ¼ Fat Free Milk • ¼ Slider •
4 Optional Calories

149 Calories • 5 gm Fat • 4 gm Protein • 22 gm Carbohydrate •
180 mg Sodium • 108 mg Calcium • 1 gm Fiber

DIABETIC EXCHANGES: 1½ Starch/Carbohydrate • 1 Fat

CARB CHOICES: 1½

Brownie Fruit Pizza

They might just be America's favorite baked good—but they're rarely combined with fruit as I've done here. Don't let the long list of ingredients discourage you from enjoying these "kitchen sink" delights!   ☺   Serves 12

½ cup I Can't Believe It's Not Butter! Light Margarine
3 tablespoons Land O Lakes no-fat sour cream
1½ cups Splenda Granular
3 eggs, or equivalent in egg substitute
¼ cup Land O Lakes Fat Free Half & Half
2 teaspoons vanilla extract
1 cup + 2 tablespoons Bisquick Heart Smart Baking Mix
6 tablespoons unsweetened cocoa powder
1 (8-ounce) package Philadelphia fat-free cream cheese
2 cups Cool Whip Lite
2 cups sliced fresh strawberries
2 cups (2 medium) sliced bananas
2 (8-ounce) cans pineapple tidbits, packed in fruit juice, drained
1 (11-ounce) can mandarin oranges, rinsed and drained
6 (2½-inch) chocolate graham cracker squares, made into crumbs

Preheat oven to 375 degrees. Spray a rimmed 10-by-15-inch baking sheet with butter-flavored cooking spray. In a large bowl, combine margarine, sour cream, and Splenda using a wire whisk. Stir in eggs, half & half, and vanilla extract. Add baking mix and cocoa powder. Mix gently just to combine using a sturdy spoon. Evenly spread batter into prepared baking sheet. Bake for 10 to 14 minutes or until crust tests done in center. Place baking sheet on a wire rack and allow crust to cool completely. In a medium bowl, stir cream cheese with a sturdy spoon until soft. Stir in Cool Whip Lite. Evenly spread cream cheese mixture over cooled crust. Sprinkle strawberries, bananas, pineapple tidbits, and mandarin oranges evenly over cream cheese mixture. Evenly sprinkle chocolate graham cracker crumbs over top. Refrigerate for at least 30 minutes. Cut into 12 servings.

HINTS: 1. If you can't find tidbits, use pineapple chunks and coarsely chop.

2. A self-seal sandwich bag works great for crushing graham crackers.

Each serving equals:

HE: 1 Protein • 1 Fruit • 1 Fat • ⅔ Bread • ¼ Slider • 11 Optional Calories

244 Calories • 8 gm Fat • 7 gm Protein • 36 gm Carbohydrate • 358 mg Sodium • 98 mg Calcium • 3 gm Fiber

DIABETIC EXCHANGES: 1 Meat • 1 Fruit • 1 Fat • 1 Starch

CARB CHOICES: 2

Fiesta Fruit Pizza

This is my nominee for an utterly luscious, fabulous festive, perfect-for-a-party dessert! It's brimming with fresh fruit, it's oh-so-creamy, and it looks just lovely. ☻ Serves 8

½ cup graham cracker crumbs
½ cup (4 ounces) Philadelphia fat-free cream cheese
2 tablespoons Land O Lakes no-fat sour cream
3 tablespoons Land O Lakes Fat Free Half & Half
1 cup Bisquick Heart Smart Baking Mix
⅓ cup Splenda Granular
2 cups chopped fresh strawberries
2 cups (4 medium) peeled and chopped ripe fresh peaches
1 cup Thompson seedless grapes, halved
1 (4-serving) package Jell-O sugar-free vanilla cook-and-
    serve pudding mix
1 (4-serving) package Jell-O sugar-free orange gelatin
1¾ cups water
½ teaspoon ground cinnamon
2 tablespoons chopped pecans

Preheat oven to 400 degrees. Spray a 12-inch round pizza pan with butter-flavored cooking spray. Reserve 2 tablespoons graham cracker crumbs. In a large bowl, stir cream cheese with a sturdy spoon until soft. Stir in sour cream and half & half. Add baking mix, remaining 6 tablespoons graham cracker crumbs, and Splenda. Mix well to combine. Pat dough into prepared pizza pan. Bake for 9 to 11 minutes or until crust is golden brown. Place pizza pan on a wire rack and allow crust to cool completely. Evenly sprinkle strawberries, peaches, and grapes over cooled crust. In a medium saucepan, combine dry pudding mix, dry gelatin, and water. Cook over medium heat until mixture thickens and starts to boil, stirring constantly using a wire whisk. Remove from heat. Stir in cinnamon. Drizzle hot mixture evenly over fruit. Refrigerate for at least 1 hour. Just before serving, combine reserved 2 tablespoons graham cracker crumbs and pecans. Evenly sprinkle cracker mixture over top. Cut into 8 wedges.

HINT: Place hand in a plastic sandwich bag and lightly coat with flour before pressing dough into pan.

Each serving equals:

HE: 1 Bread • 1 Fruit • ¼ Protein • ¼ Fat • ¼ Slider • 6 Optional Calories

175 Calories • 3 gm Fat • 6 gm Protein • 31 gm Carbohydrate • 375 mg Sodium • 81 mg Calcium • 2 gm Fiber

DIABETIC EXCHANGES: 1 Starch • 1 Fruit

CARB CHOICES: 2

Banana Split Dessert Pizza

Ever since I began creating Healthy Exchanges recipes, I've included some kind of banana split dish in just about every book. My husband has loved every single one over the years, so, Cliff, this one's for you! ● Serves 8

¾ cup Bisquick Heart Smart Baking Mix
½ cup + 2 tablespoons Splenda Granular ☆
¼ cup unsweetened cocoa powder
1 teaspoon baking powder
½ teaspoon baking soda
1 cup fat-free milk
⅓ cup Land O Lakes no-fat sour cream
1 tablespoon coconut extract ☆
1 (8-ounce) package Philadelphia fat-free cream cheese
½ cup Cool Whip Free
1 (8-ounce) can crushed pineapple, packed in fruit juice, drained
2 cups (2 medium) sliced bananas
2 cups sliced fresh strawberries
2 tablespoons mini chocolate chips
2 tablespoons flaked coconut

Preheat oven to 375 degrees. Spray a 12-inch round pizza pan with butter-flavored cooking spray. In a large bowl, combine baking mix, ½ cup Splenda, cocoa powder, baking powder, and baking soda. In a small bowl, combine milk, sour cream, and 2 teaspoons coconut extract. Add milk mixture to baking mix mixture. Mix gently just to combine using a sturdy spoon. Evenly spread mixture into prepared pizza pan. Bake for 14 to 16 minutes or until crust tests done in center. Place pizza pan on a wire rack and allow crust to cool completely. In a large bowl, stir cream cheese with a sturdy spoon until soft. Stir in Cool Whip Free, remaining 1 teaspoon coconut extract, and remaining 2 tablespoons Splenda. Add pineapple. Mix gently to combine. Evenly spread cream cheese mixture over cooled crust. Sprinkle bananas and strawberries evenly over cream cheese mixture. Evenly sprinkle chocolate chips and coconut over top. Refrigerate for at least 30 minutes. Cut into 8 wedges.

HINT: To prevent bananas from turning brown, mix with 1 teaspoon lemon juice or sprinkle with Fruit Fresh.

Each serving equals:

HE: 1 Fruit • ½ Bread • ½ Protein • ½ Slider • 8 Optional Calories

203 Calories • 3 gm Fat • 8 gm Protein • 36 gm Carbohydrate •
430 mg Sodium • 190 mg Calcium • 3 gm Fiber

DIABETIC EXCHANGES: 1 Fruit • 1 Starch/Carbohydrate • ½ Meat

CARB CHOICES: 2½

Summer Breezes Fruit Pizza

If it's possible to take all that's wonderful about a glorious summer day and stir it into a dessert recipe, this is it! Five—count 'em, five—cups of fresh berries make this a grand choice for a patio party or any other July celebration. ☻ Serves 12

> 1 Pillsbury refrigerated unbaked 9-inch pie crust
> 1 (8-ounce) package Philadelphia fat-free cream cheese
> 1 teaspoon vanilla extract
> 2 tablespoons Splenda Granular
> 2 cups sliced fresh strawberries
> 1½ cups fresh blueberries
> 1½ cups fresh raspberries
> 1 cup (1 medium) sliced banana
> 2 (8-ounce) cans pineapple tidbits, packed in fruit juice,
>   drained and ½ cup liquid reserved
> 1 (4-serving) package Jell-O sugar-free vanilla cook-and-
>   serve pudding mix
> 1 (4-serving) package Jell-O sugar-free strawberry gelatin
> 1¼ cups water
> 1½ cups Cool Whip Lite
> ¼ cup chopped pecans

Preheat oven to 425 degrees. Let pie crust warm to room temperature. Spray a 12-inch round pizza pan with butter-flavored cooking spray. Gently pat pie crust into prepared pizza pan. Evenly prick bottom of crust with tines of a fork. Bake for 8 to 10 minutes or until crust is golden brown. Place pizza pan on a wire rack and allow crust to cool completely. In a large bowl, stir cream cheese with a sturdy spoon until soft. Add vanilla extract and Splenda. Mix well to combine. Evenly spread cream cheese mixture over cooled crust. Sprinkle strawberries, blueberries, raspberries, banana, and pineapple tidbits evenly over cream cheese mixture. In a large saucepan, combine dry pudding mix, dry gelatin, reserved pineapple liquid, and water. Cook over medium heat until mixture thickens and starts to boil, stirring often using a wire whisk. Drizzle hot mixture evenly over fruit. Refrigerate for at least 1 hour. Cut into 12 pieces. When serving, top each piece with 2 tablespoons Cool Whip Lite and 1 teaspoon pecans.

Each serving equals:

HE: 1 Fruit • ⅔ Bread • ⅔ Fat • ⅓ Protein • ¼ Slider • 11 Optional Calories

208 Calories • 8 gm Fat • 4 gm Protein • 30 gm Carbohydrate • 217 mg Sodium • 70 mg Calcium • 2 gm Fiber

DIABETIC EXCHANGES: 1 Fruit • 1 Starch/Carbohydrate • 1 Fat

CARB CHOICES: 2

Trade Winds Fruit Pizza Dessert

"Bad news," the captain says, "we've been blown off course. The good news is, we're heading for Tahiti, and we've got a special taste-of-the-tropics dessert for dinner!"   ☾   Serves 12

1 (8-ounce) can Pillsbury Reduced Fat Crescent
   Rolls
1 (8-ounce) package Philadelphia fat-free cream cheese
2 tablespoons Splenda Granular
1 (8-ounce) can crushed pineapple, packed in fruit juice,
   drained
1 teaspoon coconut extract
2 cups (2 medium) sliced bananas
2 (11-ounce) cans mandarin oranges, rinsed and drained
1 cup Thompson seedless grapes, halved
1 (4-serving) package Jell-O sugar-free vanilla cook-and-
   serve pudding mix
1 (4-serving) package Jell-O sugar-free lemon gelatin
1½ cups water
2 tablespoons flaked coconut

Preheat oven to 425 degrees. Spray a rimmed 9-by-13-inch baking sheet with butter-flavored cooking spray. Unroll crescent rolls and carefully pat into prepared baking sheet, being sure to seal perforations. Bake for 8 to 10 minutes or until crust is golden brown. Place baking sheet on a wire rack and allow crust to cool completely. In a medium bowl, stir cream cheese with a sturdy spoon until soft. Stir in Splenda, pineapple, and coconut extract. Evenly spread cream cheese mixture over cooled crust. Sprinkle bananas, mandarin oranges, and grapes evenly over cream cheese mixture. In a medium saucepan, combine dry pudding mix, dry gelatin, and water. Cook over medium heat until mixture thickens and starts to boil, stirring constantly using a wire whisk. Drizzle hot mixture evenly over fruit. Refrigerate for at least 1 hour. Just before serving, sprinkle coconut evenly over top. Cut into 12 servings.

Each serving equals:

HE: 1 Fruit • ⅔ Bread • ⅓ Protein

147 Calories • 3 gm Fat • 5 gm Protein • 25 gm Carbohydrate •
308 mg Sodium • 62 mg Calcium • 2 gm Fiber

DIABETIC EXCHANGES: 1 Fruit • 1 Starch

CARB CHOICES: 1½

Tropical Sunset Dessert Pizza

There's something so captivating about the colors of the sky as the fierce, bright sun starts to slip behind the nearest mountains or into the sea. Light some candles, put your feet up, and take a bite of this lip-smacking dessert! ☻ Serves 12

1 (8-ounce) package Pillsbury Reduced Fat Crescent Rolls
2 (8-ounce) packages Philadelphia fat-free cream cheese
¼ cup unsweetened orange juice
½ cup Splenda Granular
1 teaspoon coconut extract
¼ cup chopped pecans ☆ ·
3 cups (3 medium) diced bananas
2 (11-ounce) cans mandarin oranges, rinsed and drained
1 (8-ounce) can pineapple tidbits, packed in fruit juice,
     drained and ¼ cup liquid reserved
1 (4-serving) package Jell-O sugar-free vanilla cook-and-
     serve pudding mix
1 (4-serving) package Jell-O sugar-free orange gelatin
1¼ cups Diet Mountain Dew
3 tablespoons graham cracker crumbs
3 tablespoons flaked coconut

Preheat oven to 375 degrees. Spray a rimmed 9-by-13-inch baking sheet with butter-flavored cooking spray. Unroll crescent rolls and carefully pat into prepared baking sheet, being sure to seal perforations. Bake for 8 to 10 minutes or until crust is golden brown. Place baking sheet on a wire rack and allow crust to cool completely. In a medium bowl, stir cream cheese with a sturdy spoon until soft. Add orange juice, Splenda, and coconut extract. Mix well to combine. Stir in 2 tablespoons pecans. Evenly spread cream cheese mixture over cooled crust. Sprinkle diced bananas evenly over cream cheese mixture. Sprinkle mandarin oranges and pineapple tidbits evenly over bananas. In a medium saucepan, combine dry pudding mix, dry gelatin, Diet Mountain Dew, and reserved pineapple liquid. Cook over medium heat until mixture thickens and starts to boil, stirring constantly using a wire whisk. Drizzle hot mixture evenly over fruit. Refrigerate for at least 1 hour. In a small bowl, combine graham cracker crumbs, coconut, and remaining 2 tablespoons pecans. Sprinkle crumb mixture evenly over top. Cut into 12 servings.

HINT: To prevent bananas from turning brown, mix with 1 teaspoon lemon juice or sprinkle with Fruit Fresh.

Each serving equals:

HE: 1 Fruit • ¾ Bread • ⅔ Protein • ⅓ Fat • ¼ Slider • 1 Optional Calorie

205 Calories • 5 gm Fat • 8 gm Protein • 32 gm Carbohydrate • 410 mg Sodium • 118 mg Calcium • 2 gm Fiber

DIABETIC EXCHANGES: 1 Fruit • 1 Starch/Carbohydrate • 1 Meat • 1 Fat

CARB CHOICES: 2

Hawaiian Strawberry Pizza

When I finally got to visit Maui in all its lush splendor, I thought, Everything they say about this paradise is true. Now even when I've only got memories to fill my mind, I can take a bite of this luxurious delight and head straight back there!   ☯   Serves 8

1 (8-ounce) can Pillsbury Reduced Fat Crescent
    Rolls
1 (8-ounce) package Philadelphia fat-free cream cheese
1 (8-ounce) can crushed pineapple, packed in fruit juice,
    drained and ¼ cup liquid reserved
1 teaspoon coconut extract
4 cups chopped fresh strawberries
2 (4-serving) packages Jell-O sugar-free vanilla cook-and-
    serve pudding mix
1 (4-serving) package Jell-O sugar-free strawberry
    gelatin
2¼ cups water
2 tablespoons flaked coconut
1 cup Cool Whip Lite

Preheat oven to 375 degrees. Spray a rimmed 9-by-13-inch baking sheet with butter-flavored cooking spray. Unroll crescent rolls and carefully pat into prepared baking sheet, being sure to seal perforations. Bake for 8 to 10 minutes or until crust is golden brown. Place baking sheet on a wire rack and allow crust to cool completely. In a medium bowl, stir cream cheese with a sturdy spoon until soft. Add pineapple and coconut extract. Mix well to combine. Spread cream cheese mixture evenly over cooled crust. Evenly arrange strawberries over cream cheese mixture. In a medium saucepan, combine dry pudding mixes, dry gelatin, water, and reserved pineapple juice. Cook over medium heat until mixture thickens and starts to boil, stirring constantly using a wire whisk. Drizzle hot mixture evenly over strawberries. Refrigerate for at least 1 hour. Sprinkle coconut evenly over top. Cut into 8 servings. When serving, top each piece with 2 tablespoons Cool Whip Lite.

Each serving equals:

HE: 1 Bread • ¾ Fruit • ½ Protein • ¼ Slider • 19 Optional Calories

198 Calories • 6 gm Fat • 7 gm Protein • 29 gm Carbohydrate • 460 mg Sodium • 94 mg Calcium • 3 gm Fiber

DIABETIC EXCHANGES: 1 Starch • 1 Fruit • 1 Fat

CARB CHOICES: 2

Orange-Chocolate Pizza Dessert

For my friend Barbara, I always like to create a treat that blends these two delicious tastes, in memory of a New York ice cream parlor she loved and a dish called Swiss Orange Chip. The shop is no more, but the irresistible flavor endures!   ☻   Serves 8

1 (8-ounce) can Pillsbury Reduced Fat Crescent Rolls
1 cup orange marmalade spreadable fruit
1 tablespoon Diet Mountain Dew
6 tablespoons mini chocolate chips
¼ cup chopped pecans

Preheat oven to 375 degrees. Spray a rimmed 9-by-13-inch baking sheet with butter-flavored cooking spray. Unroll crescent rolls and carefully pat into prepared baking sheet, being sure to seal perforations. Bake for 5 minutes or until crust is light golden brown. In a small bowl, combine spreadable fruit and Diet Mountain Dew. Mix well until spreadable fruit is of spreading consistency. Spread mixture evenly over partially baked crust. Sprinkle chocolate chips and pecans evenly over top. Continue baking for 6 to 8 minutes or until crust is golden brown. Place baking sheet on a wire rack and allow to cool completely. Cut into 8 servings.

HINT: Raspberry, peach, or apricot spreadable fruit is also good on this dessert pizza.

Each serving equals:

HE: 1½ Fruit • 1 Bread • ½ Fat • ¼ Slider • 8 Optional Calories

233 Calories • 9 gm Fat • 3 gm Protein • 35 gm Carbohydrate •
233 mg Sodium • 4 mg Calcium • 1 gm Fiber

DIABETIC EXCHANGES: 1½ Fruit • 1 Starch • 1 Fat

CARB CHOICES: 2

Maui Dessert Pizza

What is it about Hawaii that simply takes your breath away? Is it the profusion of exotic flowers and their exquisite scent? Is it the fresh-from-the-ocean-or-garden food? Is the warmth of the people who live there year-round? In a word, yes!   ☻   Serves 12

1 (8-ounce) can Pillsbury Reduced Fat Crescent Rolls
1 (8-ounce) package Philadelphia fat-free cream cheese
2 tablespoons Splenda Granular
1 tablespoon lemon juice
1 teaspoon coconut extract
2 eggs, or equivalent in egg substitute
2 (8-ounce) cans crushed pineapple, packed in fruit juice,
    well drained
3 tablespoons flaked coconut
2 tablespoons chopped pecans

Preheat oven to 375 degrees. Spray a rimmed 9-by-13-inch baking sheet with butter-flavored cooking spray. Unroll crescent rolls and carefully pat into prepared pan, being sure to seal perforations. Bake for 5 minutes or until crust is light golden brown. In a medium bowl, stir cream cheese with a sturdy spoon until soft. Add Splenda, lemon juice, coconut extract, and eggs. Mix well to combine. Stir in pineapple. Evenly spread mixture over partially baked crust. Sprinkle coconut and pecans evenly over top. Continue baking for 16 to 18 minutes or until filling is set and crust is golden brown. Place baking sheet on a wire rack and allow to cool completely. Cut into 12 servings.

Each serving equals:

HE: ⅔ Bread • ½ Protein • ⅓ Fruit • 5 Optional Calories

121 Calories • 5 gm Fat • 5 gm Protein • 14 gm Carbohydrate • 260 mg Sodium • 62 mg Calcium • 1 gm Fiber

DIABETIC EXCHANGES: 1 Starch/Carbohydrate • 1 Fat • ½ Meat

CARB CHOICES: 1

Big Island Banana Dessert Pizza

You really understand what it means to eat a tropical fruit that's just been picked when you go to Hawaii. The bananas are astonishingly sweet and tender, and you just want to enjoy them all day long!

◑ Serves 8

> 1 (8-ounce) can Pillsbury Reduced Fat Crescent
>   Rolls
> 1 (8-ounce) package Philadelphia fat-free
>   cream cheese
> 2 tablespoons Hershey's Sugar Free Chocolate
>   Syrup
> 2 tablespoons Splenda Granular
> 1 teaspoon coconut extract
> 3 cups (3 medium) sliced bananas
> 1 (4-serving) package Jell-O sugar-free vanilla
>   cook-and-serve pudding mix
> 1 (4-serving) package Jell-O sugar-free orange
>   gelatin
> 1¾ cups water
> 2 tablespoons mini chocolate chips
> 2 tablespoons flaked coconut
> 2 tablespoons chopped pecans

Preheat oven to 375 degrees. Spray a rimmed 9-by-13-inch baking sheet with butter-flavored cooking spray. Unroll crescent rolls and carefully pat into prepared baking sheet, being sure to seal perforations. Bake for 8 to 10 minutes or until crust is golden brown. Place baking sheet on a wire rack and allow to cool completely. In a medium bowl, stir cream cheese with a sturdy spoon until soft. Add chocolate syrup, Splenda, and coconut extract. Mix gently just to combine. Evenly spread cream cheese mixture over cooled crust. Sprinkle banana slices evenly over cream cheese mixture. In a medium saucepan, combine dry pudding mix, dry gelatin, and water. Cook over medium heat until mixture thickens and starts to boil, stirring constantly using a wire whisk. Drizzle hot mixture evenly over bananas. Refrigerate for at least 1 hour. In a small bowl, combine chocolate chips, coconut, and pecans. Sprinkle mixture evenly over top. Cut into 8 servings.

HINT: To prevent bananas from turning brown, mix with 1 teaspoon lemon juice or sprinkle with Fruit Fresh.

Each serving equals:

HE: 1 Bread • ¾ Fruit • ½ Protein • ¼ Fat • ¼ Slider • 17 Optional Calories

219 Calories • 7 gm Fat • 7 gm Protein • 32 gm Carbohydrate • 470 mg Sodium • 85 mg Calcium • 2 gm Fiber

DIABETIC EXCHANGES: 1 Starch/Carbohydrate • 1 Fruit • 1 Meat • 1 Fat

CARB CHOICES: 2

Banana Cookie Pizza

Babies love them, kids gobble them down pretending to be monkeys, and most adults I know enjoy them all their lives. Bananas are such a rich source of nutrients, and because they come to us enrobed in a skin that protects us from pesticides, we can feel confident that we're making healthy choices when we eat them.

● Serves 8

⅓ cup I Can't Believe It's Not Butter! Light Margarine ☆
6 tablespoons Land O Lakes no-fat sour cream ☆
2 cups Splenda Granular ☆
1 egg, or equivalent in egg substitute
2 tablespoons Land O Lakes Fat Free Half & Half
2 teaspoons vanilla extract ☆
1 cup cake flour
½ cup purchased graham cracker crumbs
½ teaspoon baking powder
½ teaspoon baking soda
¼ cup mini chocolate chips
1 (1-ounce) unsweetened chocolate square
2 cups (2 medium) sliced bananas
1 cup Cool Whip Lite

Preheat oven to 400 degrees. Spray a 12-inch round pizza pan with butter-flavored cooking spray. In a large bowl, combine ¼ cup margarine and ¼ cup sour cream using a wire whisk. Stir in ¾ cup Splenda, egg, half & half, and 1 teaspoon vanilla extract. Add cake flour, graham cracker crumbs, baking powder, and baking soda. Mix gently just to combine, using a sturdy spoon. Fold in chocolate chips. Pat mixture into prepared pizza pan, using a clean spatula sprayed with butter-flavored cooking spray. Bake for 5 minutes or until crust is light golden brown. Place pizza pan on a wire rack and allow crust to cool completely. In a medium saucepan, melt remaining 4 teaspoons margarine and chocolate square, stirring constantly using a wire whisk. Remove from heat. Stir in remaining 2 tablespoons sour cream, remaining 1 teaspoon vanilla extract, and remaining 1¼ cups Splenda. Drizzle warm mixture evenly over cooled crust. Evenly arrange banana slices over top. Cut into 8 wedges. When serving, top each with 2 tablespoons Cool Whip Lite.

HINT: To prevent bananas from turning brown, mix with 1 teaspoon lemon juice or sprinkle with Fruit Fresh.

Each serving equals:

HE: 1 Bread • 1 Fat • ½ Fruit • ½ Slider • 9 Optional Calories

158 Calories • 6 gm Fat • 2 gm Protein • 24 gm Carbohydrate • 148 mg Sodium • 27 mg Calcium • 1 gm Fiber

DIABETIC EXCHANGES: 1½ Starch/Carbohydrate • 1 Fat

CARB CHOICES: 1½

Apple Crumb Pizza

Here's my all-American candidate for culinary sainthood, the cozy and beloved apple pie transformed into a dessert pizza that looks and tastes splendidly homemade! While we may not always eat that prescribed "apple a day," with dishes like this to tempt us, we just might start to! ● Serves 12

30 (2½-inch) graham cracker squares ☆
4 cups (4 medium) cored, peeled, and chopped cooking
    apples
2 (4-serving) packages Jell-O sugar-free vanilla cook-and-
    serve pudding mix
1 (4-serving) package Jell-O sugar-free lemon gelatin
1 cup unsweetened apple juice
1¼ cups water
1 teaspoon apple pie spice
6 tablespoons Bisquick Heart Smart Baking Mix
¼ cup Splenda Granular
¼ cup I Can't Believe It's Not Butter! Light Margarine
¼ cup chopped walnuts

Preheat oven to 375 degrees. Spray a rimmed 10-by-15-inch baking sheet with butter-flavored cooking spray. Evenly arrange 24 graham crackers in prepared baking sheet. Sprinkle chopped apples evenly over graham crackers. In a medium saucepan, combine dry pudding mixes, dry gelatin, apple juice, water, and apple pie spice. Cook over medium heat until mixture thickens and starts to boil, stirring constantly using a wire whisk. Drizzle hot mixture evenly over apples. Finely crush remaining 6 graham crackers. In a medium bowl, combine graham cracker crumbs, baking mix, and Splenda. Add margarine. Mix well using a pastry blender or 2 forks until mixture becomes crumbly. Stir in walnuts. Sprinkle crumb mixture evenly over top. Bake for 18 to 22 minutes or until apples are tender and top is browned. Place baking sheet on a wire rack and let set for at least 10 minutes. Cut into 12 servings. Good warm or cold.

HINT: A self-seal sandwich bag works great for crushing graham crackers.

Each serving equals:

HE: 1 Bread • ⅔ Fat • ½ Fruit • 17 Optional Calories

157 Calories • 5 gm Fat • 2 gm Protein • 26 gm Carbohydrate • 252 mg Sodium • 17 mg Calcium • 2 gm Fiber

DIABETIC EXCHANGES: 1 Starch • 1 Fat • ½ Fruit

CARB CHOICES: 2

Apple Crisp Pizza

What a wonderful partnership—apples and oats! They both provide great texture and taste, crunch and satisfaction from first bite to last.　●　Serves 8

1 Pillsbury refrigerated unbaked 9-inch pie crust
½ cup water
2 teaspoons apple pie spice ☆
4 cups (4 medium) cored, peeled, and sliced cooking apples
½ cup quick oats
3 tablespoons all-purpose flour
½ cup Splenda Granular
2 tablespoons + 2 teaspoons I Can't Believe It's Not Butter!
　　Light Margarine
1 cup Cool Whip Lite

Preheat oven to 425 degrees. Let pie crust warm to room temperature. Spray a 12-inch round pizza pan with butter-flavored cooking spray. Gently pat pie crust into prepared pizza pan. Evenly prick bottom of crust with tines of a fork. Bake for 5 minutes or until crust is light golden brown. Place partially baked crust on a wire rack. Lower oven temperature to 375 degrees. In a medium saucepan, combine water and 1 teaspoon apple pie spice. Stir in apples. Cover and simmer on low for 10 minutes or just until apples start to soften, stirring occasionally. Drain and evenly spoon apple slices over partially baked crust. In a large bowl, combine oats, flour, Splenda, and remaining 1 teaspoon apple pie spice. Add margarine. Mix well using a pastry blender or 2 forks until mixture becomes crumbly. Evenly sprinkle crumb topping over apples. Continue baking for 18 to 20 minutes or until apples are tender. Place pizza pan on a wire rack and let set for at least 10 minutes. Cut into 8 servings. When serving, top each piece with 2 tablespoons Cool Whip Lite. Good warm or cold.

Each serving equals:

HE: 1⅓ Bread • 1 Fat • ½ Fruit • ¼ Slider • 10 Optional Calories

238 Calories • 10 gm Fat • 2 gm Protein • 35 gm Carbohydrate •
146 mg Sodium • 15 mg Calcium • 3 gm Fiber

DIABETIC EXCHANGES: 1½ Starch/Carbohydrate • 1½ Fat • ½ Fruit

CARB CHOICES: 2

Apple Harvest Dessert Pizza

Time to go apple picking—or maybe just head for the nearest farm-stand to get what you need for this recipe! This dish is a "triple threat"—with three apple elements to win your heart.

● Serves 12

> 1 (4-serving) package Jell-O sugar-free vanilla
>   cook-and-serve pudding mix
> 2 cups unsweetened apple juice ☆
> 1 teaspoon apple pie spice
> 4 cups (4 medium) cored, peeled, and sliced
>   Granny Smith apples
> 2/3 cup Carnation Nonfat Dry Milk Powder
> 1½ cups Bisquick Heart Smart Baking Mix
> ¼ cup Splenda Granular
> 3 tablespoons chopped pecans

Preheat oven to 375 degrees. Spray a 12-inch round pizza pan with butter-flavored cooking spray. In a medium saucepan, combine dry pudding mix, 1½ cups apple juice, and apple pie spice. Stir in apples. Cook over medium heat until mixture thickens and apples start to soften, stirring often. Place pan on a wire rack. Meanwhile, in a large bowl, combine dry milk powder and remaining ½ cup apple juice. Add baking mix, Splenda, and pecans. Mix gently to combine. Pat mixture evenly into prepared pizza pan. Evenly spoon apple mixture over top. Bake for 14 to 16 minutes or until edge is golden brown. Place pizza pan on a wire rack and let set for at least 10 minutes. Cut into 12 wedges. Good warm or cold.

HINTS: 1. Place hand in a plastic sandwich bag and lightly coat with flour before pressing dough into pan.
2. Good topped with 1 tablespoon Cool Whip Lite, but don't forget to count the few additional calories.

Each serving equals:

HE: ⅔ Bread • ⅔ Fruit • ¼ Fat • 17 Optional Calories

138 Calories • 2 gm Fat • 3 gm Protein • 27 gm Carbohydrate • 168 mg Sodium • 74 mg Calcium • 2 gm Fiber

DIABETIC EXCHANGES: 1 Starch/Carbohydrate • 1 Fruit

CARB CHOICES: 2

Apple Betty Pizza Dessert

Need a quick and festive dessert to serve to unexpected guests? If you've got the ingredients on hand, this can be prepared fast and look as if you somehow knew they were coming—and baked!

● Serves 12

> 1 (8-ounce) can Pillsbury Reduced Fat Crescent Rolls
> 2 (20-ounce) cans Lucky Leaf No Sugar Added Apple Pie
>   Filling
> ¾ cup Splenda Granular ☆
> 1½ teaspoons apple pie spice
> ¾ cup graham cracker crumbs
> ¼ cup I Can't Believe It's Not Butter! Light Margarine

Preheat oven to 375 degrees. Spray a rimmed 9-by-13-inch baking sheet with butter-flavored cooking spray. Unroll crescent rolls and carefully pat into prepared baking sheet, being sure to seal perforations. Bake for 5 minutes or until crust is light golden brown. In a medium bowl, combine both cans of apple pie filling, ¼ cup Splenda, and apple pie spice. Evenly spread apple mixture over partially baked crust. In a small bowl, combine graham cracker crumbs and remaining ½ cup Splenda. Add margarine. Mix well using a pastry blender or 2 forks until mixture becomes crumbly. Sprinkle crumb mixture evenly over apple pie filling mixture. Continue baking for 14 to 16 minutes or until topping is browned and crust is golden brown. Place baking sheet on a wire rack and let set for at least 10 minutes. Cut into 12 servings. Good warm or cold.

HINT: Good warm with Wells' Blue Bunny sugar- and fat-free ice cream or cold with Cool Whip Lite, but don't forget to count the additional calories.

Each serving equals:

HE: 1 Bread • ⅔ Fruit • ½ Fat • 6 Optional Calories

---

141 Calories • 5 gm Fat • 2 gm Protein • 22 gm Carbohydrate • 243 mg Sodium • 5 mg Calcium • 1 gm Fiber

---

DIABETIC EXCHANGES: 1 Starch • ½ Fruit • ½ Fat

CARB CHOICES: 1½

Caramel Apple Pizza Pie

This is such a kid-pleasing recipe, I bet moms everywhere will be fixing this for snacks! How can a fat-free caramel syrup look and taste as good as the regular kind? It's a marvelous mystery—and the reason this treat is out of this world! 🙂   Serves 8

> 1 Pillsbury refrigerated unbaked 9-inch pie crust
> 4 cups (4 medium) cored, peeled, and sliced Granny Smith
>   apples
> ½ cup Splenda Granular
> 1½ teaspoons apple pie spice
> ¼ cup fat-free caramel syrup
> ¼ cup chopped pecans

Preheat oven to 425 degrees. Let pie crust warm to room temperature. Spray a 12-inch round pizza pan with butter-flavored cooking spray. Gently pat pie crust into prepared pizza pan. Evenly prick bottom of crust with tines of a fork. Bake for 5 minutes or until crust is light golden brown. Place partially baked crust on a wire rack. Lower oven temperature to 375 degrees. Evenly sprinkle apples over partially baked crust. In a small bowl, combine Splenda and apple pie spice. Sprinkle mixture evenly over apples. Drizzle caramel syrup over Splenda mixture. Sprinkle pecans evenly over top. Continue baking for 6 to 8 minutes or until apples are tender. Place pizza pan on a wire rack and let set for at least 10 minutes. Cut into 8 servings. Good warm or cold.

Each serving equals:

HE: 1 Bread • 1 Fat • ½ Fruit • ¼ Slider • 11 Optional Calories

226 Calories • 10 gm Fat • 1 gm Protein • 33 gm Carbohydrate • 128 mg Sodium • 20 mg Calcium • 3 gm Fiber

DIABETIC EXCHANGES: 1½ Starch/Carbohydrate • 1½ Fat • ½ Fruit

CARB CHOICES: 2

Apple-Cranberry Dessert Pizza

My compliments to whoever started drying and sweetening all those rosy cranberries, so we could enjoy them every month of the year! They add a special tart-sweet touch to a classic apple dessert, and they're as good as they are good for us. ☻ Serves 12

1 (8-ounce) can Pillsbury Reduced Fat Crescent
    Rolls
1 (4-serving) package Jell-O sugar-free vanilla
    cook-and-serve pudding mix
1 (4-serving) package Jell-O sugar-free lemon
    gelatin
1⅓ cups water
4 cups (4 medium) cored, peeled, and diced cooking apples
¼ cup dried cranberries or craisins
1 teaspoon ground cinnamon
1 (8-ounce) package Philadelphia fat-free cream cheese
2 tablespoons Splenda Granular
1 teaspoon vanilla extract
½ cup Cool Whip Lite

Preheat oven to 375 degrees. Spray a rimmed 9-by-13-inch baking sheet with butter-flavored cooking spray. Unroll crescent rolls and carefully pat into prepared baking sheet, being sure to seal perforations. Bake for 8 to 10 minutes or until crust is golden brown. Place baking sheet on a wire rack and allow crust to cool completely. In a medium saucepan, combine dry pudding mix, dry gelatin, and water. Cook over medium heat until mixture thickens and starts to boil, stirring constantly using a wire whisk. Remove from heat. Stir in apples, dried cranberries, and cinnamon. Place saucepan on a wire rack and let set for 15 minutes. Meanwhile, in a medium bowl, stir cream cheese with a sturdy spoon until soft. Add Splenda and vanilla extract. Mix gently to combine. Fold in Cool Whip Lite. Evenly spread cream cheese mixture over cooled crust. Spread cooled apple mixture evenly over cream cheese mixture. Refrigerate for at least 1 hour. Cut into 12 servings.

Each serving equals:

HE: ⅔ Bread • ½ Fruit • ⅓ Protein • 17 Optional Calories

127 Calories • 3 gm Fat • 5 gm Protein • 20 gm Carbohydrate • 305 mg Sodium • 59 mg Calcium • 1 gm Fiber

DIABETIC EXCHANGES: 1 Starch/Carbohydrate • ½ Fruit

CARB CHOICES: 1

Mincemeat Pizza Dessert

Mincemeat is a delightful, old-fashioned holiday tradition that I love helping to sustain, and I hope you will, too. If you've never tried apple butter, you may fall in love with this smooth, cool product that is a mainstay of Amish farm families.

◐ Serves 12

> 1 Pillsbury refrigerated unbaked 9-inch pie crust
> 1 (4-serving) package Jell-O sugar-free vanilla cook-and-
>   serve pudding mix
> 1 (4-serving) package Jell-O sugar-free lemon gelatin
> 1 cup unsweetened apple juice
> 1 cup water
> 3 cups (3 medium) cored, peeled, and finely chopped cooking
>   apples
> ½ cup seedless raisins
> 1 teaspoon apple pie spice
> 1 (8-ounce) package Philadelphia fat-free cream cheese
> ½ cup apple butter
> 1½ cups Cool Whip Lite

Preheat oven to 425 degrees. Let pie crust warm to room temperature. Spray a 12-inch round pizza pan with butter-flavored cooking spray. Gently pat pie crust into prepared pizza pan. Evenly prick bottom of crust with the tines of a fork. Bake for 8 to 10 minutes or until crust is golden brown. Place pan on a wire rack and allow to cool completely. Meanwhile, in a medium saucepan, combine dry pudding mix, dry gelatin, apple juice, and water. Stir in apples, raisins, and apple pie spice. Cook over medium heat for 6 to 8 minutes or until apples are tender, stirring often. Place saucepan on a wire rack to cool. In a medium bowl, stir cream cheese with a sturdy spoon until soft. Add apple butter. Mix well to combine. Evenly spread cream cheese mixture over cooled crust. Spoon cooled apple mixture evenly over cream cheese mixture. Refrigerate for at least 30 minutes. Cut into 12 servings. When serving, top each piece with 2 tablespoons Cool Whip Lite.

Each serving equals:

HE: 1 Fruit • ⅔ Bread • ⅓ Protein • ⅓ Fat • ½ Slider • 11 Optional Calories

190 Calories • 6 gm Fat • 4 gm Protein • 30 gm Carbohydrate •
219 mg Sodium • 63 mg Calcium • 2 gm Fiber

DIABETIC EXCHANGES: 1 Fruit • 1 Starch • ½ Meat • ½ Fat

CARB CHOICES: 2

Grasshopper Pizza Dessert

I promise you, there are no crunchy little bodies in this dish, just a chocolate-mint combination that recalls sweet memories of the classic Southern cocktail made with crème de menthe! This is one of the prettiest dessert pizzas I've made. ☻ Serves 12

1 Pillsbury refrigerated unbaked 9-inch pie crust
2 (8-ounce) packages Philadelphia fat-free cream cheese
2 tablespoons Splenda Granular
2 eggs, or equivalent in egg substitute
4 to 6 drops green food coloring
¾ teaspoon mint extract ☆
2 tablespoons mini chocolate chips
1 (4-serving) package Jell-O sugar-free instant chocolate
    pudding mix
⅔ cup Carnation Nonfat Dry Milk Powder
1½ cups water
1½ cups Cool Whip Lite
2 tablespoons mini chocolate chips

Preheat oven to 425 degrees. Let pie crust warm to room temperature. Spray a 12-inch round pizza pan with butter-flavored cooking spray. Gently pat pie crust into prepared pizza pan. Evenly prick bottom of crust with tines of a fork. Bake for 5 minutes or until crust is light golden brown. Meanwhile, in a medium bowl, stir cream cheese with a sturdy spoon until soft. Add Splenda, eggs, green food coloring, and ½ teaspoon mint extract. Mix well to combine. Fold in chocolate chips. Evenly spread cream cheese mixture over partially baked crust. Continue baking for 12 to 14 minutes. Place pizza pan on a wire rack and allow crust to cool completely. In a medium bowl, combine dry pudding mix, dry milk powder, and water. Mix well using a wire whisk. Evenly spread pudding mixture over top. Refrigerate while preparing topping. In a medium bowl, combine Cool Whip Lite and remaining ¼ teaspoon mint extract. Spread evenly over pudding layer. Evenly sprinkle chocolate chips over top. Refrigerate for at least 1 hour. Cut into 12 servings.

Each serving equals:

HE: ¾ Protein • ⅔ Bread • ¾ Slider • 1 Optional Calorie

188 Calories • 8 gm Fat • 8 gm Protein • 21 gm Carbohydrate • 396 mg Sodium • 162 mg Calcium • 1 gm Fiber

DIABETIC EXCHANGES: 1 Starch/Carbohydrate • 1 Meat • 1 Fat

CARB CHOICES: 1

Maple Apple Pizza Dessert

When the snow is piled up outside your windows and the windchill dips to below zero, stay home with a good book or your favorite old movie—and enjoy a piece of this with a cup of your best coffee! Some desserts just make us feel warm and happy inside—including this one! ☻ Serves 8

> 1 Pillsbury refrigerated unbaked 9-inch pie crust
> 4 cups (4 medium) cored, unpeeled and sliced cooking apples
> ½ cup Log Cabin Sugar Free Maple Syrup ☆
> 2 tablespoons Bisquick Heart Smart Baking Mix
> ¼ cup chopped pecans

Preheat oven to 425 degrees. Let pie crust warm to room temperature. Spray a 12-inch round pizza pan with butter-flavored cooking spray. Gently pat pie crust into prepared pizza pan. Evenly prick bottom of crust with tines of a fork. Bake for 5 minutes or until crust is light golden brown. Place partially baked crust on a wire rack. Lower oven temperature to 375 degrees. In a large bowl, combine apples, ¼ cup maple syrup, and baking mix. Evenly spoon apple mixture over partially baked crust. Sprinkle pecans evenly over top. Continue baking for 10 to 12 minutes. Drizzle remaining ¼ cup maple syrup evenly over top. Place pan on a wire rack and let set for at least 10 minutes. Cut into 8 servings. Good warm or cold.

Each serving equals:

HE: 1 Bread • 1 Fat • ½ Fruit • 16 Optional Calories

206 Calories • 10 gm Fat • 1 gm Protein • 28 gm Carbohydrate • 147 mg Sodium • 8 mg Calcium • 2 gm Fiber

DIABETIC EXCHANGES: 1½ Fat • 1 Starch/Carbohydrate • ½ Fruit

CARB CHOICES: 2

Pistachio Brownie Pizza Dessert

The pistachio, like so many Americans, is an immigrant, originating in Asia and planted here for the first time in the 1850s. It has one of the most unique nutty flavors and makes for an unusual but beloved pudding flavor. ☽ Serves 8

¾ cup Bisquick Heart Smart Baking Mix
¼ cup unsweetened cocoa powder
½ cup Splenda Granular
¼ cup Land O Lakes no-fat sour cream
1½ cups water ☆
1 teaspoon vanilla extract
1 (8-ounce) package Philadelphia fat-free cream cheese
1 (4-serving) package Jell-O sugar-free instant pistachio pudding mix
⅔ cup Carnation Nonfat Dry Milk Powder
1 cup Cool Whip Free
2 tablespoons mini chocolate chips

Preheat oven to 375 degrees. Spray a 12-inch round pizza pan with butter-flavored cooking spray. In a large bowl, combine baking mix, cocoa powder, and Splenda. Add sour cream, ½ cup water, and vanilla extract. Mix gently to combine using a sturdy spoon. Evenly spread batter into prepared pizza pan. Bake for 14 to 16 minutes or until crust tests done in center. Place pizza pan on a wire rack and allow crust to cool completely. In a large bowl, stir cream cheese with a sturdy spoon until soft. Add dry pudding mix, dry milk powder, and remaining 1 cup water. Mix well using a wire whisk. Blend in Cool Whip Free. Evenly spread cream cheese mixture over cooled crust. Evenly sprinkle chocolate chips over top. Refrigerate for at least 30 minutes. Cut into 8 wedges.

Each serving equals:

HE: ½ Bread • ½ Protein • ¼ Fat Free Milk • ¾ Slider • 2 Optional Calories

150 Calories • 2 gm Fat • 8 gm Protein • 25 gm Carbohydrate •
477 mg Sodium • 180 mg Calcium • 1 gm Fiber

DIABETIC EXCHANGES: 1½ Starch/Carbohydrate • ½ Meat

CARB CHOICES: 1½

Chocolate Cheesecake Dessert Pizza

Good news—you don't have to go to Brooklyn to taste the real thing when it comes to chocolate cheesecake! Actually, there are terrific varieties of this eastern classic all over the United States, and now here's a pizza-style version to try. ☾ Serves 8

¾ cup Bisquick Heart Smart Baking Mix
¼ cup unsweetened cocoa powder
1 teaspoon baking powder
½ cup Splenda Granular
⅓ cup Land O Lakes no-fat sour cream
¼ cup Land O Lakes Fat Free Half & Half
1¾ cups water ☆
2 teaspoons vanilla extract
1 (8-ounce) package Philadelphia fat-free cream cheese
1 (4-serving) package Jell-O sugar-free instant white
    chocolate or cheesecake pudding mix
⅔ cup Carnation Nonfat Dry Milk Powder
⅓ cup Cool Whip Free
2 tablespoons Hershey's Sugar Free Chocolate Syrup
2 tablespoons mini chocolate chips

Preheat oven to 375 degrees. Spray a 12-inch round pizza pan with butter-flavored cooking spray. In a large bowl, combine baking mix, cocoa powder, baking powder, and Splenda. In a small bowl, combine sour cream, half & half, ¾ cup water, and vanilla extract. Add sour cream mixture to baking mix mixture. Stir gently just to combine using a sturdy spoon. Evenly spread batter into prepared pizza pan. Bake for 12 to 16 minutes or until crust tests done in center. Place pizza pan on a wire rack and allow crust to cool completely. In a large bowl, stir cream cheese with a sturdy spoon until soft. Add dry pudding mix, dry milk powder, and remaining 1 cup water. Mix well using a wire whisk. Blend in Cool Whip Free. Evenly spread cream cheese mixture over cooled crust. Drizzle chocolate syrup evenly over cream cheese mixture. Evenly sprinkle chocolate chips over top. Refrigerate for at least 30 minutes. Cut into 8 wedges.

Each serving equals:

HE: ½ Bread • ½ Protein • ¼ Fat Free Milk • ½ Slider • 12 Optional Calories

146 Calories • 2 gm Fat • 8 gm Protein • 24 gm Carbohydrate •
532 mg Sodium • 210 mg Calcium

DIABETIC EXCHANGES: 1½ Starch/Carbohydrate • ½ Meat

CARB CHOICES: 1½

Chocolate Holiday Pizza

It's that time of year when neighbors drop by, friends stop over, and you just never know how many people you'll be entertaining—so it's a great idea to have a rich dessert ready and waiting for guests! This pretty delight fits right in with the colorful decorations of the season. ☾ Serves 12

½ cup I Can't Believe It's Not Butter! Light Margarine
¾ cup Splenda Granular
1 egg, or equivalent in egg substitute
2 teaspoons vanilla extract ☆
1 cup all-purpose flour
¾ cup quick oats
½ teaspoon baking soda
¼ teaspoon table salt
½ cup mini chocolate chips ☆
1 (4-serving) package Jell-O sugar-free instant chocolate
   pudding mix
⅔ cup Carnation Nonfat Dry Milk Powder
1 cup water
¾ cup Dannon plain fat-free yogurt
1¼ cups Cool Whip Free ☆
6 maraschino cherries, halved

Preheat oven to 375 degrees. Spray a 12-inch round pizza pan with butter-flavored cooking spray. In a large bowl, combine margarine and Splenda using a wire whisk. Stir in egg and 1 teaspoon vanilla extract. Add flour, oats, baking soda, and salt. Mix well to combine using a sturdy spoon. Fold in 6 tablespoons chocolate chips. Shape dough into a ball and place in center of prepared pizza pan. Evenly pat dough into an 11-inch circle. Bake for 12 to 16 minutes or until crust tests done in center. Place pizza pan on a wire rack and allow crust to cool completely. In a medium bowl, combine dry pudding mix, dry milk powder, and water. Mix well using a wire whisk. Blend in yogurt, ¼ cup Cool Whip Free, and remaining 1 teaspoon vanilla extract. Evenly spread pudding mixture over cooled crust. Refrigerate for 10 minutes. Carefully spread remaining 1 cup Cool Whip Free over set pudding mixture. Evenly sprinkle remaining 2 tablespoons chocolate chips over top and garnish with cherry halves. Refrigerate for at least 30 minutes. Cut into 12 wedges.

HINT: Place hand in a plastic sandwich bag and lightly coat with flour before pressing dough into pan.

Each serving equals:

HE: 1 Fat • ¾ Bread • ¼ Fat Free Milk • ¾ Slider • 10 Optional Calories

191 Calories • 7 gm Fat • 5 gm Protein • 27 gm Carbohydrate • 342 mg Sodium • 80 mg Calcium • 2 gm Fiber

DIABETIC EXCHANGES: 2 Starch/Carbohydrate • 1 Fat

CARB CHOICES: 2

Ultimate Chocolate Dessert Pizza

This is one of those "Look no further, you've found the one you can't live without" desserts—or at least, that's what my taste testers said! I don't use the word "ultimate" lightly. This is so good, so creamy, so sweetly sensational, you'll probably have to sit down to take it all in.   ☻   Serves 12

¾ cup Bisquick Heart Smart Baking Mix
¼ cup unsweetened cocoa powder
½ teaspoon baking powder
¾ cup Splenda Granular ☆
1 cup fat-free milk
2 teaspoons coconut extract ☆
1 (8-ounce) package Philadelphia fat-free cream cheese
1½ cups Cool Whip Free ☆
1 (4-serving) package Jell-O sugar-free instant chocolate
    pudding mix
⅔ cup Carnation Nonfat Dry Milk Powder
1¼ cups water
3 tablespoons mini chocolate chips
2 tablespoons chopped pecans
2 tablespoons flaked coconut

Preheat oven to 375 degrees. Spray a 12-inch pizza pan with butter-flavored cooking spray. In a large bowl, combine baking mix, cocoa powder, baking powder, and ½ cup Splenda. Add milk and 1 teaspoon coconut extract. Mix gently to combine using a sturdy spoon. Evenly spread batter into prepared pizza pan. Bake for 12 to 16 minutes or until crust tests done in center. Place pizza pan on a wire rack and allow crust to cool completely. In a medium bowl, stir cream cheese with a sturdy spoon until soft. Add remaining ¼ cup Splenda, ½ cup Cool Whip Free, and remaining 1 teaspoon coconut extract. Mix gently to combine. Spread cream cheese mixture evenly over cooled crust. In a large bowl, combine dry pudding mix, dry milk powder, and water. Mix well using a wire whisk. Evenly spread pudding mixture over cream cheese mixture. Refrigerate for 10 minutes. Evenly spread remaining 1 cup Cool Whip

Free over set pudding mixture. Sprinkle chocolate chips, pecans, and coconut evenly over top. Refrigerate for at least 30 minutes. Cut into 12 wedges.

Each serving equals:

HE: ⅓ Bread • ⅓ Protein • ¼ Fat Free Milk • ¼ Fat • ½ Slider •
5 Optional Calories

131 Calories • 3 gm Fat • 6 gm Protein • 20 gm Carbohydrate •
342 mg Sodium • 150 mg Calcium • 1 gm Fiber

DIABETIC EXCHANGES: 1½ Starch/Carbohydrate

CARB CHOICES: 1

Rocky Road Dessert Pizza

Named for the way it looks, all bumps and "rocks," this flavor has drawn attention in ice cream form, as a brownie, and as a memorable cookie. I'm thrilled to introduce you to this pizza. I promise happy trails when you leave the driving to us! ☻ Serves 8

¼ cup I Can't Believe It's Not Butter! Light Margarine
¼ cup Land O Lakes no-fat sour cream
¾ cup Splenda Granular
2 eggs, or equivalent in egg substitute
1 teaspoon vanilla extract
1 cup cake flour
½ teaspoon baking powder
½ teaspoon baking soda
1 cup miniature marshmallows
½ cup mini chocolate chips
¼ cup chopped dry-roasted peanuts
¼ cup Hershey's Sugar Free Chocolate Syrup

Preheat oven to 375 degrees. Spray a 12-inch round pizza pan with butter-flavored cooking spray. In a large bowl, combine margarine and sour cream using a wire whisk. Stir in Splenda, eggs, and vanilla extract. Add flour, baking powder, and baking soda. Mix gently just to combine using a sturdy spoon. Pat mixture evenly into prepared pizza pan. Bake for 8 minutes. Place partially baked crust on a wire rack. Evenly sprinkle marshmallows, chocolate chips, and peanuts over top of partially baked crust. Drizzle chocolate syrup evenly over top. Continue baking for 5 to 6 minutes or until marshmallows and crust are golden brown. Place pizza pan on a wire rack and let set for at least 10 minutes. Cut into 8 wedges. Good warm or cold.

HINT: 1. Place hand in a plastic sandwich bag and lightly coat with flour before pressing dough into pan.
        2. Good served with Wells' Blue Bunny sugar- and fat-free vanilla ice cream, or any sugar- and fat-free ice cream, but don't forget to count the additional calories.

Each serving equals:

HE: 1 Fat • ⅔ Bread • ¼ Protein • ¾ Slider • 14 Optional Calories

204 Calories • 8 gm Fat • 5 gm Protein • 28 gm Carbohydrate •
191 mg Sodium • 39 mg Calcium • 1 gm Fiber

DIABETIC EXCHANGES: 1½ Starch/Carbohydrate • 1½ Fat

CARB CHOICES: 2

Peanut Buster Dessert Pizza

I don't know about you, but my heart leaps when I see peanut butter on a list of ingredients! This delectable indulgence is fun to make and fun to eat, so go and have some fun!

⏺ Serves 12

¾ cup Bisquick Heart Smart Baking Mix
½ cup + 2 tablespoons Splenda Granular ☆
¼ cup unsweetened cocoa powder
½ teaspoon baking powder
⅓ cup Land O Lakes no-fat sour cream
¼ cup Land O Lakes Fat Free Half & Half
¾ cup water
1 tablespoon vanilla extract ☆
1 (8-ounce) package Philadelphia fat-free cream cheese
½ cup Peter Pan reduced-fat peanut butter
2 tablespoons fat-free milk
2 tablespoons Hershey's Sugar Free Chocolate Syrup
2 tablespoons chopped dry-roasted peanuts
2 tablespoons mini chocolate chips

Preheat oven to 375 degrees. Spray a 12-inch round pizza pan with butter-flavored cooking spray. In a large bowl, combine baking mix, ½ cup Splenda, cocoa powder, and baking powder. In a small bowl, combine sour cream, half & half, water, and 2 teaspoons vanilla extract. Add sour cream mixture to baking mix mixture. Stir gently just to combine using a wire whisk. Spread mixture evenly into prepared pizza pan. Bake for 14 to 16 minutes or until crust tests done in center. Place pizza pan on a wire rack and allow crust to cool completely. In a large bowl, stir cream cheese with a sturdy spoon until soft. Add peanut butter, remaining 2 tablespoons Splenda, remaining 1 teaspoon vanilla extract, and milk. Mix well to combine. Spread mixture evenly over cooled crust. Evenly drizzle chocolate syrup over peanut butter mixture. Sprinkle peanuts and chocolate chips evenly over top. Cut into 12 wedges.

Each serving equals:

HE: 1 Protein • ¾ Fat • ⅓ Bread • ¼ Slider • 8 Optional Calories

150 Calories • 6 gm Fat • 7 gm Protein • 17 gm Carbohydrate •
305 mg Sodium • 91 mg Calcium • 2 gm Fiber

DIABETIC EXCHANGES: 1 Meat • 1 Fat • 1 Starch/Carbohydrate

CARB CHOICES: 1

Peanut Brownie Pizza

The great thing about baking with peanuts—and with mini chocolate chips, too—is that you don't need a lot to taste a lot of flavor. With just one tablespoon of peanut butter per person, I bet I'll convince you you're eating so much more!   ☺   Serves 8

½ cup Peter Pan or Skippy reduced-fat peanut butter ☆
¼ cup Land O Lakes no-fat sour cream
⅓ cup fat-free milk
1½ teaspoons vanilla extract ☆
¾ cup cake flour
½ cup + 2 tablespoons Splenda Granular ☆
¼ cup unsweetened cocoa powder
1 teaspoon baking powder
½ teaspoon baking soda
1 (8-ounce) package Philadelphia fat-free cream cheese
¼ cup mini chocolate chips
2 tablespoons chopped dry-roasted peanuts
¼ cup Hershey's Sugar Free Chocolate Syrup

Preheat oven to 375 degrees. Spray a 12-inch round pizza pan with butter-flavored cooking spray. In a large bowl, combine ¼ cup peanut butter, sour cream, milk, and 1 teaspoon vanilla extract. Add flour, ½ cup Splenda, cocoa powder, baking powder, and baking soda. Mix gently just to combine. Evenly spread mixture into prepared pizza pan. Bake for 8 minutes or until crust tests done in center. Place pan on a wire rack and let set for 5 minutes. In a medium bowl, stir cream cheese with a sturdy spoon until soft. Stir in remaining ¼ cup peanut butter, remaining 2 tablespoons Splenda, and remaining ½ teaspoon vanilla extract. Spread cream cheese mixture evenly over partially cooled crust. Evenly sprinkle chocolate chips and peanuts over cream cheese mixture. Drizzle chocolate syrup evenly over top. Cut into 8 wedges.

HINT: Good with sugar- and fat-free vanilla ice cream or Cool Whip Lite, but don't forget to count the additional calories.

Each serving equals:

HE: 1½ Protein • 1 Fat • ½ Bread • ½ Slider • 9 Optional Calories

224 Calories • 8 gm Fat • 10 gm Protein • 28 gm Carbohydrate •
368 mg Sodium • 107 mg Calcium • 2 gm Fiber

DIABETIC EXCHANGES: 1½ Starch/Carbohydrate • 1 Meat • 1 Fat

CARB CHOICES: 2

Chocolate Caramel Dessert Pizza

"Me first!" "No, me first!" When I asked for volunteers to try this recipe, I almost got knocked over—well, no, I'm exaggerating, but that's how it felt. The enthusiasm of my staff for this scrumptious extravagance was inspiring. ☾ Serves 12

1½ cups all-purpose flour
2 teaspoons baking powder
½ teaspoon table salt
½ cup I Can't Believe It's Not Butter! Light Margarine
2 tablespoons Land O Lakes no-fat sour cream
2 cups Splenda Granular
1 egg, or equivalent in egg substitute
2 teaspoons vanilla extract ☆
2 (8-ounce) packages Philadelphia fat-free cream cheese
¼ cup fat-free caramel syrup
¼ cup Hershey's Sugar Free Chocolate Syrup
½ cup mini chocolate chips
¼ cup chopped pecans

Spray a rimmed 9-by-13-inch baking sheet with butter-flavored cooking spray. In a medium bowl, combine flour, baking powder, and salt. In a large bowl, combine margarine, sour cream, and Splenda using a wire whisk. Stir in egg and 1 teaspoon vanilla extract. Add flour mixture to margarine mixture. Mix gently just to combine using a sturdy spoon. Cover and refrigerate dough for at least 1 hour. Preheat oven to 375 degrees. Carefully pat dough into prepared baking sheet. In a medium bowl, stir cream cheese with a sturdy spoon until soft. Stir in caramel syrup and remaining 1 teaspoon vanilla extract. Carefully spread cream cheese mixture over crust. Drizzle chocolate syrup evenly over cream cheese mixture. Evenly sprinkle chocolate chips and pecans over top. Bake for 18 to 22 minutes or until crust is golden brown. Place baking sheet on a wire rack and let set for at least 10 minutes. Cut into 12 servings.

HINTS: 1. Place hand in a plastic sandwich bag and lightly coat with flour before pressing dough into pan.

2. Good warm with Wells' Blue Bunny sugar- and fat-free ice cream or cold with Cool Whip Lite, but don't forget to count the additional calories.

Each serving equals:

HE: 1⅓ Fat • ¾ Protein • ⅔ Bread • ¾ Slider • 10 Optional Calories

216 Calories • 8 gm Fat • 8 gm Protein • 28 gm Carbohydrate • 483 mg Sodium • 165 mg Calcium • 1 gm Fiber

DIABETIC EXCHANGES: 1½ Fat • 1½ Starch/Carbohydrate • 1 Meat

CARB CHOICES: 2

Hello Dolly! Dessert Pizza

The original Broadway show song welcomed a beloved match-maker home again, and I can't think of a better way to celebrate a homecoming (from the military, from college, or just from a long day at work) than to serve this nutty dream. 🌀 Serves 12

> 1 (8-ounce) can Pillsbury Reduced Fat Crescent Rolls
> 1 (4-serving) package Jell-O sugar-free vanilla cook-and-
>   serve pudding mix
> ¼ cup Splenda Granular
> 1½ cups water
> 1½ teaspoons coconut extract
> ½ cup chopped pecans
> ½ cup mini chocolate chips
> 6 tablespoons flaked coconut

Preheat oven to 375 degrees. Spray a rimmed 9-by-13-inch baking sheet with butter-flavored cooking spray. Unroll crescent rolls and carefully pat into prepared pan, being sure to seal perforations. Bake for 5 minutes or until crust is light golden brown. Place partially baked crust on a wire rack. Meanwhile, in a medium saucepan, combine dry pudding mix, Splenda, and water. Cook over medium heat until mixture thickens and starts to boil, stirring constantly using a wire whisk. Remove from heat. Stir in coconut extract. Spoon hot mixture evenly over partially baked crust. Sprinkle pecans, chocolate chips, and coconut evenly over top. Continue baking for 6 to 8 minutes or until crust is golden brown. Place baking sheet on a wire rack and allow to cool completely. Cut into 12 servings.

Each serving equals:

HE: ⅔ Bread • ⅔ Fat • ½ Slider • 14 Optional Calories

153 Calories • 9 gm Fat • 2 gm Protein • 16 gm Carbohydrate • 194 mg Sodium • 6 mg Calcium • 1 gm Fiber

DIABETIC EXCHANGES: 1 Starch/Carbohydrate • 1 Fat

CARB CHOICES: 1

Pizza-Inspired Delights

While it's possible to live by pizza alone (especially with the recipes in this book!), I'm eager to share with you a mélange of inventive recipes that feature pizza flavors and truly satisfy your pizza "urges"! This is where I've made a happy home for dishes to serve at breakfast, brunch, parties, and so much more. From sensational soups to superb sauces, you'll find pizza here, there, and everywhere—and there's nothing wrong with that!

For a memorable morning, serve up *Ham and Potato Brunch Pizza* or *Morning Bacon and Eggs Pizza* for the grown-ups, and *Peanut Butter and Jelly Breakfast Pizza* for the kids. On those chilly fall nights when only a bowl of comforting soup will do, *Pepperoni Pizza Soup* or *Tomato Rice Pizza Soup* will warm you through and through. And for parties that sizzle and satisfy, try *Pastrami Potato Pizza Bake*, *Pizza Party Fondue*, and a real man-pleaser: *Scalloped Pizza Potatoes*!

Can you have too much pizza? I just don't think so!

Homemade Pizza Sauce

There just is no substitute for homemade—and you can get an amazing result using great canned tomatoes and tomato sauce. (They also provide a healthy serving of lycopene, a powerful antioxidant said to help prevent some cancers.)

● Makes 2½ cups

> 1 (8-ounce) can Hunt's Tomato Sauce
> 1 (14.5-ounce) can Hunt's Tomatoes Diced in Sauce
> 2 tablespoons Splenda Granular
> ½ teaspoon dried minced garlic
> 1½ teaspoons pizza or Italian seasoning

In a medium saucepan sprayed with olive oil–flavored cooking spray, combine tomatoes, Splenda, and garlic. Stir in pizza seasoning. Cook over medium heat for 8 to 10 minutes, stirring often.

HINTS: 1. Can also be used as a breadstick dip.

2. If you really like garlic, add an additional ½ teaspoon.

Each ¼ cup serving equals:

HE: 1 Vegetable • 1 Optional Calorie

24 Calories • 0 gm Fat • 1 gm Protein • 5 gm Carbohydrate • 125 mg Sodium • 7 mg Calcium • 1 gm Fiber

DIABETIC EXCHANGES: 1 Vegetable

CARB CHOICES: 0

Homemade Pizza Dough

I usually choose to use a commercial dough because I want to save time when I'm preparing a meal. But if you've got the time and the inclination, making your own dough is fun, soothing, and tasty, too.

○ Serves 8

> 1 (¼-ounce) package active dry yeast
> ½ cup warm water
> 1½ cups all-purpose flour ☆
> 1 teaspoon olive oil
> ½ teaspoon table salt
> 1 teaspoon Splenda Granular

Reserve 2 tablespoons flour. In a large bowl, dissolve yeast in warm water. Stir in ¾ cup flour, olive oil, salt, and Splenda. Add remaining 10 tablespoons flour. Mix gently just to combine. Sprinkle reserved 2 tablespoons flour on work surface. Place dough on floured surface. Knead about 10 minutes or until dough is smooth and springy. Place dough in a large bowl sprayed with olive oil–flavored cooking spray. Turn dough so that all is coated in cooking spray. Cover with a clean cloth and let rise in a warm place for 20 minutes. When risen, gently push fist into dough to deflate. Re-cover and refrigerate for at least 2 hours or overnight. Press dough into an ungreased 12-inch round pizza pan. Press dough from center so edge is slightly thicker than center. Follow directions for whichever pizza you choose to prepare.

HINTS: 1. Place hand in a plastic sandwich bag and lightly coat with flour before pressing dough into pan.
2. Also good used as breadstick dough.

Each serving equals:

HE: 1 Bread • 8 Optional Calories

93 Calories • 1 gm Fat • 3 gm Protein • 18 gm Carbohydrate • 146 mg Sodium • 4 mg Calcium • 1 gm Fiber

DIABETIC EXCHANGES: 1 Starch

CARB CHOICES: 1

Pizza Salsa

Making your own salsa allows you to vary the ingredients to suit you and your family's personal tastes. You can also leave out items that you don't want in your food, especially preservatives and added sugar. ☻ Serves 8 (½ cup)

>   3 cups chopped fresh tomatoes
>   1 cup chopped green bell pepper
>   1 cup chopped onion
>   1 tablespoon Splenda Granular
>   1 tablespoon + 1 teaspoon vegetable oil
>   2 tablespoons reduced-sodium ketchup
>   1 tablespoon pizza or Italian seasoning

In a medium bowl, combine tomatoes, green pepper, and onion. Add Splenda, vegetable oil, ketchup, and pizza seasoning. Mix gently to combine. Cover and refrigerate for at least 30 minutes. Gently stir again just before serving.

Each serving equals:

HE: 1¼ Vegetable • ½ Fat • 5 Optional Calories

46 Calories • 2 gm Fat • 1 gm Protein • 6 gm Carbohydrate • 5 mg Sodium • 12 mg Calcium • 1 gm Fiber

DIABETIC EXCHANGES: 1 Vegetable • ½ Fat

CARB CHOICES: ½

Tomato Rice Pizza Soup

I've stirred up many versions of tomato soup over the years—and we've enjoyed them all. I thought it would be fun to change the rules for this classic by adding some pizza pizzazz, and it is!

○ Serves 4 (1 full cup)

> ½ cup finely chopped onion
> ½ cup finely chopped green bell pepper
> 1 (15-ounce) can diced tomatoes, undrained
> 1 (10¾-ounce) can Healthy Request Tomato Soup
> 1½ cups water
> 2 teaspoons pizza or Italian seasoning
> ¼ cup sliced ripe olives
> ⅛ teaspoon black pepper
> ⅔ cup uncooked Minute Rice
> ½ cup shredded Kraft reduced-fat mozzarella cheese

In a medium saucepan sprayed with olive oil–flavored cooking spray, sauté onion and green pepper for 5 minutes or until tender. Add undrained tomatoes, tomato soup, and water. Mix well to combine. Stir in pizza seasoning, olives, and black pepper. Bring mixture to a boil. Stir in uncooked instant rice. Lower heat, cover, and simmer for 6 to 8 minutes or until rice is tender, stirring occasionally. When serving, top each bowl with 2 tablespoons mozzarella cheese.

Each serving equals:

HE: 1½ Vegetable • ½ Bread • ½ Protein • ¼ Fat • ½ Slider • 5 Optional Calories

---

196 Calories • 4 gm Fat • 7 gm Protein • 33 gm Carbohydrate • 575 mg Sodium • 129 mg Calcium • 3 gm Fiber

---

DIABETIC EXCHANGES: 1½ Vegetable • 1½ Starch/Carbohydrate • ½ Fat

---

CARB CHOICES: 2

Tomato Pizza Supreme Soup

Are all pizza and Italian seasoning recipes the same? No, but many are quite similar, including oregano and basil. Some mixtures add thyme, marjoram, sage, savory, and rosemary. Experiment and try to find the one or two you like best. After all, you'll be using it a lot!

○ Serves 4

> 1 (10¾-ounce) can Healthy Request Tomato Soup
> 1 (15-ounce) can diced tomatoes, undrained
> 1 cup water
> 1 (2.5-ounce) jar sliced mushrooms, drained
> 1 teaspoon dried onion flakes
> 1½ teaspoons pizza or Italian seasoning
> ½ cup shredded Kraft reduced-fat Cheddar cheese
> ¾ cup shredded Kraft reduced-fat mozzarella cheese
> 2 slices reduced-calorie Italian or white bread, toasted and
>   cut into cubes
> ¼ cup Kraft Reduced Fat Parmesan Style Grated Topping

In a medium saucepan, combine tomato soup, undrained tomatoes, water, mushrooms, onion flakes, and pizza seasoning. Stir in Cheddar and mozzarella cheeses. Cook over medium-low heat until mixture is heated through and cheese is melted, stirring often. For each serving, place ¼ of toasted bread cubes in a bowl, spoon 1 cup soup over cubes, and sprinkle 1 tablespoon Parmesan cheese over top. Serve at once.

Each serving equals:

HE: 1½ Protein • 1¼ Vegetable • ¼ Bread • ½ Slider • 5 Optional Calories

233 Calories • 9 gm Fat • 13 gm Protein • 25 gm Carbohydrate •
787 mg Sodium • 323 mg Calcium • 3 gm Fiber

DIABETIC EXCHANGES: 1½ Meat • 1 Starch/Carbohydrate • 1 Vegetable

CARB CHOICES: 1½

Pizza Lover's Veggie-Noodle Soup

It's a vegetable soup, it's a noodle soup, and it tastes like pizza! Now tell me if there's a kid at your house who could resist this recipe for a cozy lunch? Serves 4 (1½ cups)

8 ounces extra-lean ground sirloin beef or turkey breast
½ cup chopped onion
1 (15-ounce) can diced tomatoes, undrained
1 (8-ounce) can Hunt's Tomato Sauce
1½ cups water
2 teaspoons pizza or Italian seasoning
1 tablespoon Splenda Granular
1 (2.5-ounce) jar sliced mushrooms, drained
1 cup frozen cut green beans, thawed
1 cup frozen sliced carrots, thawed
1¼ cups uncooked noodles

In a large saucepan sprayed with olive oil–flavored cooking spray, brown meat and onion. Stir in undrained tomatoes, tomato sauce, water, pizza seasoning, and Splenda. Add mushrooms, green beans, carrots, and uncooked noodles. Mix well to combine. Bring mixture to a boil. Lower heat, cover, and simmer for 20 to 25 minutes or until vegetables and noodles are tender, stirring occasionally.

HINT: Thaw green beans and carrots by rinsing in a colander under hot water for 1 minute.

Each serving equals:

HE: 3½ Vegetable • 1½ Protein • ¾ Bread • 1 Optional Calorie

232 Calories • 4 gm Fat • 17 gm Protein • 32 gm Carbohydrate • 600 mg Sodium • 65 mg Calcium • 4 gm Fiber

DIABETIC EXCHANGES: 3 Vegetable • 2 Meat • 1 Starch

CARB CHOICES: 2

Pepperoni Pizza Soup

I've never tasted a soup anywhere that contained pepperoni, but as soon as the idea awakened in my brain, I *wanted to*! Because the pepperoni is reduced-fat, you won't need to skim oil off the top of your soup. ● Serves 4 (1¼ cups)

> 1 cup chopped onion
> 1 (10¾-ounce) can Healthy Request Tomato Soup
> 1 (15-ounce) can diced tomatoes, undrained
> 1½ cups water
> 1½ teaspoons pizza or Italian seasoning
> ⅔ cup uncooked rotini pasta
> 3 ounces Hormel reduced-fat pepperoni slices, chopped
> ¼ cup Kraft Reduced Fat Parmesan Style Grated Topping

In a medium saucepan sprayed with olive oil–flavored cooking spray, sauté onion for 5 minutes. Stir in tomato soup, undrained tomatoes, water, and pizza seasoning. Add uncooked pasta and chopped pepperoni. Mix well to combine. Bring mixture to a boil. Lower heat, cover, and simmer for 20 minutes or until pasta is tender, stirring occasionally. When serving, top each bowl with 1 tablespoon Parmesan cheese.

Each serving equals:

HE: 1½ Vegetable • 1 Protein • ½ Bread • ½ Slider • 5 Optional Calories

234 Calories • 6 gm Fat • 12 gm Protein • 33 gm Carbohydrate • 936 mg Sodium • 148 mg Calcium • 3 gm Fiber

DIABETIC EXCHANGES: 1½ Vegetable • 1 Meat • 1 Starch/Carbohydrate

CARB CHOICES: 2

Fresh Tomato-Noodle Pizza Skillet

This is a summer favorite fresh from the garden, and it's a real treat for every tomato lover out there! You may want to experiment using several types of tomatoes for this recipe to enjoy the benefits of their separate and combined magic.   ☻   Serves 4 (1 cup)

3 cups peeled and coarsely chopped fresh tomatoes
1 cup chopped fresh mushrooms
1 cup chopped onion
½ cup chopped green bell pepper
1 (10¾-ounce) can Healthy Request Tomato Soup
1½ teaspoons pizza or Italian seasoning
¼ cup Kraft Reduced Fat Parmesan Style Grated Topping
¾ cup shredded Kraft reduced-fat mozzarella cheese
1½ cups hot cooked noodles, rinsed and drained

In a large skillet sprayed with olive oil–flavored cooking spray, sauté tomatoes, mushrooms, onion, and green pepper for about 10 minutes, or until vegetables are tender. Stir in tomato soup, pizza seasoning, and Parmesan and mozzarella cheeses. Add noodles. Mix well to combine. Lower heat and simmer for 5 minutes or until cheese melts, stirring occasionally.

HINT: Usually 1¼ cups uncooked noodles cook to about 1½ cups.

Each serving equals:

HE: 2 Vegetable • 1 Protein • ¾ Bread • ½ Slider • 5 Optional Calories

275 Calories • 7 gm Fat • 13 gm Protein • 40 gm Carbohydrate •
547 mg Sodium • 373 mg Calcium • 3 gm Fiber

DIABETIC EXCHANGES: 1½ Vegetable • 1½ Starch/Carbohydrate • 1 Meat

CARB CHOICES: 2½

Tomato-Zucchini Veggie Skillet

Top-of-the-stove cooking is wonderful for hot summer nights when you don't want to turn on the oven. This skillet supper is a satisfying side dish but could also double as a veggie entrée when coupled with good bread and cheese. ☻ Serves 4 (1 cup)

> 2 teaspoons olive oil
> 3 cups coarsely chopped unpeeled zucchini
> ½ cup coarsely chopped onion
> 2 cups peeled and coarsely chopped fresh tomatoes
> 1 (10¾-ounce) can Healthy Request Tomato Soup
> 1½ teaspoons pizza or Italian seasoning
> ¼ cup Kraft Reduced Fat Parmesan Style Grated Topping

In a large skillet sprayed with olive oil–flavored cooking spray, heat olive oil. Stir in zucchini and onion. Sauté for 5 to 6 minutes. Add tomatoes, tomato soup, pizza seasoning, and Parmesan cheese. Mix well to combine. Lower heat and simmer for 5 to 6 minutes or until mixture is heated through, stirring often.

Each serving equals:

HE: 2¾ Vegetable • ½ Fat • ¼ Protein • ½ Slider • 5 Optional Calories

119 Calories • 3 gm Fat • 3 gm Protein • 20 mg Carbohydrate • 295 mg Sodium • 27 mg Calcium • 3 gm Fiber

DIABETIC EXCHANGES: 2 Vegetable • ½ Fat • ½ Starch/Carbohydrate

CARB CHOICES: 1

Pizza Tomato Mozzarella Salad

It's one of the most dynamic duos on restaurant appetizer menus, so I thought I'd give it some extra sizzle by tossing the tomatoes and cheese in a lively dressing. *Salud!*   ☻   Serves 4 (½ cup)

2 cups cherry tomatoes, quartered
½ cup shredded Kraft reduced-fat mozzarella cheese
¼ cup Kraft Fat Free Ranch Dressing
1 tablespoon Kraft fat-free mayonnaise
1 tablespoon reduced-sodium ketchup
2 teaspoons Splenda Granular
1½ teaspoons pizza or Italian seasoning

In a medium bowl, combine tomatoes and mozzarella cheese. In a small bowl, combine Ranch dressing, mayonnaise, ketchup, Splenda, and pizza seasoning. Drizzle dressing mixture evenly over tomato mixture. Toss gently to combine. Cover and refrigerate for at least 15 minutes. Gently stir again just before serving.

Each serving equals:

HE: 1 Vegetable • ½ Protein • ¼ Slider • 3 Optional Calories

84 Calories • 2 gm Fat • 5 gm Protein • 11 gm Carbohydrate •
312 mg Sodium • 213 mg Calcium • 1 gm Fiber

DIABETIC EXCHANGES: 1 Vegetable • ½ Meat • ½ Other Carbohydrate

CARB CHOICES: 1

Pizza Chef's Salad

I'm not sure who the chef was who first served the classic chef's salad, with its turkey, ham, and cheese blend. Since then, cooks everywhere have "tweaked" the ingredients to give the dish a personal touch. Here's my pizza party version!

○ Serves 6 (2 cups)

6 cups finely shredded lettuce
¾ cup shredded Kraft reduced-fat mozzarella cheese
1½ cups finely diced Dubuque 97% fat-free ham or any
    extra-lean ham
½ cup diced green bell pepper
½ cup diced onion
1 cup chopped fresh mushrooms
1½ cups diced fresh tomatoes
¼ cup sliced ripe olives
½ cup Kraft Fat Free Italian Dressing
2 teaspoons olive oil
1 tablespoon Splenda Granular
¼ cup reduced-sodium ketchup
1 teaspoon pizza or Italian seasoning
3 slices reduced-calorie Italian or white bread, toasted and
    cut into ½-inch cubes

In a very large bowl, combine lettuce, mozzarella cheese, ham, green pepper, onion, mushrooms, tomatoes, and olives. In a small bowl, combine Italian dressing, olive oil, Splenda, ketchup, and pizza seasoning. Drizzle dressing mixture evenly over lettuce mixture. Toss gently to coat. Stir in toast cubes. Serve at once.

Each serving equals:

HE: 2 Vegetable • 1½ Protein • ½ Fat • ¼ Bread • ¼ Slider •
4 Optional Calories

170 Calories • 6 gm Fat • 13 gm Protein • 16 gm Carbohydrate •
722 mg Sodium • 128 mg Calcium • 2 gm Fiber

DIABETIC EXCHANGES: 2 Vegetable • 1½ Meat • ½ Fat • ½
Starch/Carbohydrate

CARB CHOICES: 1

Pizza Bread Salad

A bread salad is a popular traditional dish in Europe but isn't as well known here in the States. It's a natural when you're serving bits of cheese, herbs, and freshly chopped veggies, perfect for a summer luncheon. ☻ Serves 6 (1½ cups)

> 4 slices reduced-calorie Italian or white bread, toasted and
>   cut into ½-inch cubes
> 2 cups chopped fresh tomato
> ½ cup chopped red onion
> ½ cup chopped unpeeled zucchini
> 2 tablespoons chopped fresh basil
> ½ teaspoon dried minced garlic
> ¾ cup shredded Kraft reduced-fat Cheddar cheese
> ¾ cup shredded Kraft reduced-fat mozzarella cheese
> 3 cups purchased torn mixed salad greens
> 6 tablespoons reduced-sodium ketchup
> 2 tablespoons olive oil
> 2 tablespoons white distilled vinegar
> 2 tablespoons Splenda Granular
> 1½ teaspoons pizza or Italian seasoning

In a large bowl, combine toast cubes, tomato, onion, zucchini, basil, and garlic. Stir in Cheddar and mozzarella cheeses. Add salad greens. Mix gently to combine. In a small bowl, combine ketchup, olive oil, vinegar, Splenda, and pizza seasoning. Drizzle dressing mixture evenly over salad mixture. Toss gently to coat. Serve at once.

Each serving equals:

HE: 1½ Vegetable • 1 Protein • 1 Fat • ⅓ Bread • 17 Optional Calories

185 Calories • 9 gm Fat • 11 gm Protein • 15 gm Carbohydrate • 192 mg Sodium • 350 mg Calcium • 2 gm Fiber

DIABETIC EXCHANGES: 1½ Vegetable • 1 Meat • 1 Fat • ½ Starch/Carbohydrate

CARB CHOICES: 1

Tomato and Mozzarella Pizza Pasta Salad

This pasta salad sparkles with lots of crunchy veggies and cheese, made luxurious by its creamy and tangy dressing. In just thirty minutes, you've got a winner!   ☉   Serves 4 (1 cup)

1½ cups cold cooked rotini pasta, rinsed and drained
1½ cups diced fresh tomatoes
¼ cup chopped green bell pepper
¼ cup chopped red onion
¾ cup shredded Kraft reduced-fat mozzarella cheese
½ cup Kraft fat-free mayonnaise
2 tablespoons Land O Lakes Fat Free Half & Half
1 tablespoon pizza or Italian seasoning

In a large bowl, combine rotini pasta, tomatoes, green pepper, onion, and mozzarella cheese. Add mayonnaise, half & half, and pizza seasoning. Mix well to combine. Cover and refrigerate for at least 30 minutes. Gently stir again just before serving.

HINT: Usually 1 cup uncooked rotini pasta cooks to about 1½ cups.

Each serving equals:

HE: 1 Vegetable • ¾ Bread • ¾ Protein • ¼ Slider • 4 Optional Calories

176 Calories • 4 gm Fat • 10 gm Protein • 25 gm Carbohydrate • 405 mg Sodium • 322 mg Calcium • 3 gm Fiber

DIABETIC EXCHANGES: 1½ Starch/Carbohydrate • 1 Vegetable • 1 Meat

CARB CHOICES: 1½

Pasta Pizza Salad

Invite friends over for supper and to watch an episode of *The Sopranos*, and everyone will relish getting into the culinary spirit of the evening! If you don't have rotini on hand, this is also good with shells or other shaped pastas. ☺ Serves 6 (1 cup)

> ⅓ cup Kraft fat-free mayonnaise
> ¼ cup Kraft Fat Free Italian Dressing
> 1½ teaspoons pizza or Italian seasoning
> 2¼ cups cold cooked rotini pasta, rinsed and drained
> 1 cup chopped fresh tomatoes
> ½ cup chopped fresh mushrooms
> ¼ cup sliced ripe olives
> ¾ cup shredded Kraft reduced-fat mozzarella cheese
> 6 tablespoons shredded Kraft reduced-fat Cheddar cheese

In a large bowl, combine mayonnaise, Italian dressing, and pizza seasoning. Add rotini pasta, tomatoes, and mushrooms. Mix well to combine. Fold in olives, and mozzarella and Cheddar cheeses. Cover and refrigerate for at least 30 minutes. Gently stir again just before serving.

HINT: Usually 1½ cups uncooked rotini pasta cooks to about 2¼ cups.

Each serving equals:

HE: ¾ Bread • ¾ Protein • ½ Vegetable • 14 Optional Calories

143 Calories • 3 gm Fat • 8 gm Protein • 21 gm Carbohydrate • 399 mg Sodium • 217 mg Calcium • 2 gm Fiber

DIABETIC EXCHANGES: 1 Starch • 1 Meat • ½ Vegetable

CARB CHOICES: 1

Pepperoni Macaroni Salad

I feel like "rhymin' Simon" with this inventively named recipe! (I could add that it's *sono buoni*, meaning "so good," too.) Whatever the name, the taste's the thing—and blending chopped pepperoni into a sparkling pasta salad is a winning strategy for lunch anytime.

◐ Serves 4 (1¼ cups)

> 1½ cups cold cooked shell macaroni, rinsed and drained
> 1 cup diced fresh tomatoes
> 3 ounces Hormel reduced-fat pepperoni, chopped
> ¾ cup shredded Kraft reduced-fat Cheddar cheese
> ¼ cup sliced ripe olives
> ½ cup chopped onion
> ½ cup chopped green bell pepper
> 1 cup chopped celery
> ⅓ cup Kraft fat-free mayonnaise
> 2 tablespoons reduced-sodium ketchup
> 1½ teaspoons pizza or Italian seasoning
> ⅛ teaspoon black pepper

In a large bowl, combine macaroni, tomatoes, pepperoni, Cheddar cheese, olives, onion, green pepper, and celery. Add mayonnaise, ketchup, pizza seasoning, and black pepper. Mix well to combine. Cover and refrigerate for at least 15 minutes. Gently stir again just before serving.

HINT: Usually 1 cup uncooked shell macaroni cooks to about 1½ cups.

Each serving equals:

HE: 1½ Protein • 1½ Vegetable • ¾ Bread • ¼ Fat • ¼ Slider • 3 Optional Calories

197 Calories • 5 gm Fat • 11 gm Protein • 27 gm Carbohydrate • 602 mg Sodium • 110 mg Calcium • 3 gm Fiber

DIABETIC EXCHANGES: 1½ Meat • 1½ Vegetable • 1 Starch • ½ Fat

CARB CHOICES: 2

Potato Pizza Hash

It's an idea whose time has definitely come—a hash brown recipe flavored with pizza's panache! Some people like this dish extra crusty and golden brown, so you decide when it's time to turn off the burner and serve this yummy side dish.

⊙ Serves 4 (1 cup)

> 3 cups shredded loose-packed frozen potatoes, slightly
>   thawed
> ½ cup finely chopped onion
> 1 (15-ounce) can diced tomatoes, undrained
> 1 (2.5-ounce) jar sliced mushrooms, drained
> ¼ cup sliced ripe olives
> 2 teaspoons pizza or Italian seasoning
> ½ cup shredded Kraft reduced-fat mozzarella cheese
> ½ cup shredded Kraft reduced-fat Cheddar cheese

In a large skillet sprayed with olive oil–flavored cooking spray, combine potatoes and onion. Brown mixture for 5 minutes, stirring often. Stir in undrained tomatoes, mushrooms, olives, and pizza seasoning. Cover and continue cooking over medium heat for 10 minutes, stirring occasionally. Add mozzarella and Cheddar cheeses. Mix well to combine. Continue cooking for 2 to 3 minutes or until cheese is melted, stirring often. Serve at once.

HINT: Mr. Dell's frozen shredded potatoes are a good choice or raw shredded potatoes, rinsed and patted dry, may be used in place of frozen potatoes.

Each serving equals:

HE: 1½ Vegetable • 1 Protein • ½ Bread • ¼ Fat

170 Calories • 6 gm Fat • 11 gm Protein • 18 gm Carbohydrate •
361 mg Sodium • 344 mg Calcium • 3 gm Fiber

DIABETIC EXCHANGES: 1½ Vegetable • 1 Meat • ½ Starch • ½ Fat

CARB CHOICES: 1

Scalloped Pizza Potatoes

It's amazing how a little Parmesan cheese can turn an everyday potato dish into a supersonic flight to Rome! The time this dish spends in the oven brings luscious results. ☻ Serves 6

1 (10¾-ounce) can Healthy Request Cream of Mushroom
    Soup
¼ cup Kraft Reduced Fat Parmesan Style Grated Topping
1 (8-ounce) can tomatoes, finely chopped and drained
1 tablespoon pizza or Italian seasoning
⅛ teaspoon black pepper
4½ cups frozen loose-packed hash brown potatoes
½ cup finely chopped onion
1 (4.5-ounce) jar sliced mushrooms, drained and finely
    chopped
1 cup shredded Kraft reduced-fat Cheddar cheese ☆
1 cup shredded Kraft reduced-fat mozzarella cheese ☆

Preheat oven to 350 degrees. Spray an 8-by-8-inch baking dish with olive oil–flavored cooking spray. In a large bowl, combine mushroom soup, Parmesan cheese, tomatoes, pizza seasoning, and black pepper. Stir in potatoes, onion, and mushrooms. Add ¾ cup Cheddar cheese and ¾ cup mozzarella cheese. Mix well to combine. Evenly spread mixture into prepared baking dish. Sprinkle remaining ¼ cup Cheddar cheese and ¼ cup mozzarella cheese over top. Bake for 45 to 50 minutes. Place baking dish on a wire rack and let set for 5 minutes. Divide into 6 servings.

HINT: Mr. Dell's frozen shredded potatoes are a good choice or raw shredded potatoes, rinsed and patted dry, may be used in place of frozen potatoes.

Each serving equals:

HE: 1½ Protein • ½ Bread • ½ Vegetable • ¼ Slider • 8 Optional Calories

193 Calories • 9 gm Fat • 13 gm Protein • 15 gm Carbohydrate •
554 mg Sodium • 496 mg Calcium • 2 gm Fiber

DIABETIC EXCHANGES: 1½ Meat • 1 Starch/Carbohydrate • ½ Vegetable

CARB CHOICES: 1

Pastrami Potato Pizza Bake

This oven-baked indulgence brims with beloved flavors, from the deli delight of pastrami to the generous flavor of three great cheeses. It can be served for supper or even a weekend brunch for friends. ☻ Serves 6

1 (8-ounce) can Hunt's Tomato Sauce
1 (15-ounce) can diced tomatoes, undrained
1½ teaspoons pizza or Italian seasoning
1 tablespoon Splenda Granular
¼ cup Kraft Reduced Fat Parmesan Style Grated Topping
1 (2.5-ounce) jar sliced mushrooms, drained
2 (2.5-ounce) packages Carl Buddig lean pastrami, shredded
½ cup shredded Kraft reduced-fat Cheddar cheese
½ cup shredded Kraft reduced-fat mozzarella cheese
4½ cups frozen loose-packed shredded hash brown potatoes

Preheat oven to 350 degrees. Spray an 8-by-8-inch baking dish with olive oil–flavored cooking spray. In a large bowl, combine tomato sauce, undrained tomatoes, pizza seasoning, Splenda, and Parmesan cheese. Stir in mushrooms, pastrami, and Cheddar and mozzarella cheeses. Add potatoes. Mix well to combine. Evenly spread mixture into prepared baking dish. Bake for 55 to 60 minutes. Place baking dish on a wire rack and let set for 5 minutes. Divide into 6 servings.

HINTS: 1. 1 (5-ounce) package Hillshire Farm Deli Select Pastrami can be used instead of Carl Buddig.
2. Mr. Dell's frozen shredded potatoes are a good choice or raw shredded potatoes, rinsed and patted dry, may be used in place of frozen potatoes.

Each serving equals:

HE: 1⅔ Protein • 1½ Vegetable • ½ Bread • 1 Optional Calorie

182 Calories • 6 gm Fat • 13 gm Protein • 19 gm Carbohydrate •
746 mg Sodium • 259 mg Calcium • 3 gm Fiber

DIABETIC EXCHANGES: 1½ Meat • 1½ Vegetable • 1 Starch

CARB CHOICES: 1

Bountiful Harvest Pizza Quiche

Quiche had its heyday quite a few years ago, but it just won't go away even as other culinary traditions have tried to take its place. I'll tell you why I think it's a perennial winner: the cheese, the crust, the freedom to blend in whatever veggies and proteins you enjoy. Oh, and it's so neat when you serve it!   ☻   Serves 6

1½ cups shredded carrots
1 cup chopped unpeeled zucchini
½ cup chopped onion
¼ cup Kraft Reduced Fat Parmesan Style Grated Topping
½ cup shredded Kraft reduced-fat Cheddar cheese
½ cup shredded Kraft reduced-fat mozzarella cheese
1 (12-fluid-ounce) can Carnation Evaporated Fat Free Milk
1 egg, or equivalent in egg substitute
¾ cup Bisquick Heart Smart Baking Mix
2 teaspoons pizza seasoning
⅛ teaspoon black pepper

Preheat oven to 375 degrees. Spray a deep dish 10-inch pie plate or quiche dish with olive oil–flavored cooking spray. Evenly layer carrots, zucchini, and onion into prepared pie plate. Sprinkle Parmesan, Cheddar, and mozzarella cheeses evenly over vegetables. In a medium bowl, combine evaporated milk, egg, baking mix, pizza seasoning, and black pepper using a wire whisk. Pour mixture evenly over top. Bake for 35 to 45 minutes or until a knife inserted in center comes out clean. Place pie plate on a wire rack and let set for 5 minutes. Cut into 6 servings.

Each serving equals:

HE: 1 Protein • 1 Vegetable • ⅔ Bread • ½ Fat Free Milk

202 Calories • 6 gm Fat • 12 gm Protein • 25 gm Carbohydrate • 416 mg Sodium • 412 mg Calcium • 1 gm Fiber

DIABETIC EXCHANGES: 1 Meat • 1 Vegetable • 1 Starch • ½ Fat Free Milk

CARB CHOICES: 1½

Pizza Quiche

This dish is so easy when you use a ready-made crust, you can put it on the menu often! Keep the oven door closed while it's baking, even if the aroma begs you to take a peek!

● Serves 8

> 1 Pillsbury refrigerated unbaked 9-inch pie crust
> ½ cup shredded Kraft reduced-fat mozzarella cheese
> ½ cup shredded Kraft reduced-fat Cheddar cheese
> 1 tablespoon all-purpose flour
> 3 eggs, beaten, or equivalent in egg substitute
> 1 cup fat-free milk
> ½ cup Land O Lakes Fat Free Half & Half
> 1 (2.5-ounce) jar sliced mushrooms, drained
> ½ cup finely chopped onion
> 1 tablespoon pizza or Italian seasoning ☆
> 1 (8-ounce) can Hunt's Tomato Sauce
> 1 tablespoon Splenda Granular

Preheat oven to 450 degrees. Place pie crust in a 9-inch pie plate and flute edges. In a large bowl, combine mozzarella and Cheddar cheeses, and flour. Spoon mixture evenly into pie crust. In same bowl, combine eggs, milk, and half & half. Stir in mushrooms, onion, and 1 teaspoon pizza seasoning. Carefully pour egg mixture into pie crust. Bake for 10 minutes. Lower oven temperature to 325 degrees and continue baking for 30 to 35 minutes or until a knife inserted in center comes out clean. Place pie plate on a wire rack and let set for 5 minutes. Meanwhile, in a small saucepan, combine tomato sauce, Splenda, and remaining 2 teaspoons pizza seasoning. Cook over medium heat for 5 minutes or until heated through, stirring often. Cut warm quiche into 8 servings. When serving, top each piece with 1 tablespoon warm sauce mixture.

Each serving equals:

HE: 1 Bread • 1 Protein • ¾ Vegetable • ½ Fat • ¼ Slider •
10 Optional Calories

210 Calories • 10 gm Fat • 10 gm Protein • 20 gm Carbohydrate •
417 mg Sodium • 183 mg Calcium • 1 gm Fiber

DIABETIC EXCHANGES: 1 Starch • 1 Meat • 1 Fat • ½ Vegetable

CARB CHOICES: 1

Tomato and Mushroom Pizza Quiche

If you've been washing your mushrooms, STOP! Getting these veggies wet can destroy their texture in seconds, so instead you should be wiping them with a damp towel or mushroom brush just to remove the dry, sterilized dirt that may still cling.

☻ Serves 6

2½ cups peeled and chopped fresh tomatoes
½ cup chopped onion
1½ cups chopped fresh mushrooms
½ cup shredded Kraft reduced-fat mozzarella cheese
1 (12-fluid-ounce) can Carnation Evaporated Fat Free Milk
¾ cup Bisquick Heart Smart Baking Mix
3 eggs, or equivalent in egg substitute
¼ cup Kraft Reduced Fat Parmesan Style Grated Topping
2 teaspoons pizza or Italian seasoning

Preheat oven to 375 degrees. Spray a deep dish 9-inch pie plate or quiche dish with olive oil–flavored cooking spray. Layer tomatoes, onion, and mushrooms evenly into prepared pie plate. Sprinkle mozzarella cheese evenly over vegetables. In a blender container, combine evaporated milk, baking mix, eggs, Parmesan cheese, and pizza seasoning. Cover and process on BLEND for 15 seconds or until mixture is smooth. Evenly pour mixture over top. Bake for 35 to 45 minutes or until a knife inserted in center comes out clean. Place pie plate on a wire rack and let set for 5 minutes. Cut into 6 servings.

Each serving equals:

HE: 1½ Vegetable • 1 Protein • ⅔ Bread • ½ Fat Free Milk

180 Calories • 4 gm Fat • 10 gm Protein • 26 gm Carbohydrate • 408 mg Sodium • 354 mg Calcium • 2 gm Fiber

DIABETIC EXCHANGES: 1 Vegetable • 1 Meat • 1 Starch • ½ Fat Free Milk

CARB CHOICES: 2

Grecian Pizza Supper Muffins

You could create a section in your recipe box just for English muffin pizzas! There are just many fun possibilities, including this speedy visit to Greece that is ready in just minutes.

❍ Serves 4

> 1 cup chopped red bell pepper
> ½ cup chopped onion
> ½ teaspoon dried minced garlic
> ¼ cup reduced-sodium ketchup
> 2 tablespoons Kraft Fat Free Italian Dressing
> 2 English muffins, split and lightly toasted
> ¼ cup sliced ripe olives
> ½ cup crumbled feta cheese

In a medium microwave-safe bowl, combine red pepper, onion, and garlic. Microwave on HIGH (100% power) for 2 minutes or until vegetables are tender. In a small bowl, combine ketchup and Italian dressing. Evenly spread about 1½ tablespoons ketchup mixture over top of each muffin half. Sprinkle vegetable mixture, olives, and feta cheese evenly over top. Place muffin halves on a paper towel and microwave on MEDIUM (50% power) for 2 to 3 minutes. Serve at once.

Each serving equals:

HE: 1 Bread • ¾ Vegetable • ½ Protein • ¼ Fat • 19 Optional Calories

165 Calories • 5 gm Fat • 6 gm Protein • 24 gm Carbohydrate •
506 mg Sodium • 163 mg Calcium • 2 gm Fiber

DIABETIC EXCHANGES: 1 Starch • ½ Vegetable • ½ Meat • ½ Fat

CARB CHOICES: 1½

Spinach Squares with Pizza Sauce

This layered casserole is rich with healthy ingredients, but what makes this a pleasure for the palate is how they all hold hands and work so well together when it's finished baking.

❂ Serves 6

> 1 (10-ounce) package frozen chopped spinach,
> thawed and thoroughly drained
> 1½ cups chopped onion ☆
> 1 cup shredded Kraft reduced-fat Cheddar
> cheese
> ½ teaspoon dried minced garlic
> 2 eggs, slightly beaten, or equivalent in egg
> substitute
> ¼ cup Land O Lakes Fat Free Half & Half
> 6 slices reduced-calorie Italian or white bread,
> made into crumbs
> 8 ounces extra-lean ground sirloin beef or turkey
> breast
> 1 (8-ounce) can Hunt's Tomato Sauce
> 1 (15-ounce) can diced tomatoes, undrained
> 1 (2.5-ounce) jar sliced mushrooms, drained
> 1½ teaspoons pizza or Italian seasoning
> 1 tablespoon Splenda Granular

Preheat oven to 350 degrees. Spray an 8-by-12-inch baking dish with olive oil–flavored cooking spray. In a large bowl, combine spinach, ½ cup onion, Cheddar cheese, garlic, eggs, half & half, and bread crumbs. Evenly pour mixture into prepared baking dish. Bake for 35 to 40 minutes. About 15 minutes before spinach mixture is through baking, brown meat and remaining 1 cup onion in a large skillet sprayed with olive oil–flavored cooking spray. Stir in tomato sauce, undrained tomatoes, mushrooms, pizza seasoning, and Splenda. Lower heat and simmer until spinach mixture is baked, stirring occasionally. When serving, cut spinach mixture into 6 servings and top each with about ½ cup meat mixture.

Each serving equals:

HE: 2¼ Vegetable • 2 Protein • ½ Bread • 7 Optional Calories

232 Calories • 8 gm Fat • 20 gm Protein • 20 gm Carbohydrate •
526 mg Sodium • 217 mg Calcium • 4 gm Fiber

DIABETIC EXCHANGES: 2 Vegetable • 2 Meat • ½ Starch

CARB CHOICES: 1

Chicken Pizza Pita

Handheld entrees are such a simple way to serve a meal, and this pita pocket "pie" is no exception. If you've resisted serving stuffed pitas because they always tear, the tip below will change your life!

☯ Serves 4

½ cup finely shredded lettuce
2 tablespoons Kraft Fat Free Italian Dressing
2 pita rounds, halved
1 full cup diced cooked chicken breast
¾ cup finely diced celery
2 tablespoons reduced-sodium ketchup
¼ cup Kraft fat-free mayonnaise
1½ teaspoons pizza or Italian seasoning

In a small bowl, combine lettuce and Italian dressing. Sprinkle about 2 tablespoons of lettuce mixture into each pita half. In a medium bowl, combine chicken and celery. Add ketchup, mayonnaise, and pizza seasoning. Mix well to combine. Spoon about ½ cup chicken mixture into bottom of each pita half. Serve at once or cover and refrigerate until ready to serve.

HINTS: 1. To make opening pita rounds easier, place pita halves on a paper towel and microwave on HIGH for 10 seconds. Remove and gently press open.
2. If you don't have leftovers, purchase a chunk of cooked chicken breast from your local deli.

Each serving equals:

HE: 1½ Protein • 1 Bread • ½ Vegetable • 17 Optional Calories

170 Calories • 2 gm Fat • 16 gm Protein • 22 gm Carbohydrate • 434 mg Sodium • 44 mg Calcium • 1 gm Fiber

DIABETIC EXCHANGES: 1½ Meat • 1½ Starch/Carbohydrate

CARB CHOICES: 1½

Pizza Skillet Patties

Instead of a pizza burger that is topped with a sauce, I've blended the ingredients in this dish together, so it's a pizza party all the way through! What an appealing way to join two favorites in one.

● Serves 6

> 16 ounces extra-lean ground sirloin beef or turkey breast
> 6 tablespoons dried fine bread crumbs
> ¾ cup shredded Kraft reduced-fat mozzarella cheese
> ½ cup finely chopped onion
> ⅛ teaspoon black pepper
> 1½ teaspoons pizza seasoning
> ¼ cup reduced-sodium ketchup
> 6 lettuce leaves
> 1 medium-sized fresh tomato, cut into 6 slices
> 6 small hamburger buns

In a large bowl, combine meat, bread crumbs, mozzarella cheese, onion, black pepper, pizza seasoning, and ketchup. Mix well to combine. Using a ⅓ cup measuring cup as a guide, form into 6 patties. Arrange patties in a large skillet sprayed with olive oil–flavored cooking spray. Brown for 4 to 5 minutes on each side or until cooked to desired doneness. For each sandwich, place a lettuce leaf and a tomato slice on bottom half of hamburger bun, arrange meat patty over tomato, and place top of hamburger bun over top. Serve at once.

Each serving equals:

HE: 2½ Protein • 1⅓ Bread • ½ Vegetable • 11 Optional Calories

239 Calories • 7 gm Fat • 20 gm Protein • 24 gm Carbohydrate • 337 mg Sodium • 116 mg Calcium • 2 gm Fiber

DIABETIC EXCHANGES: 2½ Meat • 1½ Starch

CARB CHOICES: 1½

Inside-Out Cheeseburgers with Pizza Sauce

The name of this recipe says it all—I put the cheese in the middle of the burgers instead of on top, and topped them off with a lively pizza-flavored topping. It's savory, it's fun to bite into the surprise inside, and one of these will certainly fill you up.

🍂 Serves 4

> 16 ounces extra-lean ground sirloin beef or turkey breast
> 6 tablespoons dried fine bread crumbs
> 1 tablespoon dried onion flakes
> ¼ cup Land O Lakes Fat Free Half & Half
> ½ cup shredded Kraft reduced-fat Cheddar cheese
> 1 (8-ounce) can Hunt's Tomato Sauce
> 1 (8-ounce) can tomatoes, finely chopped and undrained
> 1 tablespoon Splenda Granular
> 2 teaspoons pizza or Italian seasoning

Plug in and generously spray both sides of double-sided electric contact grill with olive oil–flavored cooking spray and preheat for 5 minutes. Meanwhile, in a medium bowl, combine meat, bread crumbs, onion flakes, and half & half. Using a ¼ cup measuring cup as a guide, form into 8 patties. For each burger, sprinkle 2 tablespoons Cheddar cheese between 2 patties, crimping edges of each to seal cheese in. Evenly arrange burgers on prepared grill. Close lid and grill for 6 to 7 minutes. Meanwhile, in a medium saucepan, combine tomato sauce, undrained tomatoes, Splenda, and pizza seasoning. Cook over medium-low heat while burgers are grilling, stirring occasionally. For each serving, place 1 burger on a plate and spoon a scant ½ cup pizza sauce over top. Serve at once.

Each serving equals:

HE: 3½ Protein • 1½ Vegetable • ½ Bread • 7 Optional Calories

256 Calories • 8 gm Fat • 29 gm Protein • 17 gm Carbohydrate •
530 mg Sodium • 159 mg Calcium • 2 gm Fiber

DIABETIC EXCHANGES: 3½ Meat • 1 Vegetable • ½ Starch

CARB CHOICES: 1

Loose Meat Pizza Sandwich

Take one Iowa tradition (loose meat), add some Italian charm, and stir—that's what I had in mind when I put the skillet on the stove and got cooking! It's a great way to take something basic and transform it fast into something pretty special.   ☻   Serves 6

> 16 ounces extra-lean ground sirloin beef or turkey breast
> 1 cup chopped onion
> ½ cup chopped green bell pepper
> 1 (2.5-ounce) jar sliced mushrooms, chopped and drained
> 1 (8-ounce) can Hunt's Tomato Sauce
> 1 (15-ounce) can diced tomatoes, undrained
> 1 tablespoon pizza or Italian seasoning
> 2 tablespoons Splenda Granular
> 6 small hamburger buns
> 6 (¾-ounce) slices Kraft reduced-fat mozzarella cheese

In a large skillet sprayed with olive oil–flavored cooking spray, brown meat, onion, and green pepper. Add mushrooms, tomato sauce, undrained tomatoes, pizza seasoning, and Splenda. Mix well to combine. Bring mixture to a boil. Lower heat and simmer for 12 to 15 minutes or until most of the liquid is absorbed, stirring occasionally. For each sandwich, spoon about ½ cup meat mixture on bottom of hamburger bun, arrange 1 slice mozzarella cheese over meat mixture, and place top of hamburger bun over cheese. Serve at once.

Each serving equals:

HE: 3 Protein • 2 Vegetable • 1 Bread • 1 Optional Calorie

279 Calories • 7 gm Fat • 25 gm Protein • 29 gm Carbohydrate • 651 mg Sodium • 205 mg Calcium • 2 gm Fiber

DIABETIC EXCHANGES: 2½ Meat • 2 Vegetable • 1 Starch

CARB CHOICES: 2

Pizza Meat Loaf Patties

These individual meat loaf delicacies are quick to make and easy to eat! I've used two great cheeses to give them just the right rich taste, and mixed in some terrific veggies to add both texture and flavor. Enjoy!   ☻   Serves 4

> 8 ounces extra-lean ground sirloin beef or turkey breast
> ¼ cup Kraft Reduced Fat Parmesan Style Grated Topping
> ½ cup shredded Kraft reduced-fat mozzarella cheese
> 3 tablespoons dried fine bread crumbs
> ¼ cup sliced ripe olives
> ½ cup chopped onion
> 1 (2.5-ounce) jar sliced mushrooms, drained
> 1 (8-ounce) can Hunt's Tomato Sauce ☆
> 1 tablespoon Splenda Granular
> 2 teaspoons pizza or Italian seasoning

Plug in and generously spray both sides of double-sided electric contact grill with olive oil–flavored cooking spray and preheat for 5 minutes. Meanwhile, in a large bowl, combine meat, Parmesan and mozzarella cheeses, bread crumbs, olives, onion, mushrooms, and 2 tablespoons tomato sauce. Using a ½ cup measuring cup as a guide, form into 4 patties. Evenly arrange patties on prepared grill. Close lid and grill for 6 to 7 minutes. Meanwhile, in a small saucepan, combine remaining tomato sauce, Splenda, and pizza seasoning. Cook over medium-low heat while patties are grilling, stirring occasionally. For each serving, place 1 meat loaf patty on a plate and drizzle a full 2 tablespoons tomato sauce over top.

Each serving equals:

HE: 2¼ Protein • 1½ Vegetable • ¼ Bread • ¼ Fat • 2 Optional Calories

195 Calories • 7 gm Fat • 18 gm Protein • 15 gm Carbohydrate • 729 mg Sodium • 276 mg Calcium • 2 gm Fiber

DIABETIC EXCHANGES: 2 Meat • 1½ Vegetable • ½ Fat

CARB CHOICES: 1

Pasta Pizza Bake

Your oven works magic in delicious ways, and here's an outstanding example of what that "hot box" can do! Baked pasta dishes appeal to kids of all ages, and they're good the next day, too.

● Serves 6

> 1 egg, slightly beaten, or equivalent in egg substitute
> ¼ cup Land O Lakes Fat Free Half & Half
> ¼ cup Kraft Reduced Fat Parmesan Style Grated Topping
> 3 cups cooked rotini pasta, rinsed and drained
> 16 ounces extra-lean ground sirloin beef or turkey breast
> 1 cup chopped onion
> 1 (15-ounce) can Hunt's Tomato Sauce
> 1 (4-ounce) can sliced mushrooms, drained
> 1½ teaspoons pizza or Italian seasoning
> 1 tablespoon Splenda Granular
> ¾ cup shredded Kraft reduced-fat mozzarella cheese

Preheat oven to 350 degrees. Spray a 13-inch round pizza pan with olive oil–flavored cooking spray. In a large bowl, combine egg, half & half, and Parmesan cheese. Stir in rotini pasta. Evenly spread mixture into prepared pizza pan. Bake for 20 minutes. Meanwhile, in a large skillet sprayed with olive oil–flavored cooking spray, brown meat and onion. Stir in tomato sauce, mushrooms, pizza seasoning, and Splenda. Lower heat and simmer while crust is baking. Spoon meat mixture evenly over crust. Sprinkle mozzarella cheese evenly over top. Continue baking for 10 to 12 minutes or until cheese is melted and mixture is heated through. Place pizza pan on a wire rack and let set for 5 minutes. Cut into 6 servings.

HINT: Usually 2 cups uncooked rotini pasta cooks to about 3 cups.

Each serving equals:

HE: 3 Protein • 1¾ Vegetable • 1 Bread • 7 Optional Calories

296 Calories • 8 gm Fat • 25 gm Protein • 31 gm Carbohydrate • 671 mg Sodium • 173 mg Calcium • 3 gm Fiber

DIABETIC EXCHANGES: 3 Meat • 1½ Vegetable • 1½ Starch

CARB CHOICES: 2

Cheese Pizza Tetrazzini

Here's an appetizing supper-in-a-skillet that's good in every season and easy to fix with just what you usually have on hand! I prefer fresh mushrooms in this recipe, but if you've only got a jar or can on your shelf, drain and pour them in. ☾ Serves 4 (1 cup)

½ cup finely chopped onion
1 cup sliced fresh mushrooms
1 (10¾-ounce) can Healthy Request Tomato Soup
¾ cup shredded Kraft reduced-fat mozzarella cheese
¾ cup shredded Kraft reduced-fat Cheddar cheese
1 (2-ounce) jar chopped pimiento, drained
1½ teaspoons pizza or Italian seasoning
2 cups hot cooked spaghetti, rinsed and drained
½ cup Land O Lakes Fat Free Half & Half
¼ cup Kraft Reduced Fat Parmesan Style Grated Topping

In a large skillet sprayed with butter-flavored cooking spray, sauté onion and mushrooms for 5 minutes. Stir in tomato soup and mozzarella and Cheddar cheeses. Add pimiento, pizza seasoning, and spaghetti. Mix well to combine. Stir in half & half and Parmesan cheese. Lower heat and simmer for 5 to 7 minutes or until mixture is heated through and cheese is melted, stirring often.

HINT: Usually 1½ cups broken uncooked spaghetti cooks to about 2 cups.

Each serving equals:

HE: 1½ Protein • 1 Bread • ½ Vegetable • ¾ Slider • 3 Optional Calories

318 Calories • 10 gm Fat • 17 gm Protein • 40 gm Carbohydrate • 618 mg Sodium • 346 mg Calcium • 3 gm Fiber

DIABETIC EXCHANGES: 2 Meat • 2 Starch • ½ Vegetable

CARB CHOICES: 2½

Chicken Pizza Pasta Skillet

Looking for something quick, inexpensive, and good to serve for Columbus Day? (It's often a day off and you don't want to spend it in the kitchen!) Here's a dish that will fit the bill and satisfy your family from the very first bite. ☺ Serves 4 (1¼ cups)

> 8 ounces skinned and boned uncooked chicken breast, cut
>   into bite-size pieces
> ¾ cup chopped onion
> ¾ cup chopped green bell pepper
> 1 cup chopped fresh mushrooms
> 1 (15-ounce) can diced tomatoes, undrained
> 1 (8-ounce) can Hunt's Tomato Sauce
> 1 tablespoon Splenda Granular
> 1½ teaspoons pizza or Italian seasoning
> 1½ cups hot cooked rotini, rinsed and drained
> ½ cup shredded Kraft reduced-fat mozzarella cheese
> ¼ cup Kraft Reduced Fat Parmesan Style Grated Topping

In a large skillet sprayed with olive oil–flavored cooking spray, sauté chicken pieces, onion, and green pepper for 6 to 8 minutes. Stir in mushrooms, undrained tomatoes, tomato sauce, Splenda, and pizza seasoning. Add rotini pasta and mozzarella cheese. Mix well to combine. Lower heat and simmer for 8 to 10 minutes, stirring occasionally. When serving, top each with 1 tablespoon Parmesan cheese.

HINT: Usually 1 full cup uncooked rotini pasta cooks to about 1½ cups.

Each serving equals:

HE: 3 Vegetable • 2¼ Protein • ¾ Bread • 2 Optional Calories

286 Calories • 6 gm Fat • 23 gm Protein • 35 gm Carbohydrate • 745 mg Sodium • 188 mg Calcium • 5 gm Fiber

DIABETIC EXCHANGES: 3 Vegetable • 2 Meat • 1 Starch

CARB CHOICES: 2

Pizza Macaroni Skillet

As soon as the aroma of this tummy-pleasing dish starts wafting from the kitchen to the family room, you'll have constant inquiries about when dinner will be served! Use your leverage—have the kids set the table while they're waiting.

◐ Serves 6 (1 full cup)

> 16 ounces extra-lean ground sirloin beef or turkey breast
> 1 cup chopped onion
> 1 cup chopped green bell pepper
> 1 (14.5-ounce) can Hunt's Tomatoes Diced in Sauce
> ¼ cup reduced-sodium ketchup
> 1 (2.5-ounce) jar sliced mushrooms, drained
> 2 teaspoons pizza or Italian seasoning
> ¾ cup shredded Kraft reduced-fat mozzarella cheese
> 2 cups hot cooked elbow macaroni, rinsed and drained

In a large skillet sprayed with olive oil–flavored cooking spray, brown meat, onion, and green pepper. Stir in tomatoes, ketchup, mushrooms, and pizza seasoning. Add mozzarella cheese and macaroni. Mix well to combine. Lower heat, cover, and simmer for 10 minutes, stirring occasionally.

HINT: Usually 1⅓ cups uncooked macaroni cooks to about 2 cups.

Each serving equals:

HE: 2½ Protein • 2 Vegetable • ⅔ Bread • 10 Optional Calories

250 Calories • 6 gm Fat • 23 gm Protein • 26 gm Carbohydrate • 371 mg Sodium • 215 mg Calcium • 3 gm Fiber

DIABETIC EXCHANGES: 2½ Meat • 2 Vegetable • 1 Starch

CARB CHOICES: 2

Pizza Pleasure Pot

The joys of slow cooking are vividly on display in this recipe, in which the savory Italian flavors deepen with every minute they spend cooking s-l-o-w-l-y. As they say in Rome, you'll be dining with "piacere." ❤ Serves 6 (1 cup)

> 8 ounces extra-lean ground sirloin beef or turkey breast
> 1 cup chopped onion
> ½ cup chopped green bell pepper
> 1 (2.5-ounce) jar sliced mushrooms, drained
> 1 (8-ounce) can Hunt's Tomato Sauce
> 1 (15-ounce) can diced tomatoes, undrained
> 2 teaspoons pizza or Italian seasoning
> 1 tablespoon Splenda Granular
> 2¼ cups cooked rotini pasta, rinsed and drained
> ¼ cup Kraft Fat Free Parmesan Style Grated Topping
> ¾ cup shredded Kraft reduced-fat Cheddar cheese
> ¾ cup shredded Kraft reduced-fat mozzarella cheese

Spray a slow cooker container with butter-flavored cooking spray. In a large skillet sprayed with olive oil–flavored cooking spray, brown meat, onion, and green pepper. Stir in mushrooms, tomato sauce, undrained tomatoes, pizza seasoning, and Splenda. Evenly spoon mixture into prepared container. Spread rotini pasta over meat mixture. Sprinkle Parmesan cheese over pasta. Layer Cheddar and mozzarella cheeses evenly over top. Cover and cook on LOW for 6 to 8 hours. Mix well before serving.

HINT: Usually 1½ cups uncooked rotini pasta cooks to about 2¼ cups.

Each serving equals:

HE: 2 Protein • 2 Vegetable • ¾ Bread • 11 Optional Calories

264 Calories • 8 gm Fat • 20 gm Protein • 28 gm Carbohydrate • 523 mg Sodium • 363 mg Calcium • 3 gm Fiber

DIABETIC EXCHANGES: 2 Meat • 2 Vegetable • 1 Starch

CARB CHOICES: 2

Creamy Pizza Bake

Here's an easy casserole that not only satisfies with every mouthful, it gets even better when it's reheated a day or two later! Bring it to work, heat it in the microwave, and don't be surprised to receive envious glances from co-workers!   ☻   Serves 4

> 8 ounces extra-lean ground sirloin beef or turkey breast
> ½ cup chopped onion
> 1 (10¾-ounce) can Healthy Request Cream of Mushroom
>   Soup
> 1 (15-ounce) can diced tomatoes, drained
> ½ cup shredded Kraft reduced-fat Cheddar cheese
> 1½ teaspoons pizza or Italian seasoning
> 1½ cups cooked rotini pasta, rinsed and drained
> 4 (¾-ounce) slices Kraft reduced-fat mozzarella cheese

Preheat oven to 350 degrees. Spray an 8-by-8-inch baking dish with olive oil–flavored cooking spray. In a large skillet sprayed with olive oil–flavored cooking spray, brown meat and onion. Stir in mushroom soup, tomatoes, Cheddar cheese, and pizza seasoning. Continue cooking until cheese melts, stirring often. Add rotini pasta. Mix well to combine. Evenly spread mixture into prepared baking dish. Bake for 30 minutes. Arrange mozzarella slices evenly over top. Continue baking for 5 to 6 minutes or until cheese starts to melt. Place baking dish on a wire rack and let set for 5 minutes. Divide into 4 servings.

HINT: Usually 1 cup uncooked rotini pasta cooks to about 1½ cups.

Each serving equals:

HE: 3 Protein • 1¼ Vegetable • ¾ Bread • ½ Slider • 1 Optional Calorie

301 Calories • 9 gm Fat • 25 gm Protein • 30 gm Carbohydrate • 507 mg Sodium • 498 mg Calcium • 3 gm Fiber

DIABETIC EXCHANGES: 3 Meat • 1½ Starch/Carbohydrate • 1 Vegetable

CARB CHOICES: 2

Pizza Spaghetti Skillet

This simple, speedy supper combines the best of both in one hot and filling dish! The preparation for cooking takes minutes, and you'll be seated at the table before you've had time to practice your Italian lessons. ☻ Serves 4 (1¼ cups)

8 ounces extra-lean ground sirloin beef or turkey breast
1 cup chopped onion
2 cups chopped fresh mushrooms
1 (15-ounce) can diced tomatoes, undrained
1 (8-ounce) can Hunt's Tomato Sauce
1 cup water
1 tablespoon pizza or Italian seasoning
1 tablespoon Splenda Granular
1 cup broken uncooked spaghetti
¼ cup sliced ripe olives
¾ cup shredded Kraft reduced-fat mozzarella cheese

In a large skillet sprayed with olive oil–flavored cooking spray, brown meat, onion, and mushrooms. Add undrained tomatoes, tomato sauce, water, pizza seasoning, and Splenda. Mix well to combine. Stir in uncooked spaghetti and olives. Lower heat, cover, and simmer for 15 minutes or until spaghetti is tender, stirring occasionally. Just before serving, stir in mozzarella cheese.

Each serving equals:

HE: 3 Vegetable • 2¼ Protein • ¾ Bread • ¼ Fat • 1 Optional Calorie

231 Calories • 7 gm Fat • 20 gm Protein • 22 gm Carbohydrate •
375 mg Sodium • 206 mg Calcium • 3 gm Fiber

DIABETIC EXCHANGES: 3 Vegetable • 2 Meat • 1 Starch

CARB CHOICES: 1½

Pizza Runzas

There's nothing like fresh-baked rolls, is there? Now that we can purchase frozen yeast dough at the supermarket, we can enjoy this luxurious pleasure at home. Set these out to rise, go out to do your errands, and you're ready to cook when you walk in the door!

☻ Serves 8

> 8 Rhodes frozen yeast dinner rolls
> 8 ounces extra-lean ground sirloin beef or
>   turkey breast
> ½ cup finely chopped onion
> ½ cup finely chopped green bell pepper
> ¼ cup reduced-sodium ketchup
> 2 teaspoons pizza or Italian seasoning
> ½ cup shredded Kraft reduced-fat Cheddar
>   cheese

Spray a 10-by-13-inch baking sheet with butter-flavored cooking spray. Evenly space frozen rolls on prepared baking sheet. Cover with a clean cloth and let thaw and rise, about 4 to 5 hours. In a large skillet sprayed with olive oil–flavored cooking spray, combine meat, onion, and green pepper. Stir in ketchup and pizza seasoning. Cook 10 to 12 minutes, stirring often. Remove from heat and place skillet on a wire rack and allow to cool completely. When rolls have risen, flatten one at a time. Stir Cheddar cheese into cooled meat mixture. Spoon a generous tablespoon of filling mixture in center of each flattened roll. Gently cover filling and form into roll. Place filled rolls seam-side down onto baking sheet. When through forming rolls, lightly spray tops with butter-flavored cooking spray. Cover with cloth again and let rolls rest for 10 to 15 minutes. Preheat oven to 400 degrees. Bake for 15 to 18 minutes or until rolls are golden brown. Remove from oven and spray again with butter-flavored cooking spray. Place baking sheet on a wire rack and let set for 2 to 3 minutes before serving.

Each serving equals:

HE: 1 Bread • 1 Protein • ¼ Vegetable • 7 Optional Calories

148 Calories • 4 gm Fat • 10 gm Protein • 18 gm Carbohydrate • 118 mg Sodium • 58 mg Calcium • 1 gm Fiber

DIABETIC EXCHANGES: 1 Starch • 1 Meat

CARB CHOICES: 1

Pizza Biscuit Ring

Here's a fun way to enjoy the spirited flavor of pizza in a healthy, cheesy snack! Just remember to let them set or you'll burn your mouth on the crusty hot cheese!   ☻   Serves 6

1 (7.5-ounce) can Pillsbury refrigerated buttermilk biscuits
⅓ cup reduced-sodium ketchup
1½ teaspoons pizza or Italian seasoning
¼ cup Kraft Reduced Fat Parmesan Style Grated Topping
¼ cup shredded Kraft reduced-fat mozzarella cheese
¼ cup shredded Kraft reduced-fat Cheddar cheese

Preheat oven to 425 degrees. Spray a 9-inch pie plate with olive oil–flavored cooking spray. Separate biscuits. Cut each biscuit into 3 pieces. In a small bowl, combine ketchup and pizza seasoning. Dip biscuit pieces into ketchup mixture, then into Parmesan cheese. Arrange coated pieces in prepared pie plate. Sprinkle any remaining Parmesan cheese and ketchup mixture evenly over biscuit pieces. Evenly sprinkle mozzarella and Cheddar cheeses over top. Bake for 15 to 20 minutes or until golden brown and cheeses are melted. Place pie plate on a wire rack and let set for at least 5 minutes. Cut into 6 wedges.

Each serving equals:

HE: 1¼ Bread • ½ Protein • 14 Optional Calories

167 Calories • 7 gm Fat • 5 gm Protein • 21 gm Carbohydrate • 459 mg Sodium • 100 mg Calcium • 1 gm Fiber

DIABETIC EXCHANGES: 1 Starch • ½ Meat • ½ Fat

CARB CHOICES: 1½

Cheesy Pizza Roll-Ups

I was never a contestant in the Pillsbury Bake-Off, though I enjoy watching it every year and marveling at the creativity of cooks from all over this country. I bet these yummy appetizers would have intrigued the judges in that category! ☻ Serves 8

> 1 (8-ounce) can Pillsbury Reduced Fat Crescent Rolls
> 1 (8-ounce) can Hunt's Tomato Sauce ☆
> 1½ teaspoons pizza or Italian seasoning ☆
> ¼ cup Kraft Reduced Fat Parmesan Style Grated Topping
> ¾ cup shredded Kraft reduced-fat mozzarella cheese
> 1 (15-ounce) can diced tomatoes, undrained
> 1 tablespoon Splenda Granular

Preheat oven to 375 degrees. Spray a rimmed 10-by-15-inch baking sheet with olive oil–flavored cooking spray. Unroll crescent rolls and press perforations together between the triangles to form 4 rectangles. In a medium bowl, combine 2 tablespoons tomato sauce, 1 teaspoon pizza seasoning, and Parmesan cheese. Add mozzarella cheese. Mix well to combine. Evenly divide mixture among the 4 rectangles, spreading to within 1 inch of edges. Roll each rectangle up jelly-roll fashion, starting with long side. Seal edges. Cut each in half and place seam-side down on prepared baking sheet. Bake for 12 to 15 minutes or until golden brown. Meanwhile, in a medium saucepan, combine undrained tomatoes, remaining 6 tablespoons tomato sauce, Splenda, and remaining ½ teaspoon pizza seasoning. Simmer over low heat while roll-ups bake, stirring occasionally. When serving, place 1 roll-up on a plate and spoon a scant ¼ cup sauce over top.

Each serving equals:

HE: 1 Bread • 1 Vegetable • ½ Protein • 1 Optional Calorie

159 Calories • 7 gm Fat • 5 gm Protein • 19 gm Carbohydrate • 576 mg Sodium • 106 mg Calcium • 2 gm Fiber

DIABETIC EXCHANGES: 1 Starch • 1 Vegetable • ½ Meat • ½ Fat

CARB CHOICES: 1

Pizza Kolaches

These were inspired by a beloved family tradition, brought by my Bohemian ancestors from Eastern Europe all those many years ago. This pastry, served open-faced with a delicious topping, are still prepared the old-fashioned way in the Czech Republic and nearby regions. Usually fruit-filled, they also work as savory delights.

◐ Serves 8 (2 each)

> 16 Rhodes frozen yeast rolls
> 8 ounces extra-lean ground sirloin beef or turkey breast
> ½ cup chopped onion
> 1 (8-ounce) can Hunt's Tomato Sauce
> 1½ teaspoons pizza or Italian seasoning
> 1 tablespoon Splenda Granular
> 1 (2.5-ounce) jar sliced mushrooms, drained
> ½ cup shredded Kraft reduced-fat Cheddar cheese
> ½ cup shredded Kraft reduced-fat mozzarella cheese

Spray 2 large baking sheets with olive oil–flavored cooking spray. Evenly space frozen rolls on prepared baking sheets. Cover with a clean cloth and let thaw and rise, about 4 to 5 hours. In a large skillet sprayed with olive oil–flavored cooking spray, brown meat and onion. Stir in tomato sauce, pizza seasoning, and Splenda. Add mushrooms. Mix well to combine. Remove from heat and place skillet on a wire rack and allow to cool completely. Make an indentation in center of each roll. Evenly spoon a full tablespoon of meat mixture into center of each roll. In a small bowl, combine Cheddar and mozzarella cheeses. Sprinkle 1 tablespoon cheese mixture over top of each. Preheat oven to 400 degrees. Let kolaches set for 10 minutes. Lightly spray top of each roll with olive oil–flavored cooking spray. Bake for 12 to 14 minutes or until rolls are golden brown. Place baking sheets on wire racks. Lightly spray tops again with olive oil–flavored cooking spray. Let set for 2 to 3 minutes before serving.

HINT: Good warm or cold.

Each serving equals:

HE: 2 Bread • 1¼ Protein • ¾ Vegetable • 1 Optional Calorie

246 Calories • 6 gm Fat • 16 gm Protein • 32 gm Carbohydrate • 454 mg Sodium • 111 mg Calcium • 2 gm Fiber

DIABETIC EXCHANGES: 2 Starch • 1½ Meat • ½ Vegetable

CARB CHOICES: 2

Popovers with Pizza Sauce

Talk about lip-smacking, smile-producing, I-just-can't-resist-'em good! The power of pizza flavor is undeniable, and these will get your dinner guests in a happy mood.   ☺   Serves 6

1 cup water
⅓ cup Carnation Nonfat Dry Milk Powder
2 eggs, or equivalent in egg substitute
1 tablespoon I Can't Believe It's Not Butter! Light Margarine
1 cups + 2 tablespoons all-purpose flour
¼ teaspoon table salt
1 (10¾-ounce) can Healthy Request Tomato Soup
1 (15-ounce) can diced tomatoes, undrained
½ cup Land O Lakes Fat Free Half & Half
1 tablespoon pizza or Italian seasoning
6 tablespoons Kraft Reduced Fat Parmesan Style Grated Topping

Preheat oven to 425 degrees. Spray 6 (8-ounce) custard cups with butter-flavored cooking spray. In a blender container, combine water, dry milk powder, and eggs. Cover and process on BLEND for 15 seconds. Add margarine, flour, and salt. Re-cover and process on BLEND for 20 seconds, or until mixture is smooth. Pour mixture evenly into prepared custard cups. Arrange custard cups on a baking sheet. Bake for 22 to 26 minutes or until popovers are puffed and brown. Pierce the side of each popover with a sharp knife to allow steam to escape. Meanwhile, in a medium saucepan sprayed with olive oil–flavored cooking spray, combine tomato soup, undrained tomatoes, half & half, and pizza seasoning. Cook over medium heat for 4 to 5 minutes or until mixture is heated through, stirring often. For each serving, place 1 popover on a plate, spoon about ½ cup pizza sauce over popover, and sprinkle 1 tablespoon Parmesan cheese over top. Serve at once.

Each serving equals:

HE: 1 Bread • ⅔ Vegetable • ½ Protein • ¼ Fat • ¾ Slider •
7 Optional Calories

217 Calories • 5 gm Fat • 8 gm Protein • 35 gm Carbohydrate •
576 mg Sodium • 138 mg Calcium • 2 gm Fiber

DIABETIC EXCHANGES: 2 Starch/Carbohydrate • 1 Vegetable • ½ Meat

CARB CHOICES: 2

Marinara Pizza Bread Casserole

Here's a lively side dish sure to appeal to everyone who loves Italian flavors—and bread! Rich in veggies and cheese, this recipe is one of those from peasant cuisine that tastes good enough to serve to nobility. ☺ Serves 4

½ cup chopped onion
½ cup chopped green bell pepper
1 (8-ounce) can Hunt's Tomato Sauce
½ cup reduced-sodium tomato juice
1 (8-ounce) can tomatoes, chopped and undrained
1 (2.5-ounce) jar sliced mushrooms, drained
¼ cup Kraft Reduced Fat Parmesan Style Grated Topping
2 teaspoons pizza or Italian seasoning
½ teaspoon dried minced garlic
1 tablespoon Splenda Granular
6 slices reduced-calorie Italian or white bread, toasted and
    cut into 1-inch cubes
¾ cup shredded Kraft reduced-fat mozzarella cheese

Preheat oven to 375 degrees. Spray an 8-by-8-inch baking dish with olive oil–flavored cooking spray. In a large skillet sprayed with olive oil–flavored cooking spray, sauté onion and green pepper for 5 minutes or until tender. Stir in tomato sauce, tomato juice, undrained tomatoes, and mushrooms. Add Parmesan cheese, pizza seasoning, garlic, and Splenda. Mix well to combine. Fold in bread pieces. Evenly spoon hot mixture into prepared baking dish. Sprinkle mozzarella cheese evenly over top. Bake for 25 to 30 minutes. Place baking dish on a wire rack and let set for 5 minutes. Divide into 4 servings.

Each serving equals:

HE: 2½ Vegetable • 1 Protein • ¾ Bread • 1 Optional Calorie

197 Calories • 5 gm Fat • 12 gm Protein • 26 gm Carbohydrate •
865 mg Sodium • 399 mg Calcium • 3 gm Fiber

DIABETIC EXCHANGES: 2 Vegetable • 1 Meat • 1 Starch

CARB CHOICES: 2

Pizzeria Biscuit Cups

Perfect for feeding the grandkids on a visit or a crowd for a party, these handheld delights are as much fun to eat as they are to bake!

◑ Serves 5 (2 each)

8 ounces extra-lean ground sirloin beef or turkey breast
¼ cup chopped onion
¼ cup chopped green bell pepper
1 (8-ounce) can Hunt's Tomato Sauce
1½ teaspoons pizza or Italian seasoning
1 tablespoon Splenda Granular
1 (7.5-ounce) can Pillsbury refrigerated biscuits
6 tablespoons shredded Kraft reduced-fat mozzarella cheese
¼ cup shredded Kraft reduced-fat Cheddar cheese

Preheat oven to 400 degrees. In a large skillet sprayed with olive oil–flavored cooking spray, brown meat, onion, and green pepper. Add tomato sauce, pizza seasoning, and Splenda. Mix well to combine. Lower heat and simmer for 5 minutes, stirring occasionally. Meanwhile, separate biscuits and place each biscuit in an ungreased muffin cup, pressing dough up sides to edge of cup. Evenly spoon a full 2 tablespoons meat mixture into each cup. Bake for 10 minutes. In a small bowl, combine mozzarella and Cheddar cheeses. Evenly sprinkle 1 tablespoon cheese mixture over top of each. Continue baking for 2 to 3 minutes or until biscuits are golden brown and cheese is melted. Place muffin pan on a wire rack and let set for 2 to 3 minutes. Serve at once.

HINT: Fill unused muffin wells with water. It protects the muffin pan and ensures even baking.

Each serving equals:

HE: 1¾ Protein • 1½ Bread • 1 Vegetable • 4 Optional Calories

209 Calories • 5 gm Fat • 16 gm Protein • 25 gm Carbohydrate • 704 mg Sodium • 110 mg Calcium • 1 gm Fiber

DIABETIC EXCHANGES: 1½ Meat • 1½ Starch • 1 Vegetable

CARB CHOICES: 1½

Popover Pizza Casserole

Here's a fun way to get all that pizza pleasure in one wonderful dish! I've taken the recipe for those air-filled pastries and joined it with a hearty pizza filling, with a splendidly tasty result.

⚬ Serves 6

> 8 ounces extra-lean ground sirloin beef or
> turkey breast
> ½ cup chopped onion
> ½ cup chopped green bell pepper
> 1 (15-ounce) can Hunt's Tomato Sauce
> 1 (8-ounce) can tomatoes, finely chopped and
> undrained
> 1 (2.5-ounce) jar sliced mushrooms, drained
> 1½ teaspoons pizza or Italian seasoning
> 1 tablespoon Splenda Granular
> 2 eggs, or equivalent in egg substitute
> ¾ cup fat-free milk
> 1 tablespoon vegetable oil
> 1 cup + 2 tablespoons all-purpose flour
> ¼ cup Kraft Reduced Fat Parmesan Style Grated
> Topping
> ¾ cup shredded Kraft reduced-fat mozzarella cheese

Preheat oven to 400 degrees. Spray an 8-by-8-inch baking dish with olive oil–flavored cooking spray. In a large skillet sprayed with olive oil–flavored cooking spray, brown meat, onion, and green pepper. Stir in tomato sauce, undrained tomatoes, mushrooms, pizza seasoning, and Splenda. Bring mixture to a boil. Lower heat and simmer for 5 minutes, stirring occasionally. Meanwhile, in a medium bowl, combine eggs, milk, and oil. Add flour and Parmesan cheese. Mix well to combine. Spoon hot meat mixture into prepared baking dish. Sprinkle mozzarella cheese evenly over meat mixture. Evenly pour batter mixture over top. Lightly spray top with olive oil–flavored cooking spray. Bake for

25 to 30 minutes or until top is puffed and golden brown. Place baking dish on a wire rack and let set for 5 minutes. Divide into 6 servings.

Each serving equals:

HE: 2 Protein • 2 Vegetable • 1 Bread • ½ Fat • 14 Optional Calories

287 Calories • 9 gm Fat • 19 gm Protein • 30 gm Carbohydrate • 706 mg Sodium • 207 mg Calcium • 3 gm Fiber

DIABETIC EXCHANGES: 2 Meat • 2 Vegetable • 1 Starch • ½ Fat

CARB CHOICES: 2

Baked Pizza Pie

"But wait," you might say, "aren't all pizzas baked?" I'll solve the mystery for you—this is actually a two-crust pie stuffed with pizza flavor. Isn't that a recipe for supreme satisfaction? Mmmm . . .

Serves 8

> 1 Pillsbury refrigerated unbaked 9-inch pie
>   crust
> 8 ounces extra-lean ground sirloin beef or
>   turkey breast
> 1 cup chopped onion
> 1 cup chopped green bell pepper
> 1 (15-ounce) can diced tomatoes, undrained
> 1 tablespoon all-purpose flour
> 1 (4-ounce) can sliced mushrooms, drained
> 1 tablespoon pizza or Italian seasoning
> ¾ cup shredded Kraft reduced-fat Cheddar cheese
> ¾ cup shredded Kraft reduced-fat mozzarella cheese

Let pie crust set at room temperature for 20 minutes, then cut in half on folded line. Preheat oven to 425 degrees. Gently roll each half into a ball. Wipe counter with a wet cloth and place a sheet of waxed paper over damp spot. Place 1 of the balls on the waxed paper. Cover with another piece of waxed paper and roll out with rolling pin. Carefully remove waxed paper on one side and place into an 8-inch pie plate. Remove other piece of waxed paper. In a large skillet sprayed with olive oil–flavored cooking spray, brown meat, onion, and green pepper. Stir in undrained tomatoes, flour, mushrooms, and pizza seasoning. Spoon hot mixture into prepared pie crust. Sprinkle Cheddar and mozzarella cheeses evenly over top. Repeat process for rolling out remaining pie crust half. Place on top of filling mixture and flute edges. Lightly spray top crust with olive oil–flavored cooking spray. Make 8 slashes to allow steam to escape. Bake for 30 minutes or until crust is golden brown. Place pie plate on a wire rack and let set for 10 minutes. Cut into 8 servings.

Each serving equals:

HE: 1½ Protein • 1¼ Vegetable • 1 Bread • ½ Fat • 4 Optional Calories

244 Calories • 12 gm Fat • 13 gm Protein • 21 gm Carbohydrate •
339 mg Sodium • 184 mg Calcium • 2 gm Fiber

DIABETIC EXCHANGES: 1½ Meat • 1 Vegetable • 1 Starch • 1 Fat

CARB CHOICES: 1½

Bubble Pizza Deluxe

This simple dish is always a hit with kids of any age, combining a biscuit crust with all the goodies that make pizza a family favorite! If you're a fan of supreme-style pizzas with all kinds of great toppings, try this unique version for a change.   ☻   Serves 6

> 8 ounces extra-lean ground sirloin beef or turkey breast
> 1 (8-ounce) can Hunt's Tomato Sauce
> 1 (15-ounce) can diced tomatoes, undrained
> 1½ teaspoons pizza or Italian seasoning
> 1 tablespoon Splenda Granular
> 3 ounces Hormel reduced-fat pepperoni, diced
> 1 (2.5-ounce) jar sliced mushrooms, drained
> 1 (7.5-ounce) can Pillsbury refrigerated biscuits
> ¾ cup shredded Kraft reduced-fat mozzarella cheese
> 6 tablespoons shredded Kraft reduced-fat Cheddar cheese

Preheat oven to 400 degrees. Spray an 8-by-8-inch baking dish with olive oil–flavored cooking spray. In a large skillet sprayed with olive oil–flavored cooking spray, brown meat. Stir in tomato sauce, undrained tomatoes, pizza seasoning, and Splenda. Add pepperoni and mushrooms. Mix well to combine. Lower heat and simmer for 5 minutes, stirring occasionally. Meanwhile, separate biscuits and cut each into 3 pieces. Evenly arrange biscuit pieces in prepared baking dish. Spoon hot meat mixture evenly over biscuit pieces. Sprinkle mozzarella and Cheddar cheeses evenly over top. Bake for 12 to 14 minutes or until biscuit pieces are done. Place baking dish on a wire rack and let set for 5 minutes. Cut into 6 servings.

Each serving equals:

HE: 2¼ Protein • 1½ Vegetable • 1¼ Bread • 1 Optional Calorie

256 Calories • 8 gm Fat • 21 gm Protein • 25 gm Carbohydrate • 959 mg Sodium • 321 mg Calcium • 3 gm Fiber

DIABETIC EXCHANGES: 2 Meat • 1 Vegetable • 1 Starch

CARB CHOICES: 1½

Pizza-Stuffed Green Peppers

How about pizza served in a pepper instead of on top of a traditional crust? I thought it was a good idea, and so I decided to try it! I'm thrilled to report that it's downright *fabuloso*!

● Serves 6

> 6 medium-sized green bell peppers
> 2 cups boiling water
> 8 ounces extra-lean ground sirloin beef or turkey breast
> ½ cup chopped onion
> 1 (14.5-ounce) can Hunt's Tomatoes Diced in Sauce
> 1 tablespoon Splenda Granular
> 2 teaspoons pizza or Italian seasoning
> ½ cup shredded Kraft reduced-fat Cheddar cheese ☆
> ½ cup shredded Kraft reduced-fat mozzarella cheese ☆
> 3 slices reduced-calorie Italian or white bread, toasted and
>   cut into 1-inch cubes

Preheat oven to 350 degrees. Cut tops from green peppers. Discard seeds and membrane. Place peppers in a large saucepan with boiling water. Cook on medium heat for 5 minutes. Drain well. Meanwhile, in a large skillet sprayed with olive oil–flavored cooking spray, brown meat and onion. Stir in tomato sauce, Splenda, and pizza seasoning. Add ¼ cup Cheddar cheese and ¼ cup mozzarella cheese. Mix well to combine. Fold in toast cubes. Evenly spoon a full ½ cup meat mixture into each green pepper. Arrange peppers in an 8-by-8-inch baking dish. Sprinkle 1½ tablespoons Cheddar cheese and 1½ tablespoons mozzarella cheese over top of each. Bake for 25 to 30 minutes. Place baking dish on a wire rack and let set for 5 minutes.

Each serving equals:

HE: 2 Vegetable • 1⅔ Protein • ¼ Bread • 14 Optional Calories

165 Calories • 5 gm Fat • 16 gm Protein • 15 gm Carbohydrate • 318 mg Sodium • 228 mg Calcium • 3 gm Fiber

DIABETIC EXCHANGES: 2 Vegetable • 1½ Meat

CARB CHOICES: 1

Mixed-Up Pizza

The challenge was this: make a pizza without a crust, and make it good. You might think that was kind of a "mixed-up" idea, but I think this jumble of ingredients baked up together is a pleasurable puzzle with a delicious solution. ☺ Serves 6

8 ounces extra-lean ground sirloin beef or turkey breast
1 (2.5-ounce) jar sliced mushrooms, drained
½ cup chopped green bell pepper
½ cup chopped onion
⅓ cup sliced ripe olives
1 (14.5-ounce) can Hunt's Tomatoes Diced in Sauce
1 tablespoon Splenda Granular
2 teaspoons pizza or Italian seasoning
6 slices reduced-calorie Italian or white bread, toasted and
    cut into ½-inch cubes
½ cup shredded Kraft reduced-fat Cheddar cheese
¼ cup shredded Kraft reduced-fat mozzarella cheese

Preheat oven to 350 degrees. Spray an 8-by-8-inch baking dish with olive oil–flavored cooking spray. In a large skillet sprayed with olive oil–flavored cooking spray, sauté meat, mushrooms, green pepper, onion, and olives. Stir in tomato sauce, Splenda, and pizza seasoning. Add toast cubes. Mix gently to combine. Evenly spoon mixture into prepared baking dish. Bake, uncovered, for 20 minutes. Sprinkle Cheddar and mozzarella cheeses evenly over top. Continue baking for 10 minutes or until cheese is melted. Place baking dish on a wire rack and let set for 5 minutes. Divide into 6 servings.

Each serving equals:

HE: 1½ Bread • 1½ Protein • 1¼ Vegetable • ¼ Fat

170 Calories • 6 gm Fat • 15 gm Protein • 14 gm Carbohydrate • 459 mg Sodium • 168 mg Calcium • 3 gm Fiber

DIABETIC EXCHANGES: 1½ Meat • 1 Vegetable • ½ Starch • ½ Fat

CARB CHOICES: 1

Pizza Lover's Strata

Layers of bread, just like layers of rock in the earth, often produce exciting results. Some compare this to a savory bread pudding, so see if you agree. ☻ Serves 4

> 8 ounces extra-lean ground sirloin beef or turkey breast
> 1 (8-ounce) can Hunt's Tomato Sauce
> 1 (15-ounce) can diced tomatoes, undrained
> 2 teaspoons pizza or Italian seasoning
> 8 slices reduced-calorie Italian or white bread ☆
> ¾ cup shredded Kraft reduced-fat mozzarella cheese ☆
> 2 eggs, or equivalent in egg substitute
> ¾ cup fat-free milk
> ¼ cup Land O Lakes Fat Free Half & Half
> 1 teaspoon dried parsley flakes

Preheat oven to 350 degrees. Spray an 8-by-8-inch baking dish with olive oil–flavored cooking spray. In a large skillet sprayed with olive oil–flavored cooking spray, brown meat. Stir in tomato sauce, undrained tomatoes, and pizza seasoning. Lower heat and simmer for 5 minutes, stirring occasionally. Remove from heat. Place 4 slices of bread in prepared baking dish. Sprinkle half of mozzarella cheese over bread. Spoon half of meat mixture over cheese. Repeat layers. In a medium bowl, beat eggs with a wire whisk. Add milk, half & half, and parsley flakes. Mix well to combine. Pour milk mixture evenly over top. Bake for 60 minutes or until edges are lightly browned and center is firm. Place baking dish on a wire rack and let set for 5 minutes. Divide into 4 servings.

HINT: Strata may be covered and refrigerated up to 24 hours before baking.

Each serving equals:

HE: 2¾ Protein • 2 Vegetable • 1 Bread • ¼ Slider • 4 Optional Calories

297 Calories • 9 gm Fat • 28 gm Protein • 26 gm Carbohydrate • 842 mg Sodium • 459 mg Calcium • 3 gm Fiber

DIABETIC EXCHANGES: 3 Meat • 2 Vegetable • 1 Starch

CARB CHOICES: 1½

Rice Pizza

Texture, texture, texture—one of the most intriguing aspects of any recipe, and a great reason for baking a pizza dish with a crust made of rice! Unusual, yes, but good.　◑　Serves 6

> 8 ounces extra-lean ground sirloin beef or
> turkey breast
> ½ cup chopped onion
> ½ cup chopped green bell pepper
> ½ teaspoon poultry seasoning
> ¼ teaspoon ground sage
> ¼ teaspoon garlic powder
> 3 cups cooked rice
> 2 eggs, beaten, or equivalent in egg substitute
> ¾ cup shredded Kraft reduced-fat mozzarella
> cheese ☆
> 1 (15-ounce) can Hunt's Tomato Sauce
> 1½ teaspoons Italian seasoning
> ¼ cup Kraft Reduced Fat Parmesan Style Grated
> Topping

Preheat oven to 450 degrees. Spray a 12-inch round pizza pan with olive oil–flavored cooking spray. In a large skillet sprayed with butter-flavored cooking spray, brown meat, onion, green pepper, poultry seasoning, sage, and garlic powder. In a medium bowl, combine rice, eggs, and ¼ cup mozzarella cheese. Evenly spread rice mixture onto prepared pizza pan. Bake for 20 minutes. In a small bowl, combine tomato sauce and Italian seasoning. Spread sauce evenly over partially baked crust and spoon browned meat mixture evenly over sauce. Sprinkle remaining ½ cup mozzarella cheese and Parmesan cheese evenly over top. Continue baking for 10 to 15 minutes or until crust is golden brown and cheese is melted. Place pan on a wire rack and let set for 5 minutes. Cut into 6 wedges.

HINT: Usually 2 cups uncooked instant or 1½ cups regular rice cooks to about 3 cups.

Each serving equals:

HE: 2 Protein • 1½ Vegetable • 1 Bread

247 Calories • 7 gm Fat • 16 gm Protein • 30 gm Carbohydrate • 574 mg Sodium • 153 mg Calcium • 2 gm Fiber

DIABETIC EXCHANGES: 2 Meat • 1½ Starch • 1 Vegetable

CARB CHOICES: 2

Pizza Meatballs

Instead of making the same meatballs you always do to serve with spaghetti or other pasta, why not stir something special into the mix? Here's a fresh and fun approach to this Italian favorite.

○ Serves 6 (3 each & ⅓ cup sauce)

> 16 ounces extra-lean ground sirloin beef or turkey breast
> ¾ cup dried fine bread crumbs
> 2 teaspoons pizza seasoning ☆
> 1 (10¾-ounce) can Healthy Request Tomato Soup ☆
> 1 (15-ounce) can diced tomatoes, undrained
> 1 cup finely chopped onion

Spray a slow cooker container with olive oil–flavored cooking spray. In a large bowl, combine meat, bread crumbs, 1½ teaspoons pizza seasoning, and ¼ cup tomato soup. Mix well to combine. Shape into 18 (1½-inch) meatballs. Gently arrange meatballs in prepared slow cooker container. In a small bowl, combine remaining tomato soup, undrained tomatoes, onion, and remaining ½ teaspoon pizza seasoning. Spoon sauce mixture evenly over meatballs. Cover and cook on LOW for 4 to 6 hours. Evenly divide into 6 servings.

HINT: Good as is or spooned over pasta, toast, or baked potato.

Each serving equals:

HE: 2 Protein • 1 Vegetable • ⅔ Bread • ¼ Slider • 10 Optional Calories

221 Calories • 5 gm Fat • 18 gm Protein • 26 gm Carbohydrate •
576 mg Sodium • 36 mg Calcium • 2 gm Fiber

DIABETIC EXCHANGES: 2 Meat • 1 Vegetable • 1 Starch/Carbohydrate

CARB CHOICES: 1½

Pizza "Steaks"

As someone once said, they're not "ham" burgers, they're made of steak, so call them what they really are! Okay, okay, I'm ready and willing to do that, especially when I can top those "steaks" with a super-savory sauce. ◑ Serves 6

16 ounces extra-lean ground sirloin beef or turkey breast
½ cup + 1 tablespoon dried fine bread crumbs
1 tablespoon pizza seasoning ☆
1 (15-ounce) can Hunt's Tomato Sauce ☆
1 cup finely chopped onion
1½ cups finely chopped fresh mushrooms
1 (15-ounce) can diced tomatoes, undrained
2 tablespoons Splenda Granular
3 (¾-ounce) slices Kraft reduced-fat mozzarella cheese

In a large bowl, combine meat, bread crumbs, 1½ teaspoons pizza seasoning, and ¼ cup tomato sauce. Mix well to combine. Using a ⅓ cup measuring cup as a guide, form into 6 "steaks." Place "steaks" in a large skillet sprayed with olive oil–flavored cooking spray. Brown for 5 to 6 minutes on each side. Meanwhile, in a medium saucepan sprayed with olive oil–flavored cooking spray, sauté onion and mushrooms for 6 to 8 minutes. Add remaining tomato sauce, undrained tomatoes, Splenda, and remaining 1½ teaspoons pizza seasoning. Mix well to combine. Lower heat and simmer until "steaks" are cooked through. Cut each slice of mozzarella cheese in half. For each serving, place 1 "steak" on a plate, arrange 1 piece of cheese over "steak," and spoon a full ¼ cup sauce over top.

Each serving equals:

HE: 2½ Protein • 2½ Vegetable • ½ Bread • 2 Optional Calories

206 Calories • 6 gm Fat • 21 gm Protein • 17 gm Carbohydrate • 483 mg Sodium • 123 mg Calcium • 3 gm Fiber

DIABETIC EXCHANGES: 2½ Meat • 2½ Vegetable • ½ Starch

CARB CHOICES: 1

Baked Philly Pizza Steaks

Take two great traditions from the city that gave us the Continental Congress and the Declaration of Independence, and you might end up with this delicious combo—a pizza-flavored Philly cheese steak.

○ Serves 4

> 4 (4-ounce) lean minute or cube steaks
> 4 (¾-ounce) slices Kraft reduced-fat mozzarella cheese
> 1 cup onion slices
> ½ cup chopped green bell pepper
> 1 (10¾-ounce) can Healthy Request Tomato Soup
> 1 (2.5-ounce) jar sliced mushrooms, drained
> 1½ teaspoons pizza seasoning

Preheat oven to 350 degrees. Spray an 8-by-8-inch baking dish with olive oil–flavored cooking spray. In a large skillet sprayed with olive oil–flavored cooking spray, brown steaks for 4 to 5 minutes on each side. Evenly arrange browned steaks in prepared baking dish. Top each with 1 slice mozzarella cheese. In same skillet, sauté onion and green pepper for 5 minutes. Stir in tomato soup, mushrooms, and pizza seasoning. Continue cooking for 2 to 3 minutes. Spoon soup mixture evenly over steaks. Cover and bake for 30 minutes. Uncover and continue baking for 10 to 15 minutes or until steaks are tender. Place baking dish on a wire rack and let set for 5 minutes. Divide into 4 servings.

Each serving equals:

HE: 4 Protein • 1 Vegetable • ½ Slider • 5 Optional Calories

284 Calories • 8 gm Fat • 35 gm Protein • 18 gm Carbohydrate • 506 mg Sodium • 321 mg Calcium • 2 gm Fiber

DIABETIC EXCHANGES: 4 Meat • 1 Vegetable • ½ Other Carbohydrate

CARB CHOICES: 1

Mozzarella Pizza Muffins

There's just something *fun* about savory entrée muffins—and you've got to admit that they're great for those times when you're eating on the run.   ☺   Serves 8

> 1½ cups Bisquick Heart Smart Baking Mix
> 2 tablespoons Splenda Granular
> 1½ teaspoons pizza or Italian seasoning
> ¾ cup shredded Kraft reduced-fat mozzarella cheese
> ½ cup fat-free milk
> 2 tablespoons Land O Lakes no-fat sour cream
> 1 tablespoon + 1 teaspoon olive oil
> 1 egg, or equivalent in egg substitute
> ¾ cup peeled and finely chopped tomatoes, very well
>   drained
> ¼ cup finely chopped onion

Preheat oven to 375 degrees. Spray 8 wells of a muffin pan with butter-flavored cooking spray or line with paper liners. In a large bowl, combine baking mix, Splenda, and pizza seasoning. Stir in mozzarella cheese. In a small bowl, combine milk, sour cream, olive oil, and egg. Add milk mixture to baking mix mixture. Stir gently just to combine. Gently fold in tomatoes and onion. Evenly spoon batter into prepared muffin wells. Bake for 20 to 25 minutes or until a toothpick inserted in center comes out clean. Place muffin pan on a wire rack and let set for 5 minutes. Remove muffins from pan and continue cooling on wire rack. Good warm or cold.

Each serving equals:

HE: 1 Bread • ½ Protein • ½ Fat • ¼ Vegetable • 10 Optional Calories

150 Calories • 6 gm Fat • 5 gm Protein • 19 gm Carbohydrate • 345 mg Sodium • 124 mg Calcium • 1 gm Fiber

DIABETIC EXCHANGES: 1 Starch • ½ Meat • ½ Fat

CARB CHOICES: 1

Pizza Loaf Bread

If you love pizza (and I figure you do, since you're holding this cookbook!), consider how much you might enjoy eating your sandwiches on pizza bread! This recipe makes it possible to savor what you adore with a myriad of toppings, from tuna to egg salad, from turkey to a BLT. ● Serves 12

½ cup fat-free milk
½ cup water
1 egg, or equivalent in egg substitute
1 cup peeled and finely chopped fresh tomatoes, very well
    drained ☆
1 tablespoon olive oil
3 cups bread flour
2 tablespoons Splenda Granular
½ cup Kraft Reduced Fat Parmesan Style Grated Topping
1½ teaspoons table salt
2 teaspoons active dry yeast
¼ cup finely chopped onion
¼ cup finely chopped green bell pepper
1½ teaspoons pizza or Italian seasoning

In a bread-machine container, combine milk, water, egg, ½ cup tomatoes, and olive oil. Add bread flour, Splenda, Parmesan cheese, and salt. Make an indentation on top of dry ingredients. Pour yeast into indentation. Follow your bread machine instructions for a 1½-pound loaf. Add remaining tomatoes, onion, green pepper, and pizza seasoning when "add ingredient" signal beeps. Continue following your machine's instructions. Remove loaf from machine and place on a wire rack to cool. Cut into 12 slices. Makes 1 (1½-pound) loaf.

Each serving equals:

HE: 1½ Bread • ¼ Protein • ¼ Fat • ¼ Vegetable • 4 Optional Calories

146 Calories • 2 gm Fat • 6 gm Protein • 26 gm Carbohydrate •
372 mg Sodium • 48 mg Calcium • 1 gm Fiber

DIABETIC EXCHANGES: 1½ Starch

CARB CHOICES: 1½

Pizza Quick Bread

No yeast to rise, no time to waste, and what a treat this bread is, because it features all those great little bits of sensational Italian cured meat. A slice of this is like eating a pizza sandwich—and nothing's wrong with *that*! ☺ Serves 8

> 1½ cups Bisquick Heart Smart Baking Mix
> ¾ cup shredded Kraft reduced-fat Cheddar cheese ☆
> 3 ounces Hormel reduced-fat pepperoni, chopped
> ½ cup fat-free milk
> 1 egg, or equivalent in egg substitute
> 2 tablespoons Land O Lakes no-fat sour cream
> 1 teaspoon pizza or Italian seasoning

Preheat oven to 350 degrees. Spray a 9-inch pie plate with olive oil–flavored cooking spray. In a large bowl, combine baking mix, ½ cup Cheddar cheese, and pepperoni. Add milk, egg, sour cream, and pizza seasoning. Mix gently must to combine. Evenly spread batter into prepared pie plate. Sprinkle remaining ¼ cup Cheddar cheese over top. Bake for 20 to 25 minutes or until a toothpick inserted in center comes out clean. Place pie plate on a wire rack and let set for 5 minutes. Cut into 8 wedges.

Each serving equals:

HE: 1 Bread • ¾ Protein • 16 Optional Calories

175 Calories • 7 gm Fat • 10 gm Protein • 18 gm Carbohydrate • 487 mg Sodium • 168 mg Calcium • 1 gm Fiber

DIABETIC EXCHANGES: 1 Starch • 1 Meat

CARB CHOICES: 1

Pizza Pepperoni Bread

It's like an culinary treasure hunt, to bite into this bread and dis-cover its valuable contents: tangy pepperoni and mouthwatering cheese!   ☻   Serves 8

1 (11-ounce) can Pillsbury refrigerated low-fat French Loaf
1 (8-ounce) Hunt's Tomato Sauce
2 tablespoons Splenda Granular
1½ teaspoons pizza or Italian seasoning
3 ounces Hormel reduced-fat pepperoni slices
1¼ cups shredded Kraft reduced-fat mozzarella cheese

Preheat oven to 375 degrees. Unroll French loaf and place on a large baking sheet. Lightly spray loaf with olive oil–flavored cook-ing spray. In a small bowl, combine tomato sauce, Splenda, and pizza seasoning. Evenly spread tomato sauce over French loaf leav-ing a 1-inch edge on all sides. Place pepperoni slices evenly over sauce mixture. Evenly sprinkle mozzarella cheese over top. Roll up jelly-roll fashion. Seal edges by pinching together. Place seam-side down. Lightly spray top with olive oil–flavored cooking spray. Bake for 23 to 25 minutes or until golden brown. Place baking sheet on a wire rack and let set for 10 minutes. Cut into 8 servings.

Each serving equals:

HE: 1 Bread • 1 Protein • ½ Vegetable • 2 Optional Calories

173 Calories • 5 gm Fat • 12 gm Protein • 21 gm Carbohydrate •
729 mg Sodium • 341 mg Calcium • 1 gm Fiber

DIABETIC EXCHANGES: 1 Starch • 1 Meat • ½ Vegetable

CARB CHOICES: 1½

Pizza Party Fondue

Quick, get on the phone and invite your nearest and dearest to come feast on a potful of fantastic fun! Dipping toasted bread in a pizza sauce mixture is my idea of heaven on a skewer!

❍ Serves 6 (½ cup)

> 8 ounces extra-lean ground sirloin beef or turkey breast
> ½ cup chopped onion
> 2 teaspoons pizza or Italian seasoning
> 1 (14.5-ounce) can Hunt's Tomato Sauce
> 1 cup reduced-sodium tomato juice
> 1 tablespoon Splenda Granular
> 1 tablespoon cornstarch
> ¼ teaspoon dried minced garlic
> ¾ cup shredded Kraft reduced-fat mozzarella cheese
> 12 slices reduced-calorie Italian or white bread, toasted and
>   cut into 1-inch cubes

In a large skillet sprayed with butter-flavored cooking spray, brown meat and onion. Stir in pizza seasoning, tomato sauce, tomato juice, Splenda, cornstarch, and garlic. Simmer for 10 minutes. Pour mixture into fondue pan. Add mozzarella cheese. Mix well to combine. For each serving, spoon ½ sauce in a saucer and use ¼ of toast cubes for dipping.

HINT: If you prefer, leave meat mixture in fondue pan when serving.

Each serving equals:

HE: 1½ Protein • 1½ Vegetable • 1 Bread • 6 Optional Calories

197 Calories • 5 gm Fat • 17 gm Protein • 21 gm Carbohydrate •
504 mg Sodium • 248 mg Calcium • 2 gm Fiber

DIABETIC EXCHANGES: 1½ Meat • 1½ Vegetable • 1 Starch

CARB CHOICES: 1½

Ham and Potato Brunch Pizza

This is a festive entrée to offer your family some dreary Sunday morning when they're expecting the usual. Instead, dazzle them with this savory combination that is well worth getting up for!

☻ Serves 8

1 (11-ounce) can Pillsbury refrigerated low-fat
    French Loaf
3 cups frozen loose-packed shredded hash brown
    potatoes
½ cup chopped red bell pepper
½ cup chopped green onion
½ cup Kraft fat-free mayonnaise
½ cup Land O Lakes no-fat sour cream
1 teaspoon dried parsley flakes
⅛ teaspoon black pepper
1½ cups diced Dubuque 97% fat-free ham or any
    extra-lean ham
¾ cup shredded Kraft reduced-fat Cheddar cheese

Preheat oven to 375 degrees. Spray a rimmed 10-by-15-inch baking sheet with butter-flavored cooking spray. Unroll French loaf and pat into prepared baking sheet and up sides of pan to form a rim. Lightly spray top of crust with butter-flavored cooking spray. Bake for 6 minutes. Meanwhile, in a large skillet sprayed with butter-flavored cooking spray, brown potatoes, red pepper, and onion for 5 to 6 minutes. In a medium bowl, combine mayonnaise, sour cream, parsley, and black pepper. Spread mayonnaise mixture evenly over crust. Spoon potato mixture and ham evenly over mayonnaise mixture. Sprinkle Cheddar cheese evenly over top. Continue baking for 6 to 8 minutes or until crust is golden brown and cheese is melted. Place baking sheet on a wire rack and let set for 2 to 3 minutes. Cut into 8 servings.

HINT: Mr. Dell's shredded potatoes are a good choice or shredded raw potatoes, rinsed and patted dry, may be used in place of frozen potatoes.

Each serving equals:

HE: 1½ Protein • 1¼ Bread • ¼ Vegetable • ¼ Slider • 5 Optional Calories

231 Calories • 7 gm Fat • 13 gm Protein • 29 gm Carbohydrate • 648 mg Sodium • 106 mg Calcium • 2 gm Fiber

DIABETIC EXCHANGES: 2 Starch • 1 Meat

CARB CHOICES: 2

Morning Bacon and Eggs Pizza

Now, I promised you pizza for breakfast, didn't I? Here it is, in all its delectable morning glory, a treat for weekend brunches or even every day.   ◑   Serves 8

  1 (11-ounce) can Pillsbury refrigerated low-fat French Loaf
  ½ cup Oscar Mayer or Hormel Real Bacon Bits
  ½ cup chopped green onion
  ½ cup peeled and chopped fresh tomato
  1 cup chopped fresh mushrooms
  ¾ cup shredded Kraft reduced-fat mozzarella cheese
  ¾ cup shredded Kraft reduced-fat Cheddar cheese
  6 eggs, or equivalent in egg substitute
  ¼ cup Land O Lakes Fat Free Half & Half
  1 teaspoon lemon pepper

Preheat oven to 375 degrees. Spray a rimmed 10-by-15-inch baking sheet with butter-flavored cooking spray. Unroll French loaf and pat into prepared baking sheet and up sides of pan to form a rim. Lightly spray top of crust with butter-flavored cooking spray. Bake for 6 minutes. Evenly sprinkle bacon bits, onion, tomato, and mushrooms over partially baked crust. Sprinkle mozzarella and Cheddar cheeses over vegetables. In a large bowl, beat eggs, half & half, and lemon pepper until frothy. Carefully pour egg mixture over top. Continue baking for 8 to 12 minutes or until eggs are set and crust is golden brown. Place baking pan on a wire rack and let set for 5 minutes. Cut into 8 servings.

Each serving equals:

HE: 2 Protein • 1 Bread • ½ Vegetable • ¼ Slider • 8 Optional Calories

242 Calories • 10 gm Fat • 18 gm Protein • 20 gm Carbohydrate • 624 mg Sodium • 198 mg Calcium • 1 gm Fiber

DIABETIC EXCHANGES: 2 Meat • 1 Starch • ½ Vegetable

CARB CHOICES: 1

Peanut Butter and Jelly Breakfast Pizza

For the next slumber party at your house, win the kids' hearts with this witty and wonderful wake-me-up! My grandkids preferred grape, so that's the official "jelly" flavor, but there are so many great choices available now. I think I'd love this with peach.

◐ Serves 8

> 1 (8-ounce) can Pillsbury Reduced Fat Crescent Rolls
> 1 (8-ounce) package Philadelphia fat-free cream cheese
> ½ cup Peter Pan or Skippy reduced-fat peanut butter
> ¾ cup grape spreadable fruit, or any flavor of your choice
> 2 tablespoons chopped dry-roasted peanuts

Preheat oven to 350 degrees. Unroll crescent rolls and separate into 8 triangles. Place triangles on a 12-inch round pizza pan with point toward center. Press triangles together to form a crust. Bake for 6 to 8 minutes or until light golden brown. Place pizza pan on a wire rack. In a medium bowl, stir cream cheese with a sturdy spoon until soft. Stir in peanut butter. Evenly spread cream cheese mixture over warm crust. In a small bowl, stir spreadable fruit until softened. Carefully spread softened fruit over cream cheese layer. Sprinkle peanuts evenly over top. Cut into 8 wedges.

Each serving equals:

HE: 1½ Protein • 1 Bread • 1 Fruit • 1 Fat • 13 Optional Calories

270 Calories • 10 gm Fat • 11 gm Protein • 34 gm Carbohydrate • 461 mg Sodium • 87 mg Calcium • 1 gm Fiber

DIABETIC EXCHANGES: 1½ Starch/Carbohydrate • 1 Meat • 1 Fruit • 1 Fat

CARB CHOICES: 2

Pizza Parties with Pizzazz!

Now you've got dozens and dozens of spectacular pizza inspirations to help you plan your year's celebrations—hey, that rhymes! Here are a few ideas to get you started superbly.

"I Love You This Much" Valentine's Day Brunch

Mediterranean Appetizers
Pizza Quiche
Rosemary Chicken Pizza
Stellar Raspberry-Chocolate Dessert Pizza

"It Might As Well be Spring" Dinner with Friends

Shrimp Cocktail Pizza Bites
Turkey Divan Pizza
Scalloped Pizza Potatoes
Pears Helene Dessert Pizza

"Summer in the City" Independence Day Party

Tomato Mozzarella Bites
Gazpacho Appetizer Pizza
Chicken Caesar Pizza
Diamond Head Blueberry Pizza Dessert

"See You in September" Back to School Splash

Cheesy Tuna Party Squares
Pasta Pizza Salad
Fajita Supreme Pizza
Tropical Sunset Dessert Pizza

"Monday Night Football" Bachelors' Buffet

Mini Mexican Pizza Appetizers
BLT Pizza Supreme
Pastrami Potato Pizza Bake
Chocolate Caramel Dessert Pizza

"Staying Up with Santa" Midnight Supper

Home for the Holidays Appetizer Pizza
Chicago-Style Cheese Lover's Pizza
Potato Pizza Hash
Apricot Nectar Dessert Pizza

Making Healthy

Exchanges Work

for You

You're ready now to begin a wonderful journey to better health. In the preceding pages, you've discovered the remarkable variety of good food available to you when you begin eating the Healthy Exchanges way. You've stocked your pantry and learned many of my food preparation "secrets" that will point you on the way to delicious success.

But before I let you go, I'd like to share a few tips that I've learned while traveling toward healthier eating habits. It took me a long time to learn how to eat *smarter*. In fact, I'm still working on it. But I am getting better. For years, I could *inhale* a five-course meal in five minutes flat—and still make room for a second helping of dessert!

Now I follow certain signposts on the road that help me stay on the right path. I hope these ideas will help point you in the right direction as well.

1. **Eat slowly** so your brain has time to catch up with your tummy. Cut and chew each bite slowly. Try putting your fork down between bites. Stop eating as soon as you feel full. Crumple your napkin and throw it on top of your plate so you don't continue to eat when you are no longer hungry.

2. **Smaller plates** may help you feel more satisfied by your food portions *and* limit the amount you can put on the plate.

3. **Watch portion size.** If you are *truly* hungry, you can always add more food to your plate once you've finished your initial serving. But remember to count the additional food accordingly.

4. **Always eat at your dining room or kitchen table.** You deserve better than nibbling from an open refrigerator or over the sink. Make an attractive place setting, even if you're eating alone. Feed your eyes as well as your stomach. By always eating at a table, you will become much more aware of your true food intake. For some reason, many of us conveniently "forget" the food we swallow while standing over the stove or munching in the car or on the run.

5. **Avoid doing anything else while you are eating.** If you read the paper or watch television while you eat, it's easy to consume too much food without realizing it, because you are concentrating on something else besides what you're eating. Then, when you look down at your plate and see that it's empty, you wonder where all the food went and why you still feel hungry.

Day by day, as you travel the path to good health, it will become easier to make the right choices, to eat *smarter*. But don't ever fool yourself into thinking that you'll be able to put your eating habits on cruise control and forget about them. Making a commitment to eat good healthy food and sticking to it takes some effort. But with all the good-tasting recipes in this Healthy Exchanges cookbook, just think how well you're going to eat—and enjoy it—from now on!

Healthy Lean Bon Appétit!

Index

almonds, 148, 159–60, 163–66
appetizers
  Bacon, Lettuce, and Tomato, 36
  Bacon Pizza Bites, Grande, 30
  Beet and Feta, 43
  Biscuit Cups, Pizzeria, 284
  Biscuit Ring, Pizza, 277
  Cheese Pita Pizza, Stuffed, 35
  Cheesy Pizza Roll-Ups, 278
  Chicken Pizza, Luau, 53–54
  Chicken Salad, Pineapple, 51–52
  Country Club Appetizer Pizza, 50
  Crab Appetizer Pizza, 49
  Egg Salad Snack Pizza, 45
  Fondue, Pizza Party, 302
  French Onion Appetizers, 42
  French Salad Pizza, 33–34
  Gazpacho Appetizer Pizza, 41
  Grande Party Appetizer Pizza,
    57–58
  Ham and Cheese Appetizers, 60
  Ham and Veggie Pizza, 61–62
  Home for the Holidays Pizza,
    55–56
  Italian Salad Appetizer Pizza, 37
  Mediterranean Appetizers, 40
  Mexican Pizza Appetizers, Mini,
    29
  Mexican Pizza Bites, 59
  Olive Pizza Appetizers, 39
  Popovers with Pizza Sauce,
    281–82
  Reuben Party Pizza, 63
  Shrimp and Feta Appetizers, 48
  Shrimp Cocktail Pizza Bites, 47
  Springtime Appetizers, 44
  Tex-Mex Appetizer Pizza, 28
  Tomato Mozzarella Bites, 38
  Tuna Party Squares, Cheesy, 46
  Vegetable-Cheese French Pizza, 31
  Veggie Pizza Appetizers, 32
Apple Betty Pizza Dessert, 211
Apple-Cranberry Dessert, 213–14
Apple Crisp Pizza, 207–08
Apple Crumb Pizza, 205–06
Apple Harvest Dessert Pizza, 209–10
apples
  Apple Betty Pizza Dessert, 211
  Apple-Cranberry Dessert, 213–14
  Apple Crisp Pizza, 207–08
  Apple Crumb Pizza, 205–06
  Apple Harvest Dessert Pizza,
    209–10
  Caramel Apple Pizza Pie, 212
  Maple Apple Dessert Pizza, 219
  Mincemeat Pizza Dessert, 215–16
Apricot Nectar Dessert, 177–78
asparagus, 44, 135
Asparagus and Ham Pizza, 135

Bacon, Lettuce, and Tomato
    Appetizer, 36
Bacon and Eggs Pizza, Morning, 305
Bacon and Tomato Pizzas, 102
Bacon Cheeseburger Pizza, 105
Baked Philly Pizza Steaks, 297
Baked Pizza Pie, 287–88
Banana Cookie Pizza, 203–04

bananas, 185–86, 189–96, 201–04
Banana Split Dessert Pizza, 189–90
Barbeque Chicken Pizza, 96
basil, 70
beans
    black, 78
    great northern, 77
    green, 243
    kidney, 57–58, 113–14, 117–18
    pinto, 79
beef
    Bacon Cheeseburger Pizza, 105
    Baked Pizza Pie, 287–88
    Biscuit Cups, Pizzeria, 284
    Bubble Pizza Deluxe, 289
    Cheeseburgers with Sauce, Inside-Out, 265
    Cheese Steak Pizza, Philly, 125
    Classic Pizza, Cliff's, 106
    Coney Island Pizza, 136
    Creamy Pizza Bake, 273
    Deep-Dish Pizza, Homemade, 111–12
    Fajita Supreme Pizza, 123–24
    Fondue, Pizza Party, 302
    Grande Party Appetizer Pizza, 57–58
    Green Peppers, Pizza-Stuffed, 290
    Individual Grande Pizzas, 120
    Jambalaya Pizza, 133–34
    Kolaches, Pizza, 279–80
    Macaroni Skillet, Pizza, 271
    Meatballs, Pizza, 295
    Meat Loaf Patties, Pizza, 267
    Meat Lover's Chunky Pizza, 110
    Meat Pizza Sandwich, Loose, 266
    Mexican Pizza Bites, 59
    Mixed-Up Pizza, 291
    Octoberfest Pizza, 143–44
    Pasta Pizza Bake, 268
    Pastrami Pizza, Deli, 141–42
    Pastrami Potato Pizza Bake, 255
    Patties, Pizza Skillet, 264
    Pepper Steak Pizza, 121–22
    Pizza Pleasure Pot, 272
    Popover Pizza Casserole, 285–86
    Rice Pizza, 293–94
    Runza Pizza, 109, 275–76
    Santa Fe Trail Pizza, 113–14

Southwestern Pizza, 119
Spaghetti Skillet, Pizza, 274
Spinach Squares with Pizza Sauce, 261–62
Spinach Supreme Pizza, 107–08
Steaks, Baked Philly Pizza, 297
"Steaks," Pizza, 296
Strata, Pizza Lover's, 292
Taco Pizza, Easy, 115–16
Tex-Mex Chili Pizza, 117–18
Veggie-Noodle Soup, 243
beef, corned
    Emerald Isle Pizza, 140
    Potato Crust Pizza, Irish, 145
    Reuben Party Pizza, 63
Beet and Feta Appetizers, 43
bierock. See Runza Pizza
Big Island Banana Dessert Pizza, 201–02
black beans, 78
Black Forest Dessert Pizza, 161
BLT Pizza Supreme, 104
blueberries, 179–82, 191–92
Blueberry Dessert, Diamond Head, 181–82
Blueberry Hill Dessert, 179–80
Bountiful Harvest Pizza Quiche, 256
bread
    Cheesy Pizza Roll-Ups, 278
    croutons, 93–94
    English muffins, 102, 260
    Grecian Pizza Supper Muffins, 260
    Marinara Pizza Bread Casserole, 283
    Mozzarella Pizza Muffins, 298
    pita, 35, 263
    Pizza Biscuit Ring, 277
    Pizza Bread Salad, 249
    Pizza Kolaches, 279–80
    Pizza Loaf Bread, 299
    Pizza Lover's Strata, 292
    Pizza Party Fondue, 302
    Pizza Pepperoni Bread, 301
    Pizza Quick Bread, 300
    Pizza Runzas, 275–76
    Pizzeria Biscuit Cups, 284
    Popover Pizza Casserole, 285–86
    rolls, 275–76, 279–80

broccoli, 32, 71, 101
Broccoli-Cheddar Pizza, 71
Brownie Fruit Pizza, 185–86
Bubble Pizza Deluxe, 289

cabbage (coleslaw), 109, 140, 145
cabbage (sauerkraut), 63, 137–38,
    141–44
Canadian Bacon and Kraut,
    137–38
caramel, 212, 233–34
Caramel Apple Pizza Pie, 212
cauliflower, 32
cheddar cheese
    Bacon Cheeseburger Pizza, 105
    Bread, Pizza Quick, 300
    Broccoli-Cheddar Pizza, 71
    Cheeseburgers with Sauce, Inside-
        Out, 265
    Cheese Lover's, Chicago-Style, 68
    Cheese Pita Pizza, Stuffed, 35
    Cheese Pizza Tetrazzini, 269
    Cheese Steak Pizza, Philly, 125
    Mushroom-Cheese Pizza, Easy, 72
    Tuna Party Squares, Cheesy, 46
cheese. See names of individual
        cheeses
Cheeseburgers with Sauce, Inside-
    Out, 265
Cheese Pizza Tetrazzini, 269
Cheesy Pizza Roll-Ups, 278
Cheesy Tuna Party Squares, 46
Cheez Whiz, 97
Chef Salad Pizza, 126
cherries, 148–50, 161
Chicago-Style Cheese Lover's, 68
chicken. See poultry
Chicken and Peppers with Fresh
    Tomato, 87–88
Chicken Bacon Ranch Pizza, 90
Chicken Caesar Pizza, 93–94
Chicken Chow Mein Pizza, 91–92
Chicken Cordon Bleu Pizza,
    83–84
Chicken Fajita Pizza, 97
Chicken Gyro Pizza, 95
Chicken Pizza Pasta Skillet, 270
Chicken Pizza Pita, 263
chili sauce, 47

chocolate
    Banana Cookie Pizza, 203–04
    Banana Dessert Pizza, Big Island,
        201–02
    Banana Split Dessert Pizza,
        189–90
    Black Forest Dessert Pizza, 161
    Brownie Dessert, Pistachio, 220
    Brownie Dessert, Pretty in Pink,
        149–50
    Brownie Fruit Pizza, 185–86
    Chocolate Caramel Dessert,
        233–34
    Chocolate Cheesecake Dessert,
        221–22
    Chocolate Dessert, Ultimate,
        225–26
    Chocolate Holiday Pizza,
        223–24
    Chocolate-Strawberry Dessert,
        165–66
    Grasshopper Pizza Dessert,
        217–18
    Hello Dolly! Dessert Pizza, 235
    Orange-Chocolate Pizza Dessert,
        199
    Peanut Brownie Pizza, 231–32
    Peanut Buster Dessert Pizza,
        229–30
    Pears Helene Dessert Pizza, 176
    Pineapple-Chocolate Dessert,
        183–84
    Raspberry-Chocolate Dessert,
        Stellar, 157–58
    Rocky Road Dessert Pizza,
        227–28
    Strawberry Brownie Pizza, 169–70
    Strawberry-Chocolate Cream,
        167–68
Chocolate Caramel Dessert, 233–34
Chocolate Cheesecake Dessert,
    221–22
Chocolate Holiday Pizza, 223–24
Chocolate-Strawberry Dessert,
    165–66
Classic Pizza, Cliff's, 106
cocoa powder. See chocolate
coconut, 153–54, 200
coleslaw, 109, 140, 145

Coney Island Pizza, 136
corn
Grande Party Appetizer Pizza,
57–58
Santa Fe Trail Pizza, 113–14
Tamale Ole Pizza, 79
Tex-Mex Appetizer Pizza, 28
Tex-Mex Chili Pizza, 117–18
Turkey Pizza, West Coast, 99–100
Country Club Appetizer Pizza, 50
Crab Appetizer Pizza, 49
cranberries, 55–56, 213–14
cream cheese
Chocolate Cheesecake Dessert,
221–22
Strawberry-Chocolate Cream,
167–68
Creamy Pizza Bake, 273
cucumber, 41
Cupid's Cherry Dessert Pizza, 148

Deli Pastrami Pizza, 141–42
dessert
Apple Betty Pizza Dessert, 211
Apple-Cranberry Dessert, 213–14
Apple Crisp Pizza, 207–08
Apple Crumb Pizza, 205–06
Apple Dessert Pizza, Maple, 219
Apple Harvest Dessert Pizza,
209–10
Apple Pizza Pie, Caramel, 212
Apricot Nectar Dessert, 177–78
Banana Cookie Pizza, 203–04
Banana Dessert Pizza, Big Island,
201–02
Banana Split Dessert Pizza,
189–90
Black Forest Dessert Pizza, 161
Blueberry Dessert, Diamond
Head, 181–82
Blueberry Hill Dessert, 179–80
Brownie Dessert, Pistachio, 220
Brownie Dessert, Pretty in Pink,
149–50
Brownie Fruit Pizza, 185–86
Cherry Dessert Pizza, Cupid's, 148
Chocolate Caramel Dessert,
233–34

Chocolate Cheesecake Dessert,
221–22
Chocolate Dessert Pizza, Ultimate,
225–26
Chocolate Holiday Pizza, 223–24
Chocolate-Strawberry Dessert,
165–66
Fruit Pizza, Fiesta, 187–88
Fruit Pizza, Summer Breezes,
191–92
Fruit Pizza Dessert, Trade Winds,
193–94
Grasshopper Pizza Dessert, 217–18
Hello Dolly! Dessert Pizza, 235
Maui Dessert Pizza, 200
Mincemeat Pizza Dessert, 215–16
Orange-Chocolate Pizza Dessert,
199
Peach Melba Dessert Pizza,
173–74
Peach Pecan Dessert Pizza, 175
Peanut Brownie Pizza, 231–32
Peanut Buster Dessert Pizza,
229–30
Pears Helene Dessert Pizza, 176
Pineapple-Chocolate Dessert,
183–84
Raspberry-Almond Pizza, 159–60
Raspberry-Chocolate Dessert,
Stellar, 157–58
Rhubarb-Coconut Pizza Dessert,
153–54
Rhubarb Pizza Dessert,
Refreshing, 151–52
Rhubarb-Raspberry Dessert, Ruby,
155–56
Rocky Road Dessert Pizza,
227–28
Strawberry Brownie Pizza, 169–70
Strawberry-Chocolate Cream,
167–68
Strawberry Peach Dessert Pizza,
171–72
Strawberry Pizza, Hawaiian,
197–98
Strawberry Pizza, Heavenly,
163–64
Strawberry Shortcake Pizza, 162

Tropical Sunset Dessert Pizza, 195–96
Dough, Homemade Pizza, 239

Easy Taco Pizza, 115–16
egg(s)
  Bacon and Eggs Pizza, Morning, 305
  Chef Salad Pizza, 126
  Egg Salad Snack Pizza, 45
  Quiche, Bountiful Harvest Pizza, 256
  Quiche, Pizza, 257–58
  Quiche, Tomato and Mushroom Pizza, 259
Egg Salad Snack Pizza, 45
Emerald Isle Pizza, 140
entrées
  Asparagus and Ham Pizza, 135
  Bacon and Tomato Pizzas, 102
  Bacon Cheeseburger Pizza, 105
  Baked Pizza Pie, 287–88
  BLT Pizza Supreme, 104
  Broccoli-Cheddar Pizza, 71
  Bubble Pizza Deluxe, 289
  Canadian Bacon and Kraut, 137–38
  Cheeseburgers with Sauce, Inside-Out, 265
  Cheese Lover's Pizza, Chicago-Style, 68
  Cheese Pizza, Mediterranean Three-, 69
  Cheese Pizza Tetrazzini, 269
  Cheese Steak Pizza, Philly, 125
  Chef Salad Pizza, 126
  Chicken and Peppers with Fresh Tomato, 87–88
  Chicken Bacon Ranch Pizza, 90
  Chicken Caesar Pizza, 93–94
  Chicken Chow Mein Pizza, 91–92
  Chicken Cordon Bleu Pizza, 83–84
  Chicken Fajita Pizza, 97
  Chicken Gyro Pizza, 95
  Chicken Pizza, Barbeque, 96
  Chicken Pizza, Grande, 85–86
  Chicken Pizza, L.A., 89

Chicken Pizza, Rosemary, 80
Chicken Pizza, Tuscany, 81–82
Chicken Pizza Pasta Skillet, 270
Chicken Pizza Pita, 263
Classic Pizza, Cliff's, 106
Coney Island Pizza, 136
Creamy Pizza Bake, 273
Deep-Dish Pizza, Homemade, 111–12
Emerald Isle Pizza, 140
Fajita Supreme Pizza, 123–24
Frankfurter Pizza, 139
Fresh Tomato Pizza, 66
Green Peppers, Pizza-Stuffed, 290
Ham Alfredo Pizza, 131–32
Ham and Pineapple Pizza, 129
Ham and Potato Brunch Pizza, 303–04
Hawaiian Luau Pizza, 130
Individual Grande Pizzas, 120
Italian Spinach Pizza, 73
Jambalaya Pizza, 133–34
Macaroni Skillet, Pizza, 271
Marinara Pizza Bread Casserole, 283
Meatballs, Pizza, 295
Meat Loaf Patties, Pizza, 267
Meat Lover's Chunky Pizza, 110
Meat Pizza Sandwich, Loose, 266
Mexican Black Bean Pizza, 78
Mixed-Up Pizza, 291
Mozzarella Pizza Muffins, 298
Mushroom-Cheese Pizza, Easy, 72
Octoberfest Pizza, 143–44
Pasta Pizza Bake, 268
Pastrami Pizza, Deli, 141–42
Patties, Pizza Skillet, 264
Pepper Steak Pizza, 121–22
Pizza Margherita, 67
Pizza Pleasure Pot, 272
Popover Pizza Casserole, 285–86
Potato Crust Pizza, Irish, 145
Rice Pizza, 293–94
Runza Pizza, 109, 275–76
Santa Fe Trail Pizza, 113–14
Southwestern Pizza, 119
Spaghetti Skillet, Pizza, 274

entrées (*cont.*)
Spinach and Bacon Pizza, 103
Spinach Squares with Pizza Sauce,
261–62
Spinach Supreme Pizza, 107–08
Steaks, Baked Philly Pizza, 297
"Steaks," Pizza, 296
Strata, Pizza Lover's, 292
Sub Sandwich Pizza, 127–28
Sunshine State Pizza, 76
Taco Pizza, Easy, 115–16
Tamale Ole Pizza, 79
Tex-Mex Chili Pizza, 117–18
Tomato-Basil Pizza, 70
Tomato Florentine Pizza, 74
Tomato-Zucchini Veggie Skillet,
246
Turkey Club Pizza, 98
Turkey Divan Pizza, 101
Turkey Pizza, West Coast, 99–100
Tuscan Pizza, 77
Zucchini-Mozzarella Pizza, 75

Fajita Supreme Pizza, 123–24
feta cheese
Beet and Feta Appetizers, 43
Cheese Pizza, Mediterranean
Three-, 69
Chicken Gyro Pizza, 95
Grecian Pizza Supper Muffins,
260
Mediterranean Appetizers, 40
Shrimp and Feta Appetizers, 48
Springtime Appetizers, 44
Fiesta Fruit Pizza, 187–88
Fondue, Pizza Party, 302
Frankfurter Pizza, 139
French Onion Appetizers, 42
French Salad Pizza Appetizers,
33–34
Fresh Tomato–Noodle Pizza
Skillet, 245
Fresh Tomato Pizza, 66
fruit. *See names of individual fruits*

Gazpacho Appetizer Pizza, 41
Grande Bacon Pizza Bites, 30
Grande Chicken Pizza, 85–86
Grande Party Appetizer Pizza, 57–58

grapes, seedless, 187–88, 193–94
Grasshopper Pizza Dessert, 217–18
great northern beans, 77
Grecian Pizza Supper Muffins, 260

Ham Alfredo Pizza, 131–32
Ham and Cheese Appetizers, 60
Ham and Pineapple Pizza, 129
Ham and Potato Brunch Pizza,
303–04
Ham and Veggie Pizza Appetizers,
61–62
Hawaiian Luau Pizza, 130
Hawaiian Strawberry Pizza,
197–98
Healthy Exchanges, 8, 15–17
Healthy Request. *See* soup
Heavenly Strawberry Pizza, 163–64
Hello Dolly! Dessert Pizza, 235
holiday, 55–56, 223–24
Home for the Holidays Appetizer,
55–56
Homemade Deep-Dish Pizza,
111–12
Homemade Pizza Dough, 239
Homemade Pizza Sauce, 238

Individual Grande Pizzas, 120
ingredients
analysis, 26
brands, 9–11
measurements, 20–21
Inside-Out Cheeseburgers with
Sauce, 265
Irish Potato Crust Pizza, 145
Italian Salad Appetizer Pizza, 37
Italian Spinach Pizza, 73

Jambalaya Pizza, 133–34
jams and jellies, 306
juice
apple, 205–06, 209–10, 215–16
orange, 55–56, 195–96
tomato, 283, 302

kidney beans, 57–58, 113–14,
117–18
kielbasa sausage, 143–44
Kolaches, Pizza, 279–80

L.A. Chicken Pizza, 89
Loose Meat Pizza Sandwich, 266
Luau Chicken Appetizer Pizza,
    53–54

mandarin oranges, 53–54, 185–86,
    193–96
Maple Apple Dessert Pizza, 219
Marinara Pizza Bread Casserole, 283
marshmallows, 227–28
Maui Dessert Pizza, 200
measurements, 15–17, 20–21
Meat Lover's Chunky Pizza, 110
Mediterranean Appetizers, 40
Mediterranean Three-Cheese Pizza,
    69
Mexican Black Bean Pizza, 78
Mexican Pizza Appetizers, Mini, 29
Mexican Pizza Bites, 59
Mincemeat Pizza Dessert, 215–16
Mixed-Up Pizza, 291
Morning Bacon and Eggs Pizza,
    305
mozzarella cheese
    Bread, Pizza Pepperoni, 301
    Cheese Lover's Pizza, Chicago-
        Style, 68
    Cheese Pizza, Mediterranean
        Three-, 69
    Cheese Pizza Tetrazzini, 269
    Cheese Steak Pizza, Philly, 125
    Cheesy Pizza Roll-Ups, 278
    Mozzarella Pizza Muffins, 298
    Mushroom-Cheese Pizza, Easy, 72
    Steaks, Baked Philly Pizza, 297
    Tomato and Mozzarella Pasta
        Salad, 250
    Tomato Mozzarella Bites, 38
    Tomato Mozzarella Salad, Pizza,
        247
    Zucchini-Mozzarella Pizza, 75
Mozzarella Pizza Muffins, 298
Mushroom-Cheese Pizza, Easy, 72
mushrooms
    Ham and Veggie Pizza Appetizers,
        61–62
    Mushroom-Cheese Pizza, Easy, 72
    Quiche, Tomato and Mushroom
        Pizza, 259

noodles. See pasta
nutritional information, 25
nuts. See names of individual nuts

oats, 207–08, 223–24
Octoberfest Pizza, 143–44
Olive Pizza Appetizers, 39
onions, 42, 123–24
Orange-Chocolate Pizza Dessert,
    199
orange juice, 55–56, 195–96
oranges, mandarin, 53–54, 185–86,
    193–96

parmesan cheese, 69, 72, 278
pasta
    Cheese Pizza Tetrazzini, 269
    Chicken Pizza Pasta Skillet, 270
    Creamy Pizza Bake, 273
    Macaroni Skillet, Pizza, 271
    Pasta Pizza Bake, 268
    Pasta Pizza Salad, 251
    Pepperoni Macaroni Salad, 252
    Pepperoni Pizza Soup, 244
    Pizza Pleasure Pot, 272
    Spaghetti Skillet, Pizza, 274
    Tomato and Mozzarella Pasta
        Salad, 250
    Tomato–Noodle Pizza Skillet,
        Fresh, 245
    Veggie-Noodle Soup, Pizza
        Lover's, 243
Pasta Pizza Bake, 268
Pasta Pizza Salad, 251
Pastrami Pizza, Deli, 141–42
Pastrami Potato Pizza Bake, 255
peaches, 171–75, 187–88
Peach Melba Dessert Pizza, 173–74
Peach Pecan Dessert Pizza, 175
Peanut Brownie Pizza, 231–32
Peanut Buster Dessert Pizza, 229–30
peanut butter, 229–32, 306
Peanut Butter and Jelly Breakfast
    Pizza, 306
peanuts, 227–32, 306
Pears Helene Dessert Pizza, 176
peas, 33–34, 91–92
pecans
    Apple Dessert Pizza, Maple, 219

pecans (*cont.*)
  Apple Harvest Dessert Pizza,
    209–10
  Apple Pizza Pie, Caramel, 212
  Apricot Nectar Dessert, 177–80
  Banana Dessert Pizza, Big Island,
    201–02
  Blueberry Hill Dessert, 179–80
  Chicken Salad Appetizers,
    Pineapple, 51–52
  Chocolate Caramel Dessert,
    233–34
  Chocolate Dessert, Ultimate,
    225–26
  Fruit Pizza, Fiesta, 187–88
  Fruit Pizza, Summer Breezes,
    191–92
  Hello Dolly! Dessert Pizza, 235
  Maui Dessert Pizza, 200
  Orange-Chocolate Pizza Dessert,
    199
  Peach Pecan Dessert Pizza,
    175
  Rhubarb Pizza Dessert,
    Refreshing, 151–52
  Tropical Sunset Dessert Pizza,
    195–96
peppers, 87–88, 121–24, 290
Pepperoni Macaroni Salad, 252
Pepperoni Pizza Soup, 244
Pepper Steak Pizza, 121–22
Philly Cheese Steak Pizza, 125
pie filling, 148–50, 161, 211
pimiento, 33–34, 107–08, 269
pineapple
  Banana Split Dessert Pizza,
    189–90
  Blueberry Dessert, Diamond
    Head, 181–82
  Brownie Fruit Pizza, 185–86
  Chicken Appetizer Pizza, Luau,
    53–54
  Chicken Salad Appetizers,
    Pineapple, 51–52
  Fruit Pizza, Summer Breezes,
    191–92
  Fruit Pizza Dessert, Trade Winds,
    193–94
  Ham and Pineapple Pizza, 129

Hawaiian Luau Pizza, 130
  Maui Dessert Pizza, 200
  Pineapple-Chocolate Dessert,
    183–84
  Strawberry Pizza, Hawaiian,
    197–98
  Tropical Sunset Dessert Pizza,
    195–96
Pineapple Chicken Salad Appetizers,
  51–52
Pineapple-Chocolate Dessert,
  183–84
pinto beans, 79
Pistachio Brownie Dessert, 220
pita bread, 35, 263
pizza, about, 2–7
Pizza, Cheesy Roll-Ups, 278
Pizza, Stuffed Cheese Pita, 35
Pizza Biscuit Ring, 277
Pizza Bread Salad, 249
Pizza Chef's Salad, 248
Pizza Dough, Homemade, 239
Pizza Kolaches, 279–80
Pizza Loaf Bread, 299
Pizza Lover's Strata, 292
Pizza Lover's Veggie-Noodle Soup,
  243
Pizza Macaroni Skillet, 271
Pizza Margherita, 67
Pizza Meatballs, 295
Pizza Meat Loaf Patties, 267
Pizza Party Fondue, 302
Pizza Pepperoni Bread, 301
Pizza Pleasure Pot, 272
Pizza Quiche, 257–58
Pizza Quick Bread, 300
Pizza Runza, 275–76
Pizza Salsa, 240
Pizza Sauce, Homemade, 238
Pizza Skillet Patties, 264
Pizza Spaghetti Skillet, 274
Pizza "Steaks," 296
Pizza-Stuffed Green Peppers, 290
Pizza Tomato Mozzarella Salad, 247
Pizzeria Biscuit Cups, 284
pop, 171–74, 179–82, 195–96,
  199
Popover Pizza Casserole, 285–86
Popovers with Pizza Sauce, 281–82

pork
  Asparagus and Ham Pizza, 135
  Bacon and Eggs Pizza, Morning,
    305
  Bacon and Tomato Pizzas, 102
  Bacon Cheeseburger Pizza, 105
  Bacon, Lettuce, and Tomato
    Appetizers, 36
  Bacon Pizza Bites, Grande, 30
  BLT Pizza Supreme, 104
  Bread, Pizza Pepperoni, 301
  Bread, Pizza Quick, 300
  Bubble Pizza Deluxe, 289
  Canadian Bacon and Kraut,
    137–38
  Chef Salad Pizza, 126
  Chicken Appetizer Pizza, Luau,
    53–54
  Chicken Bacon Ranch Pizza, 90
  Chicken Cordon Bleu Pizza,
    83–84
  Coney Island Pizza, 136
  Country Club Appetizer Pizza, 50
  Frankfurter Pizza, 139
  Ham Alfredo Pizza, 131–32
  Ham and Cheese Appetizers, 60
  Ham and Pineapple Pizza, 129
  Ham and Potato Brunch Pizza,
    303–04
  Ham and Veggie Pizza Appetizers,
    61–62
  Hawaiian Luau Pizza, 130
  Jambalaya Pizza, 133–34
  Pepperoni Macaroni Salad, 252
  Pepperoni Pizza Soup, 244
  Pizza Chef's Salad, 248
  Spinach and Bacon Pizza, 103
  Springtime Appetizers, 44
  Sub Sandwich Pizza, 127–28
  Turkey Club Pizza, 98
potato, 145, 253–55, 303–04
Potato Pizza Hash, 253
poultry
  Bacon Cheeseburger Pizza, 105
  Baked Pizza Pie, 287–88
  Biscuit Cups, Pizzeria, 284
  Bubble Pizza Deluxe, 289
  Cheeseburgers with Sauce, Inside-
    Out, 265

Chef Salad Pizza, 126
Chicken and Peppers with Fresh
  Tomato, 87–88
Chicken Appetizer Pizza, Luau,
  53–54
Chicken Bacon Ranch Pizza, 90
Chicken Caesar Pizza, 93–94
Chicken Chow Mein Pizza, 91–92
Chicken Cordon Bleu Pizza,
  83–84
Chicken Fajita Pizza, 97
Chicken Gyro Pizza, 95
Chicken Pizza, Barbeque, 96
Chicken Pizza, Grande, 85–86
Chicken Pizza, L.A., 89
Chicken Pizza, Luau, 53–54
Chicken Pizza, Rosemary, 80
Chicken Pizza, Tuscany, 81–82
Chicken Pizza Pasta Skillet, 270
Chicken Pizza Pita, 263
Chicken Salad Appetizers,
  Pineapple, 51–52
Classic Pizza, Cliff's, 106
Coney Island Pizza, 136
Country Club Appetizer Pizza,
  50
Cream of Chicken, Healthy
  Request, 85–86
Creamy Pizza Bake, 273
Deep-Dish Pizza, Homemade,
  111–12
Fajita Supreme Pizza, 123–24
Fondue, Pizza Party, 302
Grande Party Appetizer Pizza,
  57–58
Green Peppers, Pizza-Stuffed, 290
Home for the Holidays Appetizer,
  55–56
Individual Grande Pizzas, 120
Kolaches, Pizza, 279–80
Macaroni Skillet, Pizza, 271
Meatballs, Pizza, 295
Meat Loaf Patties, Pizza, 267
Meat Lover's Chunky Pizza, 110
Meat Pizza Sandwich, Loose, 266
Mexican Pizza Bites, 59
Mixed-Up Pizza, 291
Pasta Pizza Bake, 268
Patties, Pizza Skillet, 264

poultry (*cont.*)
    Pizza Pleasure Pot, 272
    Popover Pizza Casserole, 285–86
    Rice Pizza, 293–94
    Runza Pizza, 109, 275–76
    Santa Fe Trail Pizza, 113–14
    Southwestern Pizza, 119
    Spaghetti Skillet, Pizza, 274
    Spinach Squares with Pizza Sauce,
      261–62
    Spinach Supreme Pizza, 107–08
    "Steaks," Pizza, 296
    Strata, Pizza Lover's, 292
    Taco Pizza, Easy, 115–16
    Tex-Mex Chili Pizza, 117–18
    Turkey Club Pizza, 98
    Turkey Divan Pizza, 101
    Turkey Pizza, West Coast,
      99–100
    Veggie-Noodle Soup, Pizza
      Lover's, 243
    Pretty in Pink Brownie Dessert,
      149–50

quiche
    Quiche, Bountiful Harvest Pizza,
      256
    Quiche, Pizza, 257–58
    Quiche, Tomato and Mushroom
      Pizza, 259

raisins, 215–16
raspberries, 155–60, 173–74,
    191–92
Raspberry-Almond Pizza, 159–60
recipe. *See also* ingredients
    alterations, 20–21
    symbols, 26
    tips, 13–14, 19–21
Refreshing Rhubarb Pizza Dessert,
    151–52
Reuben Party Pizza, 63
Rhodes frozen dinner rolls, 275–76,
    279–80
rhubarb, 151–56
Rhubarb-Coconut Pizza Dessert,
    153–54
rice, 241, 293–94
Rice Pizza, 293–94

Rocky Road Dessert Pizza, 227–28
Rosemary Chicken Pizza, 80
Ruby Rhubarb-Raspberry Dessert,
    155–56
Runza Pizza, 109

salad
    Chef Salad Pizza, 126
    Chicken Salad Appetizers,
      Pineapple, 51–52
    Egg Salad Snack Pizza, 45
    Emerald Isle Pizza, 140
    French Salad Pizza Appetizers,
      33–34
    Italian Salad Appetizer Pizza, 37
    Pasta Pizza Salad, 251
    Pepperoni Macaroni Salad, 252
    Pizza Bread Salad, 249
    Pizza Chef's Salad, 248
    Potato Crust Pizza, Irish, 145
    Runza Pizza, 109
    Tomato and Mozzarella Pasta
      Salad, 250
    Tomato Mozzarella Salad, Pizza,
      247
salad dressing
    caesar, 93–94
    catalina, 89
    french, 33–34
    italian, 37, 73, 77, 251, 260
    ranch, 83–84, 90, 247
    thousand island, 63, 126, 140
Salsa, Pizza, 240
Santa Fe Trail Pizza, 113–14
sauce
    Homemade Pizza Sauce, 238
    Inside-Out Cheeseburgers with,
      265
    Popovers with Pizza Sauce, 281–82
    Spinach Squares with Pizza Sauce,
      261–62
sauerkraut, 63, 137–38, 141–44
Scalloped Pizza Potatoes, 254
seafood
    Crab Appetizer Pizza, 49
    Jambalaya Pizza, 133–34
    Shrimp and Feta Appetizers, 48
    Shrimp Cocktail Pizza Bites, 47
    Tuna Party Squares, Cheesy, 46

Shrimp and Feta Appetizers, 48
Shrimp Cocktail Pizza Bites, 47
soda, 171–74, 179–82, 195–96, 199
soup
    Cream of Chicken, Healthy
        Request, 85–86, 91–92
    Cream of Mushroom, Healthy
        Request, 109, 254, 273
    Pepperoni Pizza Soup, 244
    Tomato, Healthy Request, 241–42,
        244–46, 269, 281–82, 295,
        297
    Tomato Pizza Supreme Soup,
        242
    Tomato Rice Pizza Soup, 241
    Veggie-Noodle Soup, Pizza
        Lover's, 243
Southwestern Pizza, 119
spinach
    Crab Appetizer Pizza, 49
    Italian Spinach Pizza, 73
    Mediterranean Appetizers, 40
    Spinach and Bacon Pizza, 103
    Spinach Squares with Pizza Sauce,
        261–62
    Spinach Supreme Pizza, 107–08
    Tomato Florentine Pizza, 74
Spinach and Bacon Pizza, 103
Spinach Squares with Pizza Sauce,
    261–62
Spinach Supreme Pizza, 107–08
Springtime Appetizers, 44
squash, 69, 75–76, 246, 249, 256
Stellar Raspberry-Chocolate Dessert,
    157–58
strawberries
    Banana Split Dessert Pizza,
        189–90
    Brownie Fruit Pizza, 185–86
    Chocolate-Strawberry Dessert,
        165–66
    Fruit Pizza, Fiesta, 187–88
    Fruit Pizza, Summer Breezes,
        191–92
    Strawberry Brownie Pizza, 169–70
    Strawberry-Chocolate Cream,
        167–68
    Strawberry Peach Dessert Pizza,
        171–72

Strawberry Pizza, Hawaiian,
    197–98
Strawberry Pizza, Heavenly,
    163–64
Strawberry Shortcake Pizza, 162
Strawberry Brownie Pizza, 169–70
Strawberry-Chocolate Cream,
    167–68
Strawberry Peach Dessert Pizza,
    171–72
Strawberry Shortcake Pizza, 162
Stuffed Cheese Pita Pizza Snacks,
    35
Sub Sandwich Pizza, 127–28
Summer Breezes Fruit Pizza, 191–92
Sunshine State Pizza, 76
Swiss cheese, 42, 60–63, 83–84,
    127–28, 141–42
syrup, 219, 221–22, 227–34

Tamale Ole Pizza, 79
Tex-Mex Appetizer Pizza, 28
Tex-Mex Chili Pizza, 117–18
Tomato and Mozzarella Pasta Salad,
    250
Tomato and Mushroom Pizza
    Quiche, 259
Tomato-Basil Pizza, 70
tomatoes
    Bacon and Tomato Pizzas, 102
    Bacon, Lettuce, and Tomato
        Appetizers, 36
    BLT Pizza Supreme, 104
    Bread, Pizza Loaf, 299
    Chicken and Peppers with Fresh
        Tomato, 87–88
    Fresh Tomato Pizza, 66
    Marinara Pizza Bread Casserole,
        283
    Pizza Salsa, 240
    Quiche, Tomato and Mushroom
        Pizza, 259
    Tomato and Mozzarella Pasta
        Salad, 250
    Tomato-Basil Pizza, 70
    Tomato Florentine Pizza, 74
    Tomato Mozzarella Bites, 38
    Tomato Mozzarella Salad, Pizza,
        247

tomatoes (*cont.*)
  Tomato–Noodle Pizza Skillet,
    Fresh, 245
  Tomato Pizza Supreme Soup, 242
  Tomato Rice Pizza Soup, 241
  Tomato-Zucchini Veggie Skillet,
    246
Tomato Florentine Pizza, 74
Tomato Mozzarella Bites, 38
Tomato Pizza Supreme Soup, 242
Tomato Rice Pizza Soup, 241
Tomato-Zucchini Veggie Skillet, 246
tortilla chips, 115–16
Trade Winds Fruit Pizza Dessert,
    193–94
Tropical Sunset Dessert Pizza,
    195–96
tuna, 46
turkey. *See* poultry
Turkey Club Pizza, 98
Turkey Divan Pizza, 101
Tuscan Pizza, 77
Tuscany Chicken Pizza, 81–82

Ultimate Chocolate Dessert Pizza,
    225–26

Vegetable-Cheese French Pizza
    Snacks, 31
vegetables. *See names of individual
    vegetables*
Veggie Pizza Appetizers, 32

walnuts, 55–56, 149–50, 161, 176,
    205–06
West Coast Turkey Pizza, 99–100

yeast, 239, 279–80, 299
yogurt, 95, 223–24

zucchini
  Cheese Pizza, Mediterranean
    Three-, 69
  Pizza Bread Salad, 249
  Quiche, Bountiful Harvest Pizza,
    256
  Sunshine State Pizza, 76
  Tomato-Zucchini Veggie Skillet,
    246
  Zucchini-Mozzarella Pizza, 75

We want to hear from you . . .

The love of Joanna's life was creating "common folk" healthy recipes and solving everyday cooking questions in *The Healthy Exchanges Way*. Everyone who uses her recipes is considered part of the Healthy Exchanges Family, so please write to Cliff and Gina if you have any questions, comments, or suggestions. We will do our best to answer. With your support, Healthy Exchanges will continue to provide recipes and cooking tips for many years to come.

Write to: Clifford Lund
c/o Healthy Exchanges, Inc.
P.O. Box 80
DeWitt, IA 52742-0080

If you prefer, you can fax us at 1-563-659-2126 or contact us via e-mail by writing to HealthyJo@aol.com. Or visit our Healthy Exchanges website at www.healthyexchanges.com.

Now That You've Seen *Pizza Anytime,* Why Not Order *The Healthy Exchanges* *Food Newsletter?*

If you enjoyed the recipes in this cookbook and would like to cook up even more of my "common folk" healthy dishes, you may want to subscribe to *The Healthy Exchanges Food Newsletter.*

This monthly 12-page newsletter contains 30-plus new recipes *every month* in such columns as:

- Reader Exchange
- Reader Requests
- Recipe Makeover
- Micro Corner
- Dinner for Two
- Crock Pot Luck
- Meatless Main Dishes
- Rise & Shine
- Our Small World
- Brown Bagging It
- Snack Attack
- Side Dishes
- Main Dishes
- Desserts

In addition to all the recipes, other regular features include:

- The Editor's Motivational Corner
- Dining Out Question & Answer
- Cooking Question & Answer
- New Product Alert
- Exercise Advice from a Cardiac Rehab Specialist
- Nutrition Advice from a Registered Dietitian
- Positive Thought for the Month

The cost for a one-year (12-issue) subscription is $25. To order, call our toll-free number and pay with any major credit card—or send a check to the address on page 321 of this book.

1-800-766-8961 for Customer Orders
1-563-659-8234 for Customer Service

Thank you for your order, and for choosing to become a part of the Healthy Exchanges Family!